The
PATH
AHEAD

The

PATH
AHEAD

TRANSFORMATIVE
IDEAS FOR INDIA

Edited by

Amitabh Kant

RUPA

Published by
Rupa Publications India Pvt. Ltd 2018
7/16, Ansari Road, Daryaganj
New Delhi 110002

Sales centres:
Allahabad Bengaluru Chennai
Hyderabad Jaipur Kathmandu
Kolkata Mumbai

ISBN: 978-93-5304-150-2

Sixth impression 2022

10 9 8 7 6

Contents

SECTION 2
Transforming Rural India

SECTION 3
Towards Inclusive Growth and Prosperity

SECTION 4
Building Brand India

Foreword

It is interesting to look at India before 1947. For thousands of years, the country had been invaded again and again. This is probably because of how fertile the peninsula has always been, and the fact that it is naturally protected on all sides—by the Himalayas in the North and by a large coastline on the other sides. It's more important than ever to remember India's history today, especially as the country reaches the milestone of being an independent state for more than 70 years. In these seven decades, the progress made by India has been immense. The country has grown to become the sixth largest economy on the global stage, millions of people have been brought out of poverty, and businesses that once had no option outside of serving local populations are expanding internationally and scaling rapidly. The level of ambition around the current reform process is an inspiration to countries all around the world.

I believe that even with this level of progress, India has not even scratched the surface of its potential. As the Chairman of the U.S.-India Strategic Partnership Forum, a non-profit organization that is committed to creating the most powerful strategic partnership between the U.S. and India, I am betting big on the country's future. Under Prime Minister Narendra Modi, who is one of the top world leaders I have ever met, India truly has no limits. In fact, I am predicting that the country will be among the top three economic powers in the world within the next 10–15 years. India will be the example for the rest of the world, not as an emerging country but as a developed country that constantly reinvents itself—and that's why I am personally invested in the future of India. I recently launched JC2 Ventures, a purpose-driven venture capital firm, where I will work with start-ups to change the world through digital transformation. India is a key market for us at JC2. We already have one India-based start-up in our portfolio and expect there to be many more in the years to come.

I think others should bet big on India as well. One of the many reasons I think Prime Minster Modi is one of the top leaders in the world is because he is a visionary who is willing to take risks through the implementation of tough—but necessary—structural and societal reforms. Just consider the digital transformation India is undergoing and supporting with programmes like 'Digital India', which Prime Minister Modi launched in 2015, that has the potential to unlock the opportunity for India to grow into a trillion-dollar economy. Further, Prime Minister Modi understands better than anyone that a holistic approach to change is needed. For example, he has supported Digital India with a number of other initiatives ranging from 'Skill India' to 'Startup India' and 'Make in India'. Even his work to implement the Goods and Services Tax (GST) and demonetize some of India's currency have helped support his vision of making India a leading global economy in the years to come. Other countries and global leaders from around the world can learn from how bold Prime Minister Modi is in everything he does.

A book like this one could not come at a more opportune time. India's journey is inspiring the political, industrial and academic elite around the world. Multiple economic and human capital reforms are laying a strong foundation for the India of tomorrow. However, even with the exciting times that undoubtedly lie ahead for India, there are many unique challenges that a country of this size, complexity and diversity faces. There is an immediate need for these challenges to be identified in the short term, and for sustainable solutions to be developed and implemented with a long-term strategy in mind. Further, the livelihood of India's citizens needs to be at the core of these strategies because people are vital in pushing the entire country forward in terms of economic growth, job creation, innovation, and much more. To be successful, this process must be a collaborative effort between government policymakers, business leaders, industrialists, and academics, among others.

I was truly honoured when I was invited to write the Foreword for a book that brings together innovative ideas to help India realize and capitalize upon its potential. This book brings the views of top industrialists, academics and young leaders to the forefront, all of whom are relevant stakeholders in the future of India's most critical sectors, from health to education to electric mobility and civil services. These stakeholders have achieved immense success in their fields because they are always ahead of the curve and predicting what will happen next before anyone else is even thinking about it. To use one of my favourite phrases, 'they are market predictors'. Having access to the views of more than 25 visionaries on the future of India in one book is rare, to say the least.

The time is ripe for India to innovate and cement its position as one of the leading economies of the twenty-first century—and beyond. I believe this book rises to the occasion. It will not only be a ready reference for today's policymakers, academics, and industry professionals and leaders, it will also serve as an inspiration for India's youth and leaders of tomorrow. Let's all bet big on the future of India!

John T. Chambers
Chairman Emeritus, Cisco Systems

Introduction

As a young civil servant in Kerala over 38 years ago and growing through the ranks, I have seen India transform—one reform at a time. While donning different hats in my varied roles, I have witnessed all that India has undergone and achieved as it has worked its way towards global relevance and now global prominence. There is little if any doubt that India has faced many challenges on an economic, climatic, or even a policy front in the last forty years, and weathering them has led to far more positive outcomes especially in the recent past. The New India we are headed towards today is the product of a variety of milestone reforms and developments, many of which I have been a part of, minor or otherwise. Today, India is a picture of confidence. Prominent on the world stage, India is rapidly achieving economic progress, sharing the stage with world leaders of the marketplace and political economy alike. What lies ahead is challenging, but exciting to the core. We are on the cusp of truly making quantum leaps through young dynamism, and an unsurpassed entrepreneurial vision. I feel that I and my generation are fortunate to have been active witnesses to this transformation. It goes without saying that the lion's share of the credit for this ongoing transformation belongs to the Indian citizen—the resilient farmer, the ingenuous entrepreneur, and the diligent salaried professionals; credit must also go to the reform process in India.

The abolishment of industrial licensing in 1991 was that watershed reform moment where the liberalization of the Indian economy began its journey towards development. Private sector initiative, the increase in Foreign Direct Investment (FDI), the massive rollback of public sector control over a large number of industries supported by measures to liberalize foreign trade, were the key drivers. Free market enterprise supported by strong regulatory mechanisms that also strengthened governance were the enablers of growth from this phase onwards. The Securities and Exchange Board of India (SEBI), set up under the aegis of the SEBI Act, 1992, had the broad stated objective to 'protect the interests of investors in securities' and also to 'promote the development of, and to regulate the securities market'. The establishing and empowering of SEBI is one of the primary reasons why in World Bank's Doing Business 2018 report, India ranks number four globally in the category 'Protecting Minority Investors'. A similar example of creating the necessary regulatory framework in a high growth industry is exemplified by the setting up of the Telecom Regulatory Authority of India (TRAI) in 1997, for the fast-expanding telecom sector. TRAI has taken numerous difficult avenues towards balancing and regulating an industry as dynamic as telecom. On the other hand, reform has also been initiated by dispensing with limiting laws or regulations, such as in the civil aviation industry, with the repealing of the Air Corporations Act, 1953. Today, the Indian civil aviation market is the fastest growing in the world, and private sector involvement in our airports and airlines is key.

On a broader economy stabilization basis, the Fiscal Responsibility and Budget Management Act, 2003, has significantly impacted the inculcating of fiscal discipline among policymakers and building confidence among the international investor community. In a reform-oriented mindset, simplicity of actions can make the ease of accomplishment far more seamless. A step like computerizing the railway reservation system has had an unimaginably significant impact on millions of people's lives.

The last few years have seen massive government-led reform and structural changes. As of 2017, 25 kilometres of roads are being built in India each day. Implementation of the Goods and Services Tax

(GST) in 2017 heralded the most significant reform ever taken in any country, giving rise to one of the largest single markets in the world. The new GST regime has led to an unprecedented increase in the number of taxpayers, systematically creating the path towards a more formal economy. The Ayushman Bharat scheme will digitally link primary and community health centres with district hospitals. Along with the ₹5 lakh health insurance, which will cover 50 crore Indians, it will ensure healthcare through a paperless, cashless, portable scheme. The health stack linked to Aadhaar will be transformational.

During my tenure in Kerala, I got a unique opportunity to work in the fisheries sector. The task was to improve the livelihood of traditional fishermen. The sector was riddled with middlemen, and fishermen were getting only 25 per cent of the market price of fish. We formed self-help groups and provided them with new technology: Fibreglass crafts, outboard motors and fishing nets to enhance their productivity. We also introduced beach-level auctions so that earnings from their daily catch could be deposited in their bank accounts. The biggest challenge was to get bank accounts opened for the fishermen. It took us 10 months of chasing physical banks and bank managers to get this done. The process of 'Know Your Customer' (KYC) was a nightmare. Contrast this with my experience last month. I walked into a bank branch and opened my account using my biometric on a hand-held device in one minute flat. From 10 months to one minute has been the paradigm shift.

In the last few years, governance in India across sectors has been redefined through business process re-engineering, technology and data analytics. Technology is reshaping the way government is designing and implementing programmes. The use of technology has brought in better systems, greater efficiency and is beginning to have a profound impact on governance. India has combined the use of unique biometric identifiers and financial inclusion for effectiveness in social benefits and to reduce the vast number of illegitimate beneficiaries under welfare programmes. The Direct Benefit Transfer (DBT) has been implemented across 437 schemes, and helped save ₹83,000 crore till date. Its implementation has led to 2.75 crore duplicate, fake or non-existent ration cards being deleted, and 3.85 crore duplicate and inactive consumers for liquefied petroleum gas (LPG) subsidy being eliminated.

The Public Financial Management System (PFMS) has led to the creation of a financial management platform for all plan schemes, a database of all recipient agencies, integration with core banking solution of banks, integration of state treasurers, and tracking of fund flow to the lowest tier of implementation of plan schemes on real-time basis. PFMS has also led to just-in-time release of funds and efficient management in the use of funds, including ultimate utilization.

Digitization has led to lower costs in collection of direct taxes. Almost 98.5 per cent of all income-tax (I-T) returns have been filed online. The I-T Department received 6.84 crore income-tax returns in 2017–18, a growth of 26 per cent, and additionally, more than one crore new tax returns.

Unified Payments Interface (UPI) and Bharat Bill Payment System (BBPS) have triggered a plethora of private sector-innovated apps, which have significantly eased citizens' bill payments towards services provided by GoI. BBPS has more than doubled the number of bills paid digitally from April 2017 when the pilot was launched. The value of bills paid on the platform has jumped by about 46 per cent during this period. According to a KPMG report, the size of the bill payments market in India will reach ₹9.4 trillion by 2020. Digital payment transactions have now become extremely simple, thanks to the Bharat Interface for Money (BHIM) UPI. We have seen the emergence of Google Tez and WhatsApp payment. In 2017–18, India has seen over a billion transactions in volume and over a trillion rupees in value. There will be increased disruption with new players and new technologies.

The rollout of the Goods and Services Tax has resulted in a 50 per cent increase in unique indirect taxpayers compared with the pre-GST system. This translates to a substantial 3.4 million new indirect taxpayers leading to a radical formalization of the economy.

In the Pro-Active Governance and Timely Implementation (PRAGATI) programme, Prime Minister Narendra Modi has used technology to cut across departmental silos and geographical boundaries to ensure speedy project implementation. He has dealt directly with senior central and state officials to monitor, review and evaluate progress of social sector schemes and infrastructure projects that were facing severe bottlenecks.

A recent study predicts that digital transformation will add $154 billion to India's GDP by 2021, increasing the growth rate by 1.0 per cent annually. In 2017, about 4 per cent of the country's GDP was derived from digital products and services created directly through the use of technologies like Cloud, IoT and AI. According to an analysis by Accenture, Artificial Intelligence (AI) has the potential to add US$957 billion, or 15 per cent of current gross value added, to India's economy in 2035. India offers challenges that can be solved by application of AI in areas that are vastly different from the western world. We are attempting to find solutions in areas such as agriculture, healthcare and education. NITI Aayog is working to implement AI solutions to improve crop productivity and soil health on farms by using remote sensing images and other data available with government. It is also exploring the inception of a natural language processing platform that can provide AI applications to do Natural Language Processing. NITI is also partnering medical institutions to build a 'bio bank'—radiological and pathological images.

Blockchain is fast becoming a new operating system for facilitating digital transactions across financial markets, supply chains and content ecosystems. Blockchain technologies offer solutions for India that can improve the ease of doing business, especially in the areas of enforcement of contracts and registering of property. It can potentially eliminate 40 lakh cases relating to land and land disputes. NITI is working on blockchain-based smart contracts which will reduce litigation, and land registry on the blockchain that will reduce corruption relating to land. It is estimated that 25 per cent of domestic medicines are fake. NITI's drug authenticity project will empower consumers to verify the genuineness of drugs sold as their manufacturing will be tracked on the blockchain. India has a billion biometrics on Aadhar. We have a unique opportunity to leverage our public identities to have many applications on the blockchain architecture.

The platform is set now for young Indians to become the makers of a New India. Enthusiasm, determination and zeal with a healthy dose of entrepreneurial vision that is enhanced by rapid strides in technology will be the difference-maker for India to truly become a global powerhouse.

Some questions do however remain. In a world where geopolitical uncertainty and at times volatility is becoming more commonplace, global trade is frequently under threat as a consequence. A technological revolution in manufacturing and services in India is imminent but choosing the right reform for the right revolution will become a slightly more delicate process given the global environment and to ensure we keep step with the rest of the world. Millions of young Indians are entering the workforce annually with a continually major shift from rural to urban areas, and a burgeoning middle class with demands and expectations of quality health and education, further increasing the dependence on sustainable, viable and continuous growth. This is an ongoing challenge and India is at a delicate juncture where the new generation of policymakers must take responsibility and initiative to adeptly work in tandem with industrialists, academicians and the common man to form impactful policies.

The book was conceptualized as a collaborative effort that borrows from the very essence of working in tandem to have meaningful discourses. Over a year in the making, this book brings together a rare combination of industry executives, domain thought leaders, and government officials. Its vision was to highlight constraints and find a way forward for key sectors that will be the cornerstone for India's future growth. The authors we asked to contribute to this critical work had been carefully selected for their individual expertise and from a macro perspective, to cover a diverse range of topics. They are leaders in every way, and have been key contributors to the India growth story.

The authors were requested to present their views on what they felt were the best strategies to promote a particular sector that they personally felt was vital for sustainable growth. Their ideas that have been captured in their respective sections are cutting-edge, unique, and focused. As a result, this body of work that has resulted from the contributions of these thought leaders is sure to be a timely and crucial ready reference for young leaders from all walks of life, including industry, government and academia. This book's true purpose would have been served if and when future leaders of our great country take inspiration from some of the ideas and solutions presented here. For over a year, we have worked on this book, and now I am glad to be able share this seminal work with all of you.

The book brings together many of my own experiences through a varied career in the bureaucracy and now as CEO at the Government of India's Think Tank. I truly believe we are on the cusp of unprecedented growth, and this book perfectly captures that sentiment. I hope you enjoy reading this as much as I enjoyed working with the dynamic leaders who helped put this together.

Amitabh Kant
CEO, NITI Aayog

SECTION 1

Human Capital Development

Approach to Indian Health Sector Reform

Nachiket Mor and Amrita Agarwal

Healthcare system is complex, dynamic and adaptive.[1] It does not seem to follow deterministic pathways and degree of control is low. Healthcare system also has a discernable trajectory with a speed and a direction which are a result of many forces. Given the many stabilizing feedback forces (loops), it may seem hard to alter the trajectory of a healthcare system from the default end state. However, a careful examination of forces involved may provide a way to alter the trajectory of the system so that it is able to move towards a more desired end state. Since the notion of systems thinking first originated in Physics, continuing with the use of language from that field, these forces may be characterized as:

- **Atomic forces** (high power required, potential for high impact in near term) are very powerful and focused, and provide the system with its core strength. Breaking these atomic and subatomic bonds is possible and sometimes essential, but requires an equally powerful force to do so. Example: Increasing government spending on health from 1 per cent to 2.5 per cent of GDP.
- **Gravitational forces** (sustained effort resulting in gradual change over time) are also strong but diffused and draw strength from the shared knowledge, attitudes and beliefs of participants in the system. These forces may sometimes become

essential to alter, but require a great deal of patience and perseverance to succeed. Example: Improving performance of human resources in health through mentoring and training.

- **Magnetic forces** (feasible, short-term small impact with potential for a large impact in the long term) have the strength and focus that lies somewhere between atomic and gravitational forces. These forces draw their power not as much from their intrinsic strength but their ability to trigger reinforcing feedback loops which over time gather momentum and build sufficient power to break atomic bonds and counter gravitational forces. Example: Set up a strong MTAB (Medical Technology Assessment Board) to improve efficiency of healthcare spending.

Reformers often fall into the trap of focusing their attention exclusively on altering atomic or gravitational forces because they seem to be the most 'logical' and visible pathways to desired outcomes, but may often be unsuccessful because of the magnitude of the effort needed in the short and medium term. Magnetic forces, on the other hand, may reveal a near-term path forward for reform, especially when the system seems 'stuck'. Magnetic forces are harder to identify, operate in oblique ways, and require a deep understanding of the inherent characteristics, structure and dynamics of the whole system. However, a careful study may reveal them and they could trigger powerful long-term waves of change.

The Indian healthcare sector is not moving along a trajectory that leads to achieving the desired goals.[2] Even the best state-level systems are stuck in a low-quality equilibrium. The arguments most often advanced on why this is so, are that the poor are not able to afford healthcare, and that there is a shortage of human and financial resources available for health—which requires atomic/gravitational forces and are hard to change in short term.

While there is undoubtedly a great deal of truth to these arguments, even if more resources were added to health it is not clear that it would lead to the desired outcomes. Many countries, such as Sri Lanka, Ghana and Thailand, with comparable or lower health spending, have better health outcomes than India[3] and even within India it is not always the case that the states with the highest per-capita health expenditures necessarily have the best outcomes.[4] Altering the very structure and dynamics of the system, and not merely the amounts of money involved, is key to the achievement of the desired health system goals. To do this, it is critical to understand the characteristics of the health system within India and to explore all the atomic, gravitational and magnetic forces that govern its behaviour, both within and outside the traditional boundaries of health systems. In the following sections, we address these, and through this we hope to start a debate on ways to initiate a health reform in India.

Healthcare System and Its Inherent Characteristics

The healthcare system can be divided into component subsystems. Following WHO, the goals and subsystems of healthcare are traditionally specified as follows:[5]

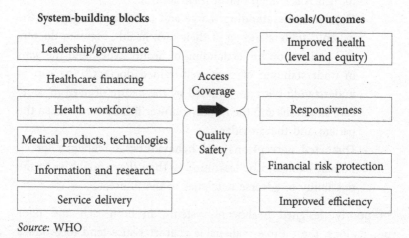

System-building blocks		Goals/Outcomes
Leadership/governance		Improved health (level and equity)
Healthcare financing	Access Coverage	
Health workforce		Responsiveness
Medical products, technologies	Quality Safety	
Information and research		Financial risk protection
Service delivery		Improved efficiency

Source: WHO

However, these traditional boundaries of the healthcare system could be expanded to include other systems such as agriculture, food systems, roads, sanitation, clean water, financial system, telecom and education (typical social determinants of health and more). Each of these systems and subsystems interact with each other and within each there are various forces at play. Creativity needs to be applied both to determine the boundary of the system as well as to identify tractable subsystems that the reformer-designer chooses to work with, to alter the direction and speed with which the system is naturally moving towards a desired one.

Within the traditional boundaries of healthcare system, there are three key inherent and unchanging characteristics[6] relating to it that any systems design will need to consider and are the key reasons why the system does not self-organize using market forces:[7]

- **Variability**: A high degree of variability in healthcare expenditures both across time for the same individual and between different individuals. Some variability is driven by random factors, but a lot of it can be traced back to genetic and environmental influences that individuals are subjected to, which are often out of their control.
- **Gaps in understanding**: Large and unbridgeable gaps in the patients' understanding of their own health, between doctors and patients on understanding of health issues, and the gaps in understanding of even well-trained doctors.[8] The gap in understanding is compounded by the nature of need in acute care situations and the resulting power imbalance between the patient and the provider.
- **Distorted perceptions and behaviours**: A tendency for all human beings to be less mindful than they should be to the possibility of adverse outcomes in the future.

In poorly designed healthcare systems, in both rich and poor populations, these three inalienable characteristics tend to produce high levels of waste, high levels of impoverishment, poor wellness levels, and low demand (and therefore supply) for preventive and primary care combined with high demand (and therefore supply) of hospital-based care. Based on experience of most countries, the only way to address the issue of variability is to ensure that health expenditures are pooled, and directed in a deliberate and forceful way to address the other two issues (gaps in understanding and distorted perceptions/behaviours). The challenge that most health system designers grapple with is how best to accomplish these goals given the realities that they find on the ground.

Trajectory

For most Indian states, the best possible 'natural' (default) end state is potentially likely to be the one in which the state of Kerala finds itself. While Kerala has had success in addressing the infant and maternal health challenges, it is not clear that it has an overall robust health system.[9] This likely best possible 'natural' (default) end state is very different from desired end state for healthcare systems— overall good health outcomes with reduced aggregate disease burden and low morbidity, no households falling into poverty because of health expenditures[10] and high level of patient satisfaction across key parameters.

Most countries have achieved the desired end state for healthcare through multiple pathways based on their social, economic and healthcare legacy context. India will have to work towards its own pathway given the local realities, and this will most likely vary across states. Health systems in states such as Bihar and Uttar Pradesh will need to accelerate their progress on their infant and maternal death rates, and all states, including Kerala, will need to alter their direction to increase the likelihood of the desired end state being realized. This will need work across multiple health subsystems.

In the following paragraphs, as an illustration, we discuss in some detail, one subsystem of healthcare financing and explore possible pathways for reform.

Healthcare Financing: Levers for Change

At its most basic, the health financing subsystem may further be subdivided into three categories of health expenditures, which would include expenditures which are:

- High-cost, low-frequency
- Low-cost, high-frequency
- Unnecessary or wasteful

Currently, these expenditures are largely[11] being financed by the government, by the people themselves, or may even not be incurred because they are out of reach for most people as care is simply not available nearby or it is unaffordable.

High-Cost, Low-Frequency Expenditures

High-cost, low-frequency expenditures on issues such as cancer, c-sections and bypass surgery, are the result of the inherent variability associated with health status of all human beings. The only way to manage the variability is by pooling small contributions from each individual and making the pool available to pay for these expenditures. Dealing with the variability through pooling is critical to protect households from financial risks associated with severe health shocks.[12] It also protects households from the financial barriers of upfront fees at the point of seeking care.

Pooling can be accomplished either by the government exercising some form of mandate such as income tax and compulsory health-related contributions, or by allowing people to voluntarily purchase some form of insurance. Most countries are a mix of all three mechanisms of pooling. Historically, India has not been able to apply these levers, with out-of-pocket health expenditures continuing to be greater than 60 per cent of total health expenditure over the last 20 years. Below, we explore the three mechanisms and opportunities they present for India.

Tax financed pooling as the dominant source is common in many countries e.g. UK, Spain, Canada. In the Indian context, a continuing low-tax-to-GDP ratio at 16.6 per cent[13] (gravitational force); and low willingness of central and state governments to allocate a higher proportion from their tax pools for healthcare[14] (atomic force) currently makes it impossible to achieve all the necessary pooling through taxation alone. The low-tax-to-GDP ratio has a diffused causality and will change only very slowly. For the second aspect (tax allocation to healthcare), while also hard to change, a sufficiently powerful reformer could find a way to break through the political reluctance as those who were driving Mahatma Gandhi National Rural Employment Guarantee Act (MGNREGA) and Food Security Act were able to do. While this will not fully address the challenge of pooling, it could go a long way in addressing many health system challenges.

While it is important to reduce out-of-pocket health spending and increase pooling, it is also important to use the pooled funds effectively. The small, fragmented and underfunded government health insurance schemes which represent between 0.01 per cent to 0.02 per cent of the GDP of any state, unsurprisingly, have not had any discernable impact on the extent of out-of-pocket expenditure or level of impoverishment, and at this level of funding, nor are they likely to in the future. However, these schemes, despite their low level of funding, could be offered to every citizen of the state, even with a minimal tertiary-care-focused basic benefits package, like the Tamil Nadu KKT scheme,[15] with a strong health informatics strategy underpinning it, along with a wide range of top-up products available for purchase by those who can afford to pay. While most states in India have some schemes, both the effectiveness (and design) of the schemes as well as the coverage needs to be strengthened substantially. A well-functioning purchasing scheme would be the first step in engaging the entire population and all the providers in the mechanism of pooling and strategic purchasing with a focus on tracking quality and outcomes. This could be a magnetic force that has good political and popular support, and costs very little. It would be self-reinforcing through several feedback loops, and would include:

- The inclusion of standard protocols and pricing for every procedure that is determined by MTAB[16] and made visible to the entire population.
- The possibility of risk-based primary care[17] (being offered through public and privately run authorized health and wellness centres).
- As the confidence and familiarity of people with insurance grows, the (atomic) resistance to mandatory purchase of one or more comprehensive 'top-up' packages would reduce.
- Strong contracting and other mechanisms to drive accountability for providers, e.g. criteria for minimum and improving standards for quality and outcomes over time.
- Payment methods moving away from fee for service/line item budget to paying for output and outcome.
- The introduction of electronic health records and health management systems which allow tracking of both the patient's wellness as well as the provider's performance.

As the benefits of the provision of good and responsive government organized healthcare grows, the political attractiveness of allocating a higher proportion of resources to health would also grow, along with the willingness to pay taxes to pay for these services—creating a positive feedback loop. National Health Protection Mission (NHPM), under Ayushman Bharat, is a good platform to start building some of the features mentioned over time, and to eventually make them available to all citizens.

Many countries have mandated social health insurance as the dominant source of pooling, e.g. Germany, South Korea and Japan. Most countries with dominant social health insurance have expanded it through the formal sector by mandated employer and employee contribution. Collecting mandatory contributions from all individuals for healthcare is a strong atomic force which is very hard to change. Switzerland could get it done only after much national debate[18] and is now the norm in most countries but the United States (US) is still struggling to ensure this, despite having the enabling legislation in place.[19] The Employee State Insurance Scheme is already a long-established scheme in India—a mandated social health insurance which covers only 'blue-collar' workers and at 50 per cent payout (vs 85 per cent for Obamacare). It has one of the lowest payout ratio for such schemes globally, thus denying much of the benefit of the scheme to the very people who contribute to it. Improving the effective benefits of the scheme by implementing strategic purchasing from the private and public providers and subsequently expanding the coverage of ESI is another magnetic force that has the potential to alter the speed and direction of the entire health sector.

Due to the phenomena of distorted perception and behaviours; and gap in understanding that are common to all human beings, not many systems have been able to get a sufficiently large number of people to purchase health insurance voluntarily. India has a small but growing voluntary insurance market. Given the macro constraints in India (high levels of informality) which slow down the potential to provide healthcare coverage through taxation or social health insurance alone, it would be critical to leverage the capacity in the commercial insurance sector—to increase pooling. A strong regulatory framework is required to help develop the voluntary health insurance in the individual market (e.g. Obamacare support to individual health insurance market).

Low-Cost, High Frequency Expenditures

Low-cost, high-frequency expenditures are those that need to be undertaken for common illnesses that occur periodically or those for the prevention and early treatment of conditions such as chronic kidney disease, cervical cancer, pre-eclampsia, suicide mortality and damage due to glaucoma. These represent small expenditures that are affordable to most people but are often not incurred by individuals either because of the twin phenomena of distorted perception and behaviour, and a gap in understanding about what they need, or because of gaps in health services delivery or access to basic financial services. Changing these preferences of individuals, which are akin to a gravitational force, through improved health education could prove to be extremely difficult and time-consuming,[20] if not impossible. Delay in seeking care and diagnosis has also been found to be a key barrier to care and reduction of India's overall disease burden. For tuberculosis,[21] a study conducted in Mumbai found that the average delay in the first care-seeking for TB patients was 24 days, mostly due to the patient's assessments of their own symptoms.

Many successful health systems, with United Kingdom (UK) being an important example, have sought to address this issue through the tool of prepayment in which significant sums additional to those required for pooling to prevent catastrophic health expenditure, are made available to the health system to fully provide comprehensive primary care. The amounts for such care are small at an individual level, and have a highly beneficial impact on the health, well-being, and productivity of populations. However, given their frequency of consumption, in terms of total cost, it can amount to greater than 50 per cent of the total health expenditure.[22] Given the low level of public financing for health, this makes such prepayment strategies to support free and universal primary care unaffordable for most, if not all, state governments of India.

Even without resources available for a comprehensive primary care package, there are a number of magnetic forces that may be deployed which can alter the trajectory of the health system. Adding a highly targeted risk-based primary care[23] benefits package becomes possible on top of even a thinly financed Universal Health Insurance and Employee State Insurance Schemes, if there are strong electronic health records and analytics deployed on top of them.[24] As more money becomes available to the health system, these services can easily be expanded. However, in the interim, several targeted low-cost campaigns can be launched. China followed this approach by enrolling all population into a thin catastrophic coverage and then expanding the benefits to an outpatient package as more money became available.[25]

There is already a great deal of work in progress to expand access to basic financial services, and even airline access to remote airports,[26] but the same cannot be said for primary healthcare services. The country needs over 300,000 health-and-wellness-centres to provide comprehensive primary care of the type described earlier. The public sector may not have the financial and supervisory capacity to build and manage all the needed centres. The Ministry of Health and Family Welfare can use some of the financial resources and knowledge, borrowing ideas from the Ministry of Civil Aviation, to incentivize and support the creation of such centres by the private sector, in addition to those being built by the public sector. The Nikshay scheme of the Ministry of Health and Family Welfare for the management of tuberculosis, which provides access to free advanced diagnostics and TB medicines to registered private doctors,[27] offer some valuable lessons on how it may be possible to unleash this magnetic force in healthcare sector, by leveraging the vast private sector for overall population health outcomes.

However, even prepayment and pooling may not be sufficient to overcome patients' distorted perceptions. This may require gravitational forces of population awareness and behavioural nudges to mitigate the distorted preferences.

Unnecessary Expenditures

In high and low frequency expenditures, driven by gap in understanding, there is a considerable degree of wasted expenditure. Few examples are: The high consumption of cough syrups[28] across the entire country, the high c-section rates in states such as Kerala, even in the public sector, the large variation in prices charged by different providers for identical services, and the high concentration of hospitals in large cities while the smaller towns struggle to offer basic emergency care services.

Health systems around the world have grappled with this problem and all successful health systems even in highly advanced market-based economies such as Germany, Japan and Switzerland, have found a way to tightly regulate the prices (atomic force), volume and the nature of all health services offered. In India, such a change, while entirely feasible, particularly given our shared history of 'command and control' and the 'license-permit-raj', would be hard to implement—given the atomic nature of the forces arrayed against such a move.

Within India, the creation of the MTAB, a powerful feedback loop, within the Directorate of Health Research[29] and the gradual adoption of its guidelines by Insurance Regulatory and Development Authority (IRDAI), Employees' State Insurance Scheme (ESIS), National Health Protection Mission (NHPM) and state schemes could start to exert a magnetic influence on the trajectory of the entire health system on this dimension. While this is not easy to do, public sectors in states such as Kerala and Tamil Nadu have been able to set reasonable price-quality benchmarks that are exerting a degree of beneficial influence on the entire private sector.

A strong information technology (IT) system, coupled with a strong purchaser can be a magnetic force in preventing unnecessary care and managing utilization. Taiwan[30] has used its National Health Insurance powerful IT to provide near real-time information on expenditures and utilization to prevent unnecessary expenditure. There is also a panel review system of medical records to keep healthcare costs down, whilst maintaining the quality of healthcare.

As we look at the healthcare system in India, the problems may seem insurmountable, complex and intractable. The general tendency is to focus on the atomic and gravitational forces which either take too long or face enormous resistance—so the system seems 'stuck'. Identifying a few magnetic forces may provide a near-term path forward close to the desired state. These magnetic forces are often not obvious, however, a careful study of the key subsystems, feedback loops, flows and boundaries may reveal them. It is critical to build institutional capacity for careful research on health systems to identify the various forces, to monitor and evaluate impact of any action, and to provide an empirical feedback loop to its design.

◆

Nachiket Mor, PhD, is an economist. Amrita Agarwal, MBA, is a specialist in Health Systems Design. Both work with the India Country Office of the Bill & Melinda Gates Foundation, but the views expressed here are strictly personal.

Endnotes

1. While the System Dynamics was born at MIT Sloan in the 1950s and developed by Prof. Emeritus Jay W. Forrester, this article lays down a practitioner's perspective of change levers in a dynamic adaptive system.
2. Desired goals of a good health system is good health outcomes, equity, financial protection and responsiveness as described by Roberts, Reich, Berman and Hsiao, https://global.oup.com/academic/product/getting-health-reform-right-9780195371505?cc=in&lang=en&
3. http://www.thehindu.com/todays-paper/tp-opinion/framing-the-right-prescription/article17547852.ece
4. https://www.brookings.edu/events/book-launch-india-transformed-25-years-of-economic-reforms/
5. http://www.wpro.who.int/health_services/health_systems_framework/en/
6. As described by Arrow, Dixon and Hsiao, https://web.stanford.edu/~jay/health_class/Readings/Lecture01/arrow.pdf
7. http://papers.ssrn.com/sol3/papers.cfm?abstract_id=2649347
8. http://www.telegraph.co.uk/news/health/10501959/Half-of-GPs-dont-refer-cancer-patients-urgently-first-league-tables-show.html
9. Kerala is at an adequate level of total health expenditure (6.5 per cent of GSDP), low infant and maternal death rates driven by social determinants of health and a largely private healthcare service delivery architecture; c-section rates in excess of 30 per cent in both the public and private sectors; a very high burden of suicide mortality, mental illness, blood pressure, cholesterol and diabetes; and over 85 per cent of expenditure being incurred by patients when they seek care, from their own pockets, source: HMIS, http://www.thehindu.com/news/national/kerala/kerala-achieves-single-digit-imr/article17388542.ece
10. In China, 42 per cent of those falling into poverty are because of health expenditure, source: Based on survey done by The State Council Leading Group Office of Poverty Alleviation and Development in 2015, China.

11. Employer contributions to health through CHGS, ESIS and voluntary insurance is a small share (less than 5 per cent) of the overall healthcare expenditure of the country.
12. http://www.thelancet.com/journals/lancet/article/PIIS0140-6736(10)61894-6/abstract
13. India tax to GDP ratio in 2015–16 was less than 10 per cent; most developed countries are at tax to GDP ratio of 30 per cent, http://indiabudget.nic.in/es2015-16/echapvol1-07.pdf; https://ourworldindata.org/taxation/
14. Central budget allocation to health is ~3.8 per cent, most state budget allocation to health is less than 5 per cent; other countries typically allocate 8–10 per cent of budget to healthcare.
15. https://www.cmchistn.com/
16. A Health Technology Assessment (HTA) body, being set up within Department of Health Research (DHR) in India, http://www.dhr.gov.in/mtab
17. Simple algorithms (e.g. Cambridge Risk Score; https://www.ncbi.nlm.nih.gov/pubmed/18515811) could be developed to identify people at high risk for hypertension, diabetes and many other lifestyle diseases and could be targeted with primary care benefits package.
18. https://www.eda.admin.ch/missions/mission-onu-geneve/en/home/manual-regime-privileges-and-immunities/introduction/manual-insurance/manual-insurance.html
19. https://www.healthcare.gov/fees/fee-for-not-being-covered/
20. https://academic.oup.com/ije/article/30/2/201/713761/Exporting-failure-Coronary-heart-disease-and
21. http://journals.plos.org/plosone/article?id=10.1371/journal.pone.0152287
22. http://planningcommission.nic.in/reports/genrep/rep_uhc0812.pdf, pages 18, 108
23. Simple algorithms (e.g. Cambridge Risk Score, https://www.ncbi.nlm.nih.gov/pubmed/18515811) could be developed to identify people at high risk for hypertension, diabetes and many other lifestyle diseases requiring primary care and then could be targeted with primary care benefits package.
24. https://academic.oup.com/fampra/article-lookup/doi/10.1093/fampra/cmn024
25. Liang L. and Langenbrunner J., World Bank UNICO series, 2013,

Washington DC.
26. http://www.pmindia.gov.in/en/news_updates/pm-launches-udan-regional-connectivity-scheme-for-civil-aviation-from-shimla/
27. http://pib.nic.in/newsite/PrintRelease.aspx?relid=159932
28. http://timesofindia.indiatimes.com/business/india-business/Cough-and-cold-drugs-still-bestsellers/articleshow/4067309.cms
29. http://www.dhr.gov.in/mtab
30. https://www.ncbi.nlm.nih.gov/pmc/articles/PMC3960712/

From Demographic Disaster to Dividend: Transforming Higher Education with EdTech

Pramath Raj Sinha

Higher education (HE) is a critical building block for national growth, social harmony and economic progress for any country. India's higher education can transform India's demographic potential into a productive force for development.

However, the challenge we face to get this right is daunting. The numbers tell a grim story. Even today, the Gross Enrolment Ratio (GER), an important metric to judge level of access, is just 24 per cent for the 18–23 age group.[1] This includes distance education students. In most advanced countries, the ratio is close to 50 per cent. Clearly, HE in India needs urgent and massive intervention.

GER is the starting point for evaluating progress in HE, but it is a limited, insufficient marker. It stops at enrolment and does not examine learning outcomes. 'Quality GER' would actually be far lower, although, unlike in primary education, there are no such standardized benchmarks for HE.

In India, neither quantity nor quality is likely to improve significantly anytime soon, considering the poor investments in education. At around 4 per cent of GDP, India's expenditure on education lags behind that of comparable economies, which typically spend at least 6 per cent of their GDP on education. Things are worse in HE, as it gets only a fraction of the overall budgetary allocation on education.[2]

For example, China spent nearly $565 billion on education in 2016, more than 60 per cent of which was government spending. Out of this, nearly $145 billion was spent on HE.[3] By contrast, the government of India spent a mere $12.5 billion on the education sector, of which about $4.5 billion was allocated for HE.[4] Even when investments are made, regulatory friction and philosophy are perennial obstacles for our HE sector.

The Stark Reality of HE

A quarter of a century after economic liberalization, the harsh truth is that HE, much like healthcare, remains trapped in unwieldy and unprogressive state control. Seventy years after Independence, we are still struggling with the right-fit regulation for our brick-and-mortar universities, particularly with regard to private players, without whom we cannot hope to make tangible progress.

The current regulatory framework begins with creating huge barriers to entry. We can fool ourselves into believing that this ensures quality; that it keeps fly-by-night operators away. Unfortunately, that is not true. The Licence Raj is very much alive and kicking in Indian HE. In fact, current regulation has created a vicious cycle. Genuine philanthropic players are scared to enter and commercial profiteers— in the garb of non-profits—who can work the system, make hay.

Private HE evokes two fears: First, it is expensive and that 'investors' will fleece students. This sentiment guides our regulation. The second justified concern is that private HE is, by definition, poor quality.

Recently, some smart thinking at the higher-quality end led to the '10+10' policy to free up ten public and private institutions from restrictive regulatory control and create 'Institutions of Eminence'.[5] This is not a new idea: China's C9 League and Russia's Project 5-100 (5top100.com) are similar and are making waves globally.

Although we must actively encourage not-for-profit philanthropic investment in HE, and improve the regulatory mechanism that governs and monitors such institutions; even the most concerted expansion and investments in this model won't suffice.

To move towards our objective of significantly raising our 'Quality GER' with any seriousness, we cannot afford to depend on traditional models of HE, mainly, large physical campuses.

Here is what is ahead of us. With more than 1.5 million schools and more than 250 million students enrolled in them, India's school system is one of the largest in the world.[6] In HE, we have the second largest student population in the world with nearly 34 million students enrolled across more than 789 universities and nearly 38,000 colleges.[7]

The nation is expected to add almost 10–12 million people to its workforce every year over the next two decades, with the working-age population crossing the 1 billion mark by 2030,[8] surpassing even China and becoming the world's largest working-age population. How can our HE system respond and prepare to skill, reskill and upskill this massive cadre?

If traditional models and methods do not work for this unprecedented problem, is there a radically different approach to education and learning that can help Indian youth achieve their aspirations, and live to their full potential? If not, our much-vaunted demographic dividend of the world's youngest population all the way to year 2050 is going to turn into a serious demographic disaster.

Can we come up with a scalable and sustainable model that enables every young Indian to get an affordable and high-quality education that leads to a tangible outcome that matches their potential?

A New Vista

Much as India has had to 'leapfrog' on mobile Internet and device access, our education solutions will have to be disruptive, non-traditional and technology-enabled. The world is gradually becoming aware of the power of technology to enrich the world of education and making it more equitable, effective and efficient.

It is only scalable, customizable technology that can deliver affordable, sustained and high-quality education to the large numbers we need to educate and make employable in a short time. As everything is going online, so is education.

Education technology, or EdTech, is an emerging trend globally. Over the past few years, there have been several experiments in using technology at the school and college level to deliver academic curriculum, test preparation and remedial subject-specific content, especially in Maths, for example.

EdTech is also increasingly being used by companies and organizations across the world for job skills training and employee-focused learning development programmes.

Several worthy businesses and EdTech ventures such as The Khan Academy, Coursera and EdX have paved the way for much experimentation in this space. In India, companies such as Byju's, Simplilearn and UpGrad have made impressive beginnings. Personalized digital learning offered by Byju's has not only found a massive number of takers in India, but has also received support from global giants such as the Zuckerberg-Chan Initiative, a not-for-profit set up by Facebook founder Mark Zuckerberg and his wife Priscilla Chan to promote and invest in education.

According to a recent article by TechCrunch, the rise of a new education and learning world has begun; and that investment in EdTech is set to reach $252 billion globally by 2020.[9] They predict that EdTech is poised to be the 'biggest and possibly most profitable digitalised sector yet'.

Education experts and observers say some of the trends powering EdTech—and the subsequent impact they might have—are like other epochal shifts, such as the introduction of professional degrees, or linking college-leaving certificates to job opportunities.

India is even more uniquely poised to benefit from the advantages and the transformational impact of EdTech. These include:

1. **Scale:** EdTech helps us build a future-ready education system with its ability for massive scale.

If our imagined future is a GER (which takes into account all enrolled students between the ages of 18–23 in higher education) closer to 50 per cent, we are looking at more than doubling the 34 million number of Indian students in higher education.

EdTech is the only way to reach this huge universe of students. It is estimated that about a billion people globally are now benefitting from EdTech. Massive Online Open Courses (MOOCs), a course of study made available over the Internet without charge to a very large number of people, has added great texture to our learning ecosystems. It has begun the process of making even pedigreed, elite education more accessible. Top universities across the world have participated in the MOOC movement and have made their faculty and content available to students online, for little or no cost.

This momentum is evident in India too. For both Coursera and Udacity, popular online learning platforms, India is the second largest market outside the United States. A recent KPMG report found that there has been a fourfold growth in education content consumption on YouTube in India. Online searches for education have doubled over the past two years; and there has been a threefold increase in education-related searches from mobile devices. Interestingly, 44 per cent of education searches are now coming from beyond the top six metros.

Currently, India is the second largest e-learning market in the world after the US. The size of India's e-learning market was $247 million, comprising 1.6 million users in 2016. The market size is set to grow eightfold to a $1.96 billion and the user base will grow by six times to 9.6 million by 2021.[10]

The uptick in Internet penetration and increased access to smartphones will create greater opportunities and build on this momentum. Today, there are nearly 400 million Internet users in India, which is expected to rise to 850 million by

2025. Smartphones are accelerating the advantages of the reach of the Internet in India. By 2021, we are estimated to add 180 million new users to the current smartphone user base of 290 million.[11]

2. **Affordability:** For students, one of the largest barriers to education is cost. Quality HE, in particular, can be expensive and difficult for many to afford. Often, the high cost doesn't lead to employment opportunities with justifiable returns. In many countries, student debt is a mounting problem. EdTech can help relieve some of the financial burden.

   The scale advantage leads to affordable 'price points' and tuition fees. Online courses are often a fraction of the cost of traditional programmes, mainly since a lot of infrastructure-related costs incurred in delivering education are bypassed here. Reduced costs and lower fees can act as a great motivator for people to explore EdTech solutions. Many of the existing platforms are based on what is referred to as a 'freemium' model, whereby basic services are provided free of charge while more advanced features must be paid for. This enables a student to experience online learning before committing more spends.

3. **Technology:** Over the past few years, EdTech platforms have matured and evolved significantly. New ventures have moved beyond the turn-of-the-century offerings of audiovisual to try and deploy virtual reality, augmented reality, artificial intelligence (AI) and several interactive technologies to make the learning experience more immersive and tangible. The new technology in the field takes into account the 'science of learning' (combination of psychology, cognitive science and other disciplines) as well as 'machine learning' (letting computers learn about the students using them by studying the data produced in the process).

   Today's EdTech efforts are being built with technologies that are more tested, intuitive and advanced. No longer does technology mean mere access to the Internet or the presence of a computer in the room.

4. **Quality:** Advancing technology to make interactivity more real and the added benefit of student analysis, by way of key business intelligence features that many EdTech platforms now offer, gives way to better quality of education.

   Think of a typical university classroom and a typical teacher. There is no way a teacher can standardize her own teaching to a baseline—batch after batch. On any given day, the quality can differ from the day before, month before or year before. That is why learning outcomes in physical classrooms are variable.

   With EdTech, it is safe to assume that quality can be *relatively better* or *much better* than what is out there. Online education helps minimize and control the variables. To begin with, everyone has access to the best teachers and the best content they have to offer. Let us take an example from the way the world of music was transformed: Long-play records made the best singers accessible to a larger base of music enthusiasts.

   It is important we articulate this quality boon effectively— to students, employers, education providers. There is a perception that EdTech-enabled programmes, much like distance learning courses and vocational education, are cheap and low-quality alternatives to traditional HE.

5. **Mass customization:** The 'factory model' of old classrooms in traditional universities, where students learn the same thing from the same teacher in the same way, isn't intuitive or useful. There is no way a teacher in a classroom can effectively adapt their speed, curriculum and rigour to each student in the class.

   The digital classroom can be a more vibrant place. The twin promise of EdTech is the possibility it offers for individual learning—at scale. It can foster mass customization and personalization.

At once, it can offer the best curriculum on a subject, designed and delivered by a talented faculty and have it accessible to any student, anywhere—at the pace, time and level at which they need it. It has, therefore, a huge upper hand on traditional education providers.

Adaptive learning makes the customization and personalization possible. First developed in the 1970s, adaptive learning is a computer-based online educational system that modifies the presentation of material in response to student performance. Essentially, it refers to the individual, in-the-moment learning experiences that are deeply personalized for every type of student to provide the right next lesson, at the right level of difficulty, at the right time. It enables the seamless integration of instruction and assessment before, during, and after each lesson. It converts group instruction into personal tuition.

6. **Flexibility and choice:** A key trend in EdTech now is competency-based education or what is also known as 'unbundling' of education. In competency-based education, students aren't trained on subjects/topics within a programme, but are rather enrolled to learn and build skills on competencies and skills, say, for example, in critical thinking, cash flow management or marketing analytics.

At its core, unbundling means breaking down education into bite-sized modules that are accessible to people as and when they need them. Think of old-world textbooks or standard degrees being replaced by a convenient 'playlist' of learning modules that is unique to each person and is selected and lined up by them.

A future-ready, well-designed EdTech venture will marry this ability to the growing suite of assessment tools and technologies that can benchmark students on functional ability, aptitude and psychometric characteristics. Students can build their individual playlists on the basis of the results gleaned from their assessments and the need-gap areas they are able to identify.

The competency-based approach disrupts the 'bundling' of traditional degrees into three/four-year programmes. With unbundling, students have much greater autonomy in enhancing their chosen competencies. They have the clear advantage of widening their course options; and deciding the subjects and competencies they want to learn, at a time and pace that is convenient for them. For example, they can learn while they earn.

The huge range of competencies available, the sequence in which they can be learnt, and the individual pace at which learning happens builds on the possibility of customization.

7. **Lifelong learning:** At its ideal, unbundling encourages constant learning and relearning. It makes it easier to be a continuous learner. This is a crucial advantage in a world economy where industries are being rapidly disrupted, some job roles are becoming extinct and there is a high premium for agile professionals who can learn new contexts quickly. The ability to be a lifelong learner is going to be an important attribute for a successful twenty-first-century professional. The era of guaranteed lifelong employment after a one-time college or professional degree at the age of 24 is on its way out. Continuous, continued learning, and the pace at which one can learn new skills, will become more significant predictors of success than a college degree.

Unleashing the Real Potential: Role of Government Policy

Despite the many inherent advantages, EdTech isn't a solved problem yet anywhere in the world. The reality is that most contemporary initiatives in this segment, and the successful business ventures that have spun off them, supplement existing programmes and curriculums. Some do go beyond merely e-enabling the current learning infrastructure by adding analytics and other features, but none of them yet substitute or transplant the dominant learning model of the physical classroom.

For EdTech to be a truly transformative agent in HE, and in primary education in India, it will need to transcend beyond being a supplementary force for existing learning systems. It will have to help us build backwards from the future.

How can government policy and thinking accelerate this objective? Can India take the lead on crafting an ambitious but pragmatic policy for online education? Most online education ventures operate in a regulatory vacuum. They are more 'companies' than education providers. Can, or should, government policy lay out guidelines and national objectives? As private players innovate on curriculum, academic delivery and learning outcomes, what innovative thinking can the government bring to EdTech policy that will enable and urge its development into a high quality, scale option? Can such a policy balance the dual objectives that confront education administrators and national governments everywhere: Excellence, on one hand, and increased access, on the other? How can such a policy encourage and incentivize adoption; yet leave private players to establish business models that are built on the market forces of win-win? How can government policy evangelize the benefits of a good-quality digital education, and create awareness around it?

The Government of India recognizes the potential and is attempting to understand the possibilities of EdTech. Swayam, the government's digital learning platform, is a worthy experiment to this end. Swayam offers personalized online education for each learner. It has an expansive array of courses; and the government hopes that the platform will be a crucial amplifier of the cardinal principles of its education policy: Access, equity and quality. The platform has already digitized courses from several leading institutions, such as the Indian Institute of Technology (IIT) at Bombay, Madras, Kanpur, Delhi and Guwahati; and Jawaharlal Nehru University (JNU), amongst others.

Swayam was launched in July 2017 so it is still too early to examine its full impact. Although many observers say that the government doesn't have the building blocks to really make it a ubiquitous learning environment for India's youth, there is no doubt it is an important and ambitious initiative.

In EdTech, local context (languages, industry focus and marketable skills) plays a hugely important role in determining the right solution. There is no global adaptive learning software that can compete with a worldwide solution to education. Since languages, curriculums and pedagogies differ significantly, EdTech has to adapt to every country's specific context and objectives.

India can build case studies and examples—whether Swayam or Byju's—that other countries can be inspired by and learn from.

We have no choice but to adopt EdTech at scale. It provides us the potential to take our challenge and convert it into an opportunity. Let us approach doing so with rigour, ambition and determination, if we want to transform our formidable human capital. India can become a leader of EdTech in the world, and build an HE system that will be a benchmark for the future.

◆

Dr Pramath Raj Sinha has been associated with the founding of some of India's leading private, philanthropic HE institutions including the Indian School of Business (ISB) and Ashoka University.

He would like to acknowledge the contributions of Shashiprabha Gupta and Shreyasi Singh.

Endnotes

1. http://timesofindia.indiatimes.com/india/share-of-spend-in-government-expenditure-gdp-on-education-falling-for-3-years/articleshow/56991039.cms
2. http://www.livemint.com/Education/tj0GgGojuEbwLN1SCc8eSJ/Indias-education-spending-needs-a-course-on-accountability.html
3. http://www.chinadaily.com.cn/china/2017-05/04/content_29203196.htm
4. http://www.livemint.com/Politics/hkjZw2CFY9u4xGHDk6QftN/Union-budget-2017-Education-outlay-increases-99-to-Rs796.html

5. http://www.hindustantimes.com/education/20-world-class-research-varsities-to-be-called-indian-institutes-of-eminence-will-come-up-soon-javadekar/story-7yRZL7neWCVhjQtTmYjphL.html
6. http://www.deccanherald.com/content/600213/overcoming-challenges-education-sector.html
7. http://www.indiaeducation.net/universities/
8. https://www.pwc.in/assets/pdfs/future-of-india/future-of-india-the-winning-leap.pdf
9. https://techcrunch.com/2016/08/13/edtech-is-the-next-fintech/
10. https://home.kpmg.com/in/en/home/insights/2017/05/internet-online-education-india.html
11. https://home.kpmg.com/in/en/home/insights/2017/05/internet-online-education-india.html

Innovative Public Procurement Policy for Fuelling ASSURED Inclusive Innovation

R.A. Mashelkar

Rising inequality is one of the greatest challenges of our time. Income inequalities, for instance, create access (education, health, public services) inequalities. This leads to social disharmony. However, reducing income inequalities takes generations. Can we create access equality despite income inequality? The answer is yes, we can.

To illustrate the point, here are some simple specific questions:

- Can we make a high-quality Hepatitis-B vaccine priced at $20 per dose available at a price that is 40 times less, not just 40 per cent?
- Can we make a high-quality artificial foot priced at $10,000 available at a price that is 300 times less, not just 30 per cent?
- Can we make a high-quality cataract eye surgery, costing $3,000, available at a price that is 100 times less, not just 100 per cent?
- Can we make a $10,000 ECG machine available at a price that is 20 times lower, and not just 20 per cent?

Incredible as it may sound, all these impossible sounding four feats have been achieved by Indian innovators—Shantha Biotechnics,[1] Jaipur Foot,[2] Aravind Eye Care[3] and Indian engineers in GE Healthcare in Bangalore[4] respectively.

All the above are ASSURED inclusive innovations, which stands for:

A (Affordable)
S (Scalable)
S (Sustainable)
U (Universal)
R (Rapid)
E (Excellent)
D (Distinctive)

Why ASSURED?

A (Affordability) is required to create access for everyone across the economic pyramid, especially the bottom. S (Scalability) is required to make real impact by reaching out to every individual in society, and not just a privileged few. S (Sustainability) is required in many contexts; environmental, economic and societal. U (Universal) implies user-friendliness, so that the innovation can be used irrespective of the skill levels of an individual citizen. R (Rapid) means speed. Acceleration in inclusive growth cannot be achieved without speed of action matching speed of innovative thoughts. E (Excellence) in technology, product quality, and service quality is required for everyone in society, since rising aspirations of resource-poor people have to be fulfilled. D (Distinctive) is required, since one does not want to promote copycat, 'me too' products and services. In fact, we should raise our ambitions and make D (Disruptive)', which will be truly game-changing, as shown in examples below.

Indian innovators have the ability to move from low performance, cheap knock-off versions of technologies in developed nations to harnessing sophisticated technological or non-technological innovations to produce affordable quality goods and services. The inevitability of such a strategic shift has been highlighted in a number of recent scholarly contributions.[5-9]

Recent Game-Changing ASSURED Inclusive Innovations

In recent times, India has witnessed two game-changing ASSURED inclusive innovations—the government-led JAM combining J (Pradhan Mantri Jan Dhan Yojna), A (Aaadhar identification and authentication) and M (mobile telecommunications)[10] and the other was private sector-led, namely Jio.[11]

JAM, with all the seven elements of ASSURED, created the fastest and largest financial inclusion in the world, with 300-million-plus bank accounts opening up in record time.

Reliance Jio[11] catapulted India from the 155th rank in mobile data transmission globally to the current number one position. More importantly, Jio moved India from missed call to video call—a shift from jugaad to systematic innovation.

Challenge in Creating ASSURED Indian Inclusive Innovation

India could have been the birthplace of many game-changing ASSURED inclusive innovations, but for the fact that some letters, pertaining to speed, scale and sustainability went missing from ASSURED.

As an illustration, let us take the case of Simputer, a product of Indian innovation launched by the Simputer Trust on 25 April, 2001, which was designed to be a low cost and portable alternative to PCs.[12] The idea was to create shared devices that permit truly simple and natural user interfaces based on sight, touch and audio. The Simputer was to read and speak in several Indian languages in its initial release.

The innovation was hailed for its 'radical simplicity for universal access'. Before the arrival of the smartphone in 2003, Simputer had anticipated some breakthrough technologies that are now commonplace in mobile devices. One of them was the accelerometer, introduced to the rest of the world for the first time in the iPhone. The other was doodle on mail, the ability to write on a phone, that became a major feature on Samsung Galaxy phones.

According to Bruce Sterling,[13] 'the most significant innovation in computer technology in 2001 was not Apple's gleaming titanium Powerbook G4 or Microsoft's Windows XP. It was the Simputer, a net-linked, radically simple portable computer, intended to bring the computer revolution to the third world...'

Despite having the key letters from ASSURED representing Affordable, Excellence, Universal (user-friendly) and Distinctive, what went missing was Rapid (speed), Scale and Sustainability! Why? No innovation-friendly public procurement policy despite many rural specific demonstrations.

Yet another bus in the same space was missed five years later.

New Millennium Indian Technology Leadership Initiative (NMITLI)-led Products

At a national level, in 2000, CSIR conceived and operationalized the New Millennium Indian Technology Leadership Initiative (NMITLI), which was based on the idea of competitive bids based on national grand challenges.[14] It was a bold public–private partnership (PPP) (India's largest so far) with the private sector getting very low interest loans (to be returned only if successful) and the public sector getting grants. The best brains in India worked together in a 'Team India' fashion.

NMITLI gave several grand challenges in the year 2000 aligned with many critical national needs. For instance, when the cost of a laptop was $2000, NMITLI gave a challenge of making it ten times cheaper, around $200. After inviting competitive bids, Vinay Deshpande from Encore in Bangalore won the bid. Mobilis, a mobile PC was launched in March 2005, meeting the price-performance demand set.

NMITLI was to focus only on the proof of concept. However, it went an extra mile to help doing the initial prototyping. Today, an improved version of Mobilis is being sold in rather limited numbers as DSK Mobiliz,[15] which is an indigenous, affordable, high performance, solar-powered mobile computer. An innovative public procurement policy in 2005 would have helped it scale rapidly, giving India a global leadership.

Public procurement in India in general has a tendency to opt for lowest cost (L_1) and low-risk solutions, low-margin players and mature technology. Innovation is not routinely welcomed or rewarded. In part, this is due to the competing objectives and bureaucratic barriers that public procurers face, which discourage risk-taking.

We must move away from this and create a bold, transparent and innovative public procurement policy for fuelling ASSURED inclusive innovation.

Fundamentals of Designing an Innovative Public Procurement Policy

Innovations are products of creative interaction of supply and demand. India has incentivized supply through creation of numerous national research and technology organizations that it funds. It has created schemes for part financing 'technology-led businesses'. Examples include NMITLI, Biotechnology Industrial Research Assistance Council,[16] Technology Development Board,[17] etc. Various financial incentives, such as weighted tax deductions have also been given to spur industry-led supply of R&D.

We also need aggressive demand side initiatives. With large procurement budgets, the Indian government can not only be the biggest, but also the most influential and demanding customer.

The government approach could be based on three pillars.

First, government could act as the 'first buyer' and an 'early user' for small, innovative firms and manage the consequent risk, thus providing the initial revenue and customer feedback they need to survive and refine their products and services so that they can later compete effectively in the global marketplace. (Interestingly, based on a survey of 1,100 innovative firms in Germany, it was found that public procurement is especially effective for smaller firms in regions under economic stress—a helpful lesson for India.)

Second, government can set up regulations that can successfully drive innovation either indirectly through altering market structure and affecting the funds available for investment, or directly through boosting or limiting demand for particular products and services.

Third, government can set standards that can create market power by generating demand for innovation. Agreed standards will ensure that the risk taken by both early adopters and innovators is lower, thus increasing investment in innovation. The standards should be set at a demanding level of functionality without specifying which solution must be followed. By not prescribing a specific route, innovation is bound to flourish.

International Experience

Many nations have set up innovative public procurement policies for boosting global competitiveness. China has set up truly aggressive policies. OECD members have also taken a big lead. Based on best practices in OECD and in partner countries, OECD recently published a report in June 2017, titled, 'Public Procurement for Innovation: Good Practices & Strategies.'[18]

Almost 80 per cent of OECD members are reported to have taken measures to support innovation procurement while 50 per cent have developed an action plan for the same.

More than a third of European companies have sold an innovative product or service as part of a public procurement contract they won since 2011.[19] More specifically, Germany[20] has created a new Agreement on Public Procurement of Innovation by which six federal ministries (interior, economics, defence, transport, environment and research) will promote innovative procurement.

Roadmap for Creating Innovative Public Procurement Policy

However, context defines the content. Indian policies will have to be based on the dynamically changing Indian context.

The following ten-point action agenda is suggested.

  1. India has progressed from a science policy resolution

(1957) to Technology Policy Statement (1983) to Science & Technology Policy (2003) to Science, Technology & Innovation Policy (2013). It is time that India@70 sets up a fully integrated National Innovation Policy; integrated, since beyond technology innovation, non-technological innovations such as social, business model, workflow, system delivery, process and policy innovations play a critical role. The policy should be such that it should propel India@75 to be among the very top innovative nations.

2. In this integrated innovation policy, inclusive innovation for accelerated inclusive growth would be a major thrust. In this agenda, affordable excellence should be an important subset with well-defined, affordable, price-high performance for public services in health, education, energy, housing and water.

3. An important component of the National Innovation Policy should be innovation-oriented public procurement policy, which should be 'for' innovation as well as 'of' innovation, thus catalyzing both the demand and supply side of the innovation equation. Public procurement of innovative goods and services can induce innovation by specifying levels of performance or functionality that are not achievable with 'off-the-shelf' products, because such exacting demand can be only met by innovation.

4. The policy (3) above should be based on the three pillars of talent, technology and trust. Transparency is a prerequisite to trust. To achieve this, a legal framework will have to be designed, which should include easily understandable definitions, guidelines and templates based on the ASSURED principles highlighted earlier. This will facilitate smooth and speedy implementation.

5. All the ministries should be mandated to publish long-term demand forecasts, engage in continuous market analysis to identify potential breakthrough solutions, offer professional

training on legal options to promote innovation, and foster a strategic dialogue and exchange of experiences between procuring agencies, end users, industry, and procurement agencies.

6. Procurement agencies from ministries should be given specific targets for innovation procurement. Provision of annual budgets, dedicated funds and stimulating financial incentives, especially for PPPs, will have to be a key part of the execution plan.

7. For speedy implementation, an 'Innovation Procurement Platform' as an online hub should be created. It will help procurers, policymakers, government authorities, innovators, and other stakeholders to fully utilize the power of public procurement of innovation. The platform could comprise a website, a procurement forum and a knowledge resource centre. The procurement forum should provide a space for procurers and related stakeholders to share, connect and interact. The resource centre should have central databases and all documents relating to public procurement policy of and for innovation.

8. Major investments will have to be made in capacity-building by way of specific training to build staff capabilities and skills, setting up multidisciplinary teams and competence centres, raising awareness by hosting workshops and seminars.

9. To reduce possible loss and damage, robust risk management and impact measurement systems will have to be put in place. Powerful e-procurement and IT tools should be used to carry out proper risk assessment.

10. Standardization should be used as a catalyst for innovation with full consultation with Indian industry. One should define the test standards, methods and the process for giving quality certificates.

Execution of Innovation-friendly Public Procurement Policy

Supply-led approach

The Prime Minister's inspiring clarion calls on 'Startup India' and 'Standup India' have stirred the nation. The government has also provided a number of remarkable incentives for start-ups. Of these, the relaxation of public procurement norms for start-ups heralds a great beginning.

But for fuelling ASSURED inclusive innovation, we need to identify start-ups that have game-changing ideas based on the solid foundation of affordable excellence.

Just as an illustration, we present here two start-ups that are the winners of the Anjani Mashelkar Inclusive Innovation Award.[21]

Mihir Shah's UE Life Sciences has developed[22] the non-invasive and painless iBreastExam, a simple, accurate and affordable palm-sized handheld device that is used for early detection of breast tumours, without mammography. The device is US FDA cleared and CE marked. It can be operated by any community health worker, and costs only ₹65 ($1) per scan!

Can we design a very simple and affordable portable ECG device, which allows the ECG to be seen by an expert from miles away?

This has been achieved by another awardee, Rahul Rastogi, who created[23] a portable matchbox size 12-lead ECG machine. The cost is just ₹5 (8 cents) per ECG test.

These are all innovations in the formal science/technology system. However, India has a huge reservoir of grassroots innovations, meaning innovations by the people and for the people. The potential of some of the select grassroots innovations, in partnership with formal science/technology institutions, can be brought to meet the ASSURED criteria too.

Demand-led approach

Within this, there could be two approaches. The first is to leverage the existing national portfolio of innovation and the second is to create new knowledge assets through grand challenges.

Consider the first approach. For instance, look at the outcome of a specific NMITLI based PPP, which has the capacity of giving India a leadership in fuel cells for electricity generation, thus dramatically reducing India's carbon footprint. This is a critical area, where technology is not available to India.

The NMITLI programme has led to successful demonstration of indigenously developed and extensively tested 1–3 kWe low-temperature Proton Exchange Membrane (PEM) fuel cell stacks. It has also led to the development of high-temperature PEM fuel cells, which are currently being scaled up to 5 kWe. Both technologies are based on successful translation of science resulting in 30-plus patent applications and 150 high-quality publications.

Most importantly, this programme has also led to the development of the entire ecosystem for PEM fuel cells comprising (a) SME vendors, who can manufacture the critical materials, components and sub-assemblies of the stacks such as the catalyst, membranes, gas diffusion layers and membrane electrode assemblies, (b) aggregators, who can assemble fuel cell systems comprising stack, balance of plant components, fuel generators, power electronics and control systems, and (c) industrial users of PEM fuel cell systems.

How can public procurement catalyze successful penetration of PEM fuel cells in Indian markets? While PEM fuel cells can be used in diverse areas such as stationary power generation, long-range electric vehicles, defence and industrial cogeneration, perhaps the first important market penetration can be in replacement of around 600,000 diesel generator sets that are presently installed with telecommunication towers to provide backup power. A PEM fuel cell provides reliable, efficient, quick start-up, low-noise and cleaner energy, as the exhaust from a fuel cell is water and not solid particulates as in diesel generators. The total cost of operation of a PEM fuel cell with an on-board compact methanol reformer to generate hydrogen is similar to that of diesel generator. It is estimated that if just 30 per cent of present towers shift to PEM fuel cells, there would be a need for 180,000 PEM fuel cell systems of 3–5 kWe rating for this one application alone resulting in the creation of 20,000 jobs in the SME sector.

A national policy[24] that incentivizes adoption of alternative power generation systems such as PEM fuel cells supported by large scale public procurement initiative can led to Indian leadership in this technology.

The second approach is to set new grand challenges aligned with critical Indian needs on the ASSURED principles enumerated earlier.

The Expert Committee set up by NITI Aayog has strongly advocated that Atal Innovation Mission (AIM) funds should be used to finance grand challenges.[25] We strongly support the identified grand challenges as also the proposed execution model.

Innovative public procurement policy for and of ASSURED inclusive innovation can greatly help India in achieving multiple objectives, including:

- **Social harmony:** It will help create equality of access despite income inequality.
- **Affordability:** It will lead to scale, thus bringing equity to large population.
- **Excellence:** On one hand, excellence will meet the rising aspirations of local populace for high-quality goods and services. On the other hand, it will open up opportunities for competitive exports to global markets.

In short, such a policy will help in creating a new India of our dreams, with a smile on the face of 1.25 billion Indians and not just a privileged few.

◆

Dr R.A. Mashelkar, National Research Professor, is the president of Global Research Alliance, a network of publicly funded R&D institutes from Asia-Pacific, Europe and USA with over 60,000 scientists.

Endnotes

1. Indian Vaccine Innovation: The Case of Shantha Biotechnics, http://www.researchgate.net

2. The Jaipur Foot, https://www.researchgate.net.

3. A Case study on Aravind Eye Care Systems—Aravind Eye Hospital, www.aravind.org.

4. Reverse Innovation at GE Healthcare, https://academilib.com

5. Prahalad, C.K. and Mashelkar, R.A., Innovation's Holy Grail, Harvard Business Review, July–August 2010.

6. Mashelkar, R.A., *Reinventing India*, Sahyadri Publications, 2011.

7. Mashelkar, R.A., 'Indovation' for affordable excellence', *Current Science*, Vol. 108, No. 1, pp 7–8, 10 January 2015.

8. Radjou Navi and Prabhu Jaideep, *Frugal Innovation: How to Do More with Less*, Profile Books Ltd, London, 2015.

9. Immelt, J.R.; Govinadrajan, V; and Trimble, C., 'How GE Is Disrupting Itself', *Harvard Business Review*, October 2009.

10. Jan Dhan 2.0, www.inspirit.in

11. 'Time to take digital innovations at grassroots level: Reliance Jio', *The Economic Times*, https://economictimes.indiatimes.com

12. The Simputer: Access Device for Masses, www.simputer.org.

13. Sterling, Bruce, 'The Year in Ideas', *The New York Times* Magazine, 9 December 2001.

14. Mashelkar, R.A., 'What will it take for Indian science, technology & innovation to make global impact', Vol. 109, pp 1021–42, 25 September 2015.

15. DSK Mobilitz, www.dskdigital.com

16. BIRAC, www.birac.nic.in

17. Technology Development Board, tdb.gov.in

18. http://www.keepeek.com/Digital-Asset/management/oecd/governance/public-procurement-for-innovation.

19. http://www.innovation-procurement.org/about-ppi/facts-figures/.

20. https://www.innovationpolicyplatform.org/content/public-procurement-innovation.

21. Anjani Mashelkar Inclusive Innovation Award, award.ilcindia.org

22. Crusco, Deanna, 'More from Less for More: One Company's Quest to Tackle Early Breast Cancer Detection in Developing Countries', Science Centre, 5 October 2017, infor@sciencecenter.org.

23. Agastsa: Sanket Life for All, www.agatsa.com.
24. http://www.trai.gov.in/sites/default/files/Consultation_Paper_16_jan_2017_0.pdf
25. Report of the Expert Committee on Innovation and Entrepreneurship, niti.gov.in

Diagnosing the Demographic
Dividend of Health

Shobana Kamineni

Health is intrinsic to the wealth of a nation; there is no exception to this rule. This powerful truth is best illustrated in the context of India's most prized asset—her people. India today is the envy of the world. While the developed world is aging, India is getting younger. By 2020, the average age of 65 per cent of our citizens will be just 29.

However, demographic dividend is not just about young people; it is about *healthy* young people.

Healthcare is a complex, multidimensional, multilayered challenge that includes not just provision of access to care centres and hospitals at different levels, but also the entire supply chain of medical education and generation of medical specialists, technicians and professionals as also diagnostic services, medical devices and equipment, pharmaceuticals and insurance. It involves special measures for addressing multiple diseases, both communicable and non-communicable, along with malnutrition, vector-borne diseases, and mental health. It addresses whole-life services from maternal and child health to geriatric care. The healthcare system must cater to different geographies across rural, urban and tribal areas, each with its own characteristics. The area of public health and preventive healthcare is an important and integral part of the sector, requiring a different set of infrastructure and competencies. Further, aspects of

R&D, digital technologies, and advances in medical equipment need to be also ensured in a holistic health sector to address and shape its future as a global leader.

I believe that the only way to holistically tackle these myriad facets of health is to think of healthcare through the prism of three 'moonshot' challenge statements—challenges that require the same single-minded focus, innovation, and mission approach that took India to the moon at the lowest cost in the world.

These challenges are:

Save over $50 billion every year in health costs.
Heal India and heal the world from India.
Create over one million jobs annually.

The Story of India's Healthcare

From a macro perspective, India seems to have the healthcare imperative heavily stacked against it. Our world health index ranking is abysmal—we were ranked 154th among 195 countries in the recent Healthcare Access and Quality Index brought out by *The Lancet*.[1] In non-communicable diseases (NCDs), we rank among top nations in incidence of cardiac illness, diabetes and cancers. In life expectancy, infant mortality, infectious diseases and access to healthcare, we might be so low so as to trigger a countrywide bout of depression!

But that is not the full story of India's healthcare. Sixty per cent of the world is cured by Indian-made pharma generics; the US and UK health systems depend significantly on doctors of Indian-origin, and nurses from India enjoy positions across the world. 'Our private healthcare serves 70 per cent of India with hospitals' outcomes comparable to the best institutions in the world. No Indian has to travel abroad for the best and the latest healthcare which is [about] 60 per cent cheaper than any developed country.'[2]

Moonshot Challenge 1: Save $50 Billion Annually in Health Costs by Making India Healthier

India spent $75 per capita for healthcare in 2014, according to the World Health Organisation (WHO), while the average for OECD countries stands at over $4,700.[3] This clearly indicates a huge current gap in our healthcare expenditure and access. Per capita cost will rise exponentially as the country becomes richer and more people require and access care. Also, the total number of senior citizens will increase, pushing up the health spend. Forecasting per capita healthcare spending required in 2025 at $500 multiplied into 1.35 billion Indians puts the potential health bill for government and private care, medicines and preventive care at a whopping $675 billion.

Cost-saving to reduce our healthcare bill by $50 billion per annum is eminently possible through a combination of different levers such as better resource allocation, managing NCDs, strengthening prevention systems, addressing nutrition, expanding health insurance, promoting education and introducing digital innovations. India will be able to deliver appropriate healthcare services at a much lower cost than most other countries, provided these measures are deployed strategically.

While India has made significant gains in human development indicators since the 1980s, its rank in the United Nations Development Programme (UNDP) Human Development Index at 131 fares poorly.[4] Just to give a few data points, an average person born in the country can expect to live up to 68.3 years, three years less than the world average. Almost 48 of every thousand babies cannot expect to reach their fifth birthdays.[5]

Apart from concerns about the individual, the Indian economy too suffers as a result of poor health outcomes, lack of immunization and high levels of malnutrition, and the gaps in access to timely, affordable and accessible healthcare. The UN estimates that NCDs alone will cost India over $6 trillion between 2012 and 2030.[6] As Dr K. Srinath Reddy, president of the Public Health Foundation of India puts it, 'Most of the non-communicable diseases, for example diabetes or heart disease, affect the person in the productive years. They cause reduced productivity and early retirement. Also, they place immense pressure on public health expenditure as in most cases, the treatment costs are higher compared to communicable diseases.[7]

As a result, it is estimated that the increasing burden of NCDs could cut down India's potential arising from its demographic dividend of a young workforce.

Recognizing that India's healthcare needs a substantive policy direction, the National Health Policy 2017 was announced with the goal of providing the highest possible level of healthcare through preventive and promotive policies, and universal access to quality, affordable care. The public sector will provide free primary care, and be the focal point for services, raising health expenditure to 2.5 per cent of GDP from the current 1.4 per cent. All public hospitals would provide free drugs, free diagnostics and free emergency care services.[8]

The National Health Policy has been an extremely good starting point, but healthcare needs much more. NITI Aayog has commenced work on these issues and drafted guidelines for PPP in three NCDs, namely, cardiology, pulmonology and oncology, at district hospitals. State governments can enter into agreements with private sector entities to provide services and operational management at select district hospitals. This is a path-breaking initiative and can deliver phenomenal results, if extended to the treatment of other illnesses.

Health insurance penetration in India is still quite low and the country represents the world's fastest growing market. At present, only 216 million people, or less than 20 per cent of the population, have some form of state or private insurance for healthcare.[9] Once this market covers over 60 per cent of the population, the entire health profile of the country will shift to prevention and outcome targeted spends, while keeping costs manageable.

Deploying New Technologies

Digital technologies can be used by the private sector effectively to reach out to patients and bridge the infrastructure and professional gaps to some extent. It is estimated that digital models driven by innovation can add to the growth impetus so that the size of the market can double in a few years. In addition, deploying digital healthcare can save India an estimated $90 billion by 2034, with required number of hospital beds coming down by over one million.[10]

Digital health would include large-scale adoption of electronic health records which would help better and evidence-based care, accurate and faster diagnosis for lower cost of treatment, predictive analytics for personalized care and better health policy outcomes. Telemedicine for remote diagnosis, monitoring and education is also rapidly evolving in the country. It has the potential to provide low-cost consultation and diagnosis services to remote areas connected through the Internet. Big data from insurers, healthcare providers and research centres is another digital trend, which, supported by Aadhar based online registrations systems, can help simplify procedures for patients. Further, e-commerce in the pharma and clinic space is also emerging as a disruptive force.

Deploying new technologies in healthcare can help meet the objectives of universal healthcare at a much lower cost to the country and with less expenditure on infrastructure.

Moonshot Challenge 2: Heal India and Heal the World from India

The central and state governments combined spent about ₹1.91 lakh crore in 2015–16, which adds up to barely 1.4 per cent of the GDP, a data point that has inched up lethargically over the last five years.[11] Almost one-third of Indians do not have access to primary healthcare facilities[12] and close to 63 million fall below the poverty line each year because of healthcare expenses. It is vital for the nation's progress and future that healthcare is universally accessible. We must ideate on partnerships that will 'Heal India' and also provide for 'Healing the World from India.'

India's medical provision is skewed towards the private sector. Households spend eight times as much in private hospitals than they do in government ones.[13] Seventy per cent of health expenditure takes place in the private sector of which over 87 per cent is out of pocket expenses. The bulk of private sector clinics is made up of small one-doctor clinics providing basic medical advice and with little equipment or infrastructure.

The private sector is required to play a vital role in the country's healthcare in (a) healthcare provision, that is, hospitals, clinics, diagnostics, web and telehealth, pharmacies, etc.; (b) pharmaceuticals industry; (c) training of doctors, technicians and specialists, and (d) research, drug development, and medical device development.

The stand-alone diagnostics facilities are almost entirely run by the private sector. There are about one lakh diagnostic clinics in the country with most of them in the unorganized sector.[14] There is need for a regulatory mechanism to encourage accreditation.

The Indian pharmaceutical industry multiplied by six times in 2005–12, going up from $6 billion to over $36 billion. The sector has captured significant space in the global generics market, and exports at $16.7 billion in 2016–17 account for 20 per cent of the world pharma exports in the generics segment in volume.[15]

India has also emerged as a notable player in drug formulations. The USFDA approved total 847 Abbreviated New Drug Application (ANDA) during 2017 which is the highest number of ANDA approvals during the last decade. The country's biotechnology sector is expected to touch $100 billion by 2025, with the biopharma sector as the largest component.[16] This affirms India's R&D strength, most of which is again led by the private sector. In fact, companies are now entering the area of preclinical development of small molecules. To further encourage and accelerate this positive trend, the government needs to step in with higher investments in pharmaceutical R&D through a special fund. With a pool of quality scientific personnel as also patients, India can be a formidable hub for R&D at low cost.

Also, medical tourism (often translating into medical diplomacy) is growing rapidly over the last few years. The government has offered a facilitative visa procedure for foreign patients, which has encouraged them to travel to India for quality healthcare at affordable rates. Hence, it has been estimated that value of medical tourism in India is likely to reach US$9 billion by 2020 as compared to US$3 billion in 2015.[17]

Wellness tourism is also a growing sector led by Ayurveda, Yoga, Siddha, Naturopathy, and other traditional processes that are increasingly sought after by a stressed population. Yoga, practised by millions of people across the world, is surging ahead with the huge impetus provided by the declaration of 21 June as International Yoga Day by the United Nations and strong promotional measures through overseas diplomatic missions.

With India seen as a source of spiritual and physical systems for healing, the brand can be further promoted overseas.

Moonshot Challenge 3: Create Over One Million Jobs Every Year

The fundamental imperative for all the diverse dimensions of healthcare is adequate availability of human resources of high capability. If there are not enough stethoscopes on the ground, so to speak, all plans for expanding services, providing quality, spreading insurance and so on are bound to be infructuous. The medical education system must be expanded and must function efficiently in order to create the large number of doctors, specialists, nurses and midwives, technicians and public health officials needed to staff our health centres at all levels. If we start now, we will be able to have the entire human resource structure of healthcare delivery in place in 6–7 years.

For every one lakh population, India has 65 doctors, 130 nurses and 130 hospital beds. An estimate by the National Skill Development Corporation (NSDC) suggests that the workforce requirement in the healthcare sector would grow from 4.7 million in 2017 to 7.3 million by 2022. Assuming that three indirect jobs are created for every well-paying job in the sector, this would translate into 7.8 million new job opportunities in a span of five years. Even if we were to realize 60–65 per cent of this potential through appropriate skilling and infrastructure, about one million jobs per year could emerge as a result of the growth of this sector between 2017 and 2022.

The other issue regarding gaps in availability of doctors, nurses and other professionals and personnel for healthcare relates to their presence in places where they are most required. In rural areas, it is challenging to staff primary health clinics on a regular basis. Absence of doctors from their posts is a recurring problem as they prefer to remain in cities. With health as a state subject, it has been seen that state governments often do not hire regular doctors and take them on contract basis at a low salary.

A twofold approach is therefore necessary—tackling availability of personnel on the one hand, and on the other, ensuring that they remain invested in the public health delivery system. In the private sector, it is necessary to encourage participation of specialty and super-specialty hospitals across districts, and grant of infrastructure status to the healthcare sector can help towards this.

Currently, India has 472 medical colleges producing about 65,000 doctors and 26,000 postgraduates each year.[18] Anecdotal evidence suggests that in many of these, adequate faculty, infrastructure and quality standards are lacking. As a result, students reaching these colleges, even after a challenging entrance exam, do not acquire the necessary skills. Similarly, in terms of nursing staff, the registered numbers of about 1.86 million nurses are insufficient to meet the requirements.

To begin with, more teaching hospitals are required to be introduced into the system. The government has several schemes for setting up new colleges and strengthening state medical colleges. For 2017–18, the central government has approved over 4,000 PG seats, taking the total to over 35,000.[19] The National Eligibility Cum Entrance Test (NEET) 2016 had some 7.31 lakh candidates with 4.1 lakhs qualifying. When the results were declared, less than 20,000 candidates gained admission in the 15 per cent all India quota seats.[20] The non-availability of medical seats has forced students to travel overseas to study medicine, often at dubious colleges. For example, India sends about 8,000 medical students to China.[21] Often, these students complete the course but are unable to pass the registration exam conducted by the Medical Council of India (MCI).

The main issue in setting up medical colleges is cost and availability of land. The state governments are expected to provide land free of cost, which often takes time. Land should be demarcated for large hospitals in district centres and small towns and this should be permitted under the Smart Cities and AMRUT schemes for urbanization.

Staffing these colleges with the right calibre of faculty is another issue to be addressed. A system similar to the national level Indian Institutes of Technology (IIT) and Indian Institutes of Management (IIM) needs to be explored to develop centres of excellence in medical teaching. Accreditation with the MCI for new colleges is a must, and for this to happen, the MCI too must undergo many changes to make it responsive to the healthcare necessity. A parliamentary panel has identified several anomalies on the part of MCI and has suggested some changes.[22] This was followed up by NITI Aayog through a committee recommending a National Medical Commission and other regulatory bodies in a draft bill.[23]

New hospitals along the lines of the All India Institute of Medical Sciences (AIIMS), a teaching cum research institution of high standards, were proposed to be set up. So far, fifteen such hospitals have been approved in the country, of which six are functional.[24] The delay in setting up these hospitals, six of which were first announced in 2004 and the remaining in 2014, shows lack of coordination for setting up new institutions and scaling up public health facilities.

The central government should also devise an all India cadre of medical services. Parity with other class-one government services will be a good incentive to attract medical professionals to join. A stringent method for selecting candidates like other services through the Union Public Services Commission (UPSC) could be considered. Government doctors through this route would have clear conditions of work and defined career paths with mandated tenures in rural areas and additional benefits for acquiring new skills.

The private sector can play a key role in developing new hospitals.

It can supplement the government's expenditure in infrastructure and training and participate in certain specified healthcare programs through a PPP approach. To attract private enterprises to invest in hospitals, which are long gestation and investment heavy, it is necessary that competitive pricing based on facilities and outcomes is encouraged in a transparent fashion. Healthcare infrastructure should be provided with infrastructure status like other infrastructure sectors.

Considerations regarding emoluments have led to a preponderance of Indian-origin doctors overseas. For example, in the UK's National Health Services, the largest number of doctors and consultants are from India at about 7 per cent of the total.[25] This can be turned from a threat to an opportunity. As the world ages rapidly, there will be a rising demand for Indian caregivers across the globe. A massive initiative for institution-building and skills training is the need of the hour to capture this opportunity and create the necessary jobs.

The three parameters where the healthcare sector's contribution is critical are GDP growth, savings and employment. The sector has the potential to contribute significantly to GDP growth rates by raising the productivity of India's labour force and enabling its judicious participation in the global economic sphere. Second, healthcare, if managed well, can help the country save as much as $50 billion annually in different ways. Third, as an important creator of employment at all skill levels, healthcare can be a key component of the national mission of creating 100 million new jobs by adding one million jobs every year.

As a dynamic sector of concern to every individual as well as to societies and economies collectively, India's healthcare ecosystem must enable the country to perform to its best and highest potential with constructive partnerships of all stakeholders. We must jointly make the moonshot challenges a reality.

◆

Shobana Kamineni is the president of the Confederation of Indian Industry (CII).

Endnotes

1. http://www.livemint.com/Politics/b9c6cJFhzDHfubCfXEEIoJ/India-ranks-154-in-global-healthcare-rankings-for-2015-Swit.html
2. Pranay Gupte, 'Healer: Dr Prathap Chandra Reddy and the Transformation of India', Portfolio 2013.
3. https://data.worldbank.org/indicator/SH.XPD.PCAP
4. United Nations Development Programme Human Development Report 2016, http://hdr.undp.org/en/countries/profiles/IND accessed on 18 August 2017
5. Economic Survey 2016–17, Vol. 2, Chapter 10, Table 4, 'India and Emerging Economies: Select Indicators', http://indiabudget.nic.in/es2016-17/echap10_vol2.pdf accessed on 18 August 2017.
6. http://economictimes.indiatimes.com/industry/healthcare/biotech/healthcare/cardiovascular-disease-diabetes-may-cost-india-6-2-trillion/articleshow/51739578.cms
7. http://timesofindia.indiatimes.com/india/Lifestyle-diseases-to-cost-India-6-trillion-study-estimates/articleshow/22385056.cms
8. National Health Policy 2017, Ministry of Health and Family Welfare, http://mohfw.nic.in/sites/default/files/9147562941489753121.pdf accessed on 19 August 2017.
9. http://timesofindia.indiatimes.com/india/Less-than-20-of-population-under-health-insurance-cover-Report/articleshow/49082784.cms
10. CII-PWC report 'The healthcare agenda: stakeholder collaboration for the way forward', December 2015.
11. Economic Survey 2016–17, Chapter 10, Table 1, 'Trends in Social Services Expenditure by General Government (Centre and States)' http://indiabudget.nic.in/es2016-17/echap10_vol2.pdf accessed on 18 August 2017.
12. CII-PWC Background Paper for 12th Health Summit, 'The healthcare agenda: Stakeholder collaboration for the way forward'. December 2015
13. http://www.thehindu.com/data/Indians-spend-8-times-more-on-private-hospitals-than-on-govt.-ones/article14593186.ece
14. http://businessworld.in/article/Aggregating-The-Fragmented-Diagnostic-Sector-In-India/09-05-2016-97780/
15. IBEF, accessed on 30 August 2017.
16. IBEF, accessed on 30 August 2017.
17. http://www.business-standard.com/article/companies/medical-tourist-

arrivals-in-india-up-25-117041900577_1.html

18. Annual Report 2016–17, Ministry of Health and Family Welfare.

19. PIB Press Release dated 2 March 2017, http://pib.nic.in/newsite/PrintRelease.aspx?relid=158806, accessed on 20 August 2017.

20. Annual Report 2016-17, Ministry of Health and Family Welfare.

21. http://indiatoday.intoday.in/education/story/sharp-increase-of-indian-students-studying-in-china/1/834857.html

22. http://www.academics-india.com/Parl_Panel_report_on_MCI.pdf

23. NITI Aayog, The National Medical Commission Bill 2016, http://niti.gov.in/writereaddata/files/new_initiatives/MCI per cent20Bill per cent20Final.pdf accessed on 21 August 2017.

24. PIB Press Release dated 19 July 2016, http://pib.nic.in/newsite/mbErel.aspx?relid=147260 accessed on 20 August 2017.

25. https://www.theguardian.com/society/2014/jan/26/nhs-foreign-nationals-immigration-health-service

Lateral Entry in Government

Urvashi Prasad, Devashish Dhar and Vaibhav Kapoor

The World Bank[1] defines governance as 'the process and institutions through which decisions are made and authority in a country is exercised'. A well-functioning civil service has a far-reaching positive impact on the development of a country. Post India's Independence, Sardar Vallabhai Patel recognized the importance of a national-level civil service for maintaining unity in the country. He famously referred to the Indian Administrative Services (IAS) as the 'Steel Frame of India'. The IAS, along with the other civil services, is responsible for designing and implementing various economic and social policies for India's citizens. It is due to the tireless efforts of bright and committed civil servants that several new programmes have been launched and mainstreamed across the country, including the MGNREGA and the Mid-Day Meal scheme, among many others. To understand civil services in our country, let us take a brief look at its history.

During the colonial rule, a permanent civil service based on merit was recommended for the first time in 1854 by the Macaulay Committee.[2] Prior to this, the system was patronage based. While the recruitment for the Indian Civil Service (ICS) became merit based in 1855, the examinations were initially held in London and the eligibility criteria required a degree from elite universities such as Oxford or Cambridge. The ICS Act was put in place in 1861. Examinations for the ICS started being held in India only after 1922.

The post-Independence avatar of the civil services retained some elements of the British version. It classified civil services into three broad categories—All India, Central and State. Members of the All India Service (AIS) serve in both the centre and state. The IAS, Indian Police Service and Indian Forest Service are part of the AIS. Article 312 of the Constitution gives powers to the Rajya Sabha for setting up AIS branches and establishing new services. Some of the objectives of AIS include[3] preserving national unity (a new recruit doesn't usually get deployed in their home state, encouraging integration), standardization of administration, neutrality, objectivity and integrity. In general, civil services at the central- and state-level are safeguarded by Articles 310 and 311 of the Constitution of India which deal with their appointment and dismissal respectively.

Civil services have played a central role in delivering the economic and social growth that India has enjoyed in the last 70 years. But as India continues to grow in a world where competition is global, it requires its steel frame to evolve as well. Global attention has turned towards us and expectations from India include delivering strong economic growth, social development (for e.g. lifting people out of poverty, getting the next billion on the Internet) and political stability to the world. In this competitive age, not only do we need our private sector to innovate, we equally need fresh perspectives in our public sector as well. Government departments in India should have the flexibility to tap into a strong workforce flush with specialists from a diverse range of sectors. In this context, lateral hires can play a critical role in complementing the functioning of the civil services and equipping it to deliver a globally competitive and sustainable growth model.

To start with, it is encouraging to note that the Indian government has explored lateral entry in the past. Many state and central government departments have engaged external advisers or consultants on fixed-term contracts. Some of the most prominent technocrats in the government have been hired laterally. Examples include Dr Manmohan Singh, Dr Montek Singh Ahluwalia, as well as various chief economic advisers to the government. Further, many of these individuals are hired at the top levels and there exists no transparent mechanism for hiring laterally at the mid- and junior-levels. In general, the process of engaging non-bureaucrats in the government has been ad-hoc at best.

In the recent past, however, several efforts have been made to institutionalize lateral entry in India. For example, in 2005, the second Administrative Reforms Commission (ARC) recommended that a transparent process should be adopted for lateral entries at the central and state levels. However, the recommendations were not implemented. NITI Aayog in its 3-Year Action Agenda[4] released in 2017 proposed lateral hiring of specialized staff to complement the skills of internal staff. The Manual for Procurement of Consultancy and Other Services 2017,[5] prepared by the Department of Expenditure, provides guidelines for the fixed-term hiring of consultants for various government departments.

Benefits of Lateral Entry Around the World

Lateral entry has several benefits. First, hiring laterally to fill government posts adds subject matter expertise and introduces outside perspectives along with dynamic thinking. Second, bringing in lateral entries would lead to knowledge sharing between civil servants and lateral hires. Third, institutionalized lateral entry will provide a platform for qualified, motivated professionals who want to take part in nation-building but have not been able to do so in a structured way in the past.

A comparative global study on the evolution of bureaucracies reveals two predominant structures of lateral entry: Position-based and career-based systems. In the early nineteenth century, the former was championed by Britain while the latter was championed by France, Prussia and Germany.[6] The position-based system focuses on filling a given position and allows open access, including scope for lateral hiring. The focus is on recruiting people best-suited for the job. In a career-based system, the entry is based on credentials and examinations. Thereafter, people are placed in positions as per the requirements of the organization.

Among the OECD countries, France, Greece, Japan, Korea, Luxembourg, and Spain exhibit strong characteristics of a career-based system, while the position-based system is followed in countries such as Finland, New Zealand, Sweden, Switzerland, US and the UK.[7,8] Countries in the latter group have demonstrated a strong inclination to reform their civil services, shifting towards a position-based system. For instance, post Brexit, the UK is planning to hire 300 specialist staff to negotiate new trade deals.[9] In Eastern Europe, countries such as Hungary and the Slovak Republic have adopted a career-based mechanism whereas the Czech Republic and Poland have preferred a position-based system. The European Commission hires Seconded National Experts from member-state administrations on a temporary basis (up to six years) to supplement the expertise of the Commission's permanent staff.

Away from the limelight of Cabinet ranks, the US has institutionalized lateral hiring at various levels in administration and governance. It has adopted a revolving door policy, allowing academics and private sector practitioners to enter public service on a regular basis.[10] For instance, the US Department of Justice hires nearly 750 experienced attorneys every year across its 40 components, making it the largest legal employer in the world.[11] In 2016, the US Digital Service (USDS) submitted a detailed report to the Congress on hiring top technical talent from the private sector. The report illustrated how USDS attracted specialized technical talent, created a customized hiring plan with reduced timelines, focused on candidate experience, adopted extensive outreach activities, and used subject matter experts for evaluation.[12] The USDS and 18F, a digital service delivery agency of the US Government, undertook high-profile talent recruitment, under the personal guidance of the then President, Barack Obama, to revamp government departments and website services for veterans, students etc.[13] Prior to the completion of his tenure, President Obama signed the Tested Ability to Leverage

Exceptional National Talent Act 2017 (Talent Act) for codifying the White House's Presidential Innovation Fellows into law. The Fellowship aims to 'enable exceptional individuals with proven track records to serve time-limited appointments in executive agencies to address some of the nation's most significant challenges and improve existing government efforts.'[14]

In Africa, several attempts have been made over the years to acquire and retain specialist talent. For instance, in the 1990s, Botswana extensively employed the use of a 'parallel progression' framework which helped the country provide career prospects to sector experts and prevent the loss of government talent to the private sector.[15]

Closer home, Singapore is often cited as one of the shining examples of civil service reform. Singapore is a good case study for India as it became independent from colonial rule around the same time as India and has transitioned from a developing to a developed country in a relatively short time frame. The civil service reforms in Singapore took place primarily in two waves, after 1959 as well as during the 1980s and 1990s. The reform process was comprehensive and included several measures[16] such as spotting and developing young talent, hiring external talent at critical bureaucratic positions etc. The Singapore government has consistently achieved high efficiency ratings primarily due to their ability to dissolve differences between technocrats and bureaucrats.[17]

Lateral Entry in Indian Government: The Way Forward

While several models for lateral entry in the government have been proposed, none of them have been implemented in a systematic manner thus far. In this context, it would be worthwhile considering the creation of a parallel hierarchy to complement the steel frame.

While some lateral entrants prefer contributing to policymaking for a shorter period of time (2–3 years), other capable candidates could be interested in contributing over longer time periods. The current system, however, provides limited opportunities for lateral hires to grow within the system and gradually take on broader or higher responsibilities.

In the proposed parallel cadre, professionals from diverse career paths would be able to enter the system at 25 years of age. Should they decide to remain in the system, subject to their achieving predefined key performance indicators at every level, they would be able to rise in the cadre till a maximum of 45 years of age. An upper age limit is important because the cadre should ideally comprise professionals who are at the cutting-edge in their respective disciplines. It will also enable those wishing to pursue opportunities outside the government system after contributing to policymaking for a substantial period of time to do so.

Selection for this cadre should be through an open recruitment process, the first stage of which would involve advertising the required academic qualifications and work experience for the concerned specialization. Following this, applicants would be shortlisted using a standardized grading system. At the final stage, the shortlisted candidates would be invited for an interview, including a personality test and a written test, if necessary, to ensure that they possess the attributes necessary for the advertised position.

In developing this cadre, it is crucial that the roles and responsibilities are spelled out clearly. This will ensure that candidates who possess the requisite academic and professional qualifications apply. Further, it will facilitate the development of performance benchmarks and clear criteria for promotions at every level of the hierarchy.

Entitlements for this cadre should be determined based on the entry-level years of experience and requisite qualifications possessed by the applicants. We should steer clear of any attempts to compare these emoluments with or establish their equivalence to those of the civil services. This is vital because the primary role of this cadre will be to complement the civil services in discharging its duties more effectively and delivering a globally competitive governance system, as opposed to competing with it.

Professionals within this cadre will have their own career path as defined by a comprehensive human resource policy covering all aspects of recruitment, retention and performance measurement. To begin with, such a structure could be piloted in a few government ministries, ideally those that deal with highly technical subject matter like the Ministry of Health & Family Welfare, Ministry of Power, Ministry of New and Renewable Energy, etc.

This cadre could complement the civil service and take the system closer to the objective of 'minimum government, maximum governance' by ensuring a blend of technical expertise and administrative know-how. Depending on the success of this cadre in the short to medium term, a model in which lateral entrants compete with career bureaucrats could be considered, in the longer term.

When Sardar Patel referred to the bureaucracy as the Steel Frame of India, he entrusted the cadre with the task of running the country and maintaining its unity. Seventy years later, no one can deny that the bureaucracy has lived up to these expectations. However, in the twenty-first century, our bureaucracy, which, to a large extent, follows the guidelines and principles set in the twentieth century, finds itself constrained in certain ways. In this context, institutionalized lateral entry is one of the instruments that can bolster the efforts of the bureaucracy in delivering a governance model equipped to cater to a fast-paced and ever-evolving world. A structured approach to lateral hiring, as enumerated above, will enable India to leverage an optimum mix of career-based and position-based forms of public service mechanisms for delivering effective governance in the twenty-first century.

◆

Urvashi Prasad, Devashish Dhar and Vaibhav Kapoor are Public Policy Specialists at NITI Aayog.

Endnotes

1. Source: http://siteresources.worldbank.org/INTWBIGOVANTCOR/Resources/1740479-1149112210081/2604389-1149699431307/edouardpresentation_munich_inwent.pdf
2. Source: http://arc.gov.in/10th/arc_10threport_ch2.pdf
3. Source: http://arc.gov.in/10th/arc_10threport_ch2.pdf
4. Source: http://niti.gov.in/writereaddata/files/coop/India_ActionAgenda.pdf
5. Source: http://doe.gov.in/sites/default/files/Manual per cent20for per cent20Procurement per cent20of per cent20Consultancy per cent20and per cent20Other per cent20Services per cent202017.pdf
6. 'Dimensions of Bureaucracy: A Cross-National Dataset on the Structure and Behaviour of Public Administration', QoG Working Paper Series 2010, The Quality Of Government Institute, University of Gothenburg, June 2010.
7. 'Modernising Government: The Way Forward', OECD, 2005.
8. 'Green Paper on a New Employment Policy for a New Public Service', May 1997, Department of Public Service and Administration, Ministry for Public Service and Administration, http://www.dpsa.gov.za/dpsa2g/documents/acts&regulations/frameworks/green-papers/employ.pdf
9. Pickard, Jim, 'Javid looks to hire hundreds of trade experts', *Financial Times*, 9 July 2016, https://www.ft.com/content/5c6b0530-4530-11e6-b22f-79eb4891c97d
10. Kovacic, William E., 'Competition Policy in the European Union and the United States: Convergence or Divergence', U.S. Federal Trade Commission, 2 June 2008, https://www.ftc.gov/sites/default/files/documents/public_statements/competition-policy-european-union-and-united-states-convergence-or-divergence/080602bateswhite.pdf
11. 'A Career Counselor's Guide to Lateral Hiring at DOJ', US Department of Justice, Office of Attorney Recruitment and Management.
12. 2016 Report to Congress, 'Hiring Top Technical Talent from the Private Sector', https://www.usds.gov/report-to-congress/2016/hiring-talent/
13. Gertner, Jon, 'Inside Obama's Stealth Startup', 15 June 2015, https://www.fastcompany.com/3046756/obama-and-his-geeks
14. H.R.39—TALENT Act of 2017, https://www.congress.gov/bill/115th-congress/house-bill/39
15. Thovoethin, Paul-Sewa, 'Techno-Bureaucratic Governance and

Developmental State in Africa: Botswana and Nigeria in Comparative Perspective, *European Scientific Journal,* August 2014.

16. Benedetto Francesco, Ballatore, 'The reform of the Public Administration in Singapore: a model to follow in Italy?' Italian Ministry of Agricultural, Food and Forestry Policies, December 2013.

17. Saadat, Syed, 'A purposeless civil service', 26 February 2018, https://www.dawn.com/news/788762

Interdisciplinary Education: Sowing the Seeds of Innovation

The business landscape is changing today at an unprecedented pace. Industries which have traditionally built products and delivered services in a certain way are increasingly finding those modes of operation to be obsolete. Eighty-eight per cent of the Fortune 500 companies have disappeared between 1955–2016.[1] Problems are becoming more and more ambiguous and rapidly shifting context. This means that with time, it is becoming more difficult for our people, processes and platforms to be prepared to deal with challenges. Education is making progress, no doubt, but despite that progress, there is an increasing gap between what the education system delivers and what the market actually demands from students. Very few people have addressed that gap.

India has a large workforce of young people who put their faith in the education system to train them in developing skills relevant for the future. The Indian education system is in good shape and is improving tremendously. Computer-based training is becoming more prevalent, and information is ubiquitous. We are exposing students to computers and the Internet very early in their lives. New subjects like analytics and data science are also a part of the curriculum in many schools today.

However, more than 60 per cent of the eight lakh engineers

graduating from technical institutions across the country remain unemployed,[2] every year. While as many as 97 per cent of graduating engineers want jobs either in software engineering or core engineering, the reality is only 3 per cent have suitable skills to be employed in the software or product market.[3]

Background and Design

The origins of engineering date back to the invention of the steam engine, which led to the industrial revolution. During the late nineteenth and early twentieth centuries, a mere 4–5 disciplines of engineering, namely mechanical, electrical, chemical and civil engineering accounted for a significant chunk of all professions. Through the course of the twentieth century, new disciplines emerged, such as electronics and telecommunications. Towards the latter part of the century, the personal computing and Internet revolution led to large-scale dissemination of data and information. This was the seed that resulted in an explosion of newer engineering disciplines capable of dealing with ambiguous, rapidly changing, interdisciplinary problems.

Take the automobile industry, for example. Traditionally, major automobile manufacturers competed with other large manufacturers. Today, automobile manufacturers compete with technology companies that are building self-driving cars, while also competing with cab aggregators who have reduced the need to purchase automobiles. Automobile engines are no longer designed based on mechanical systems alone, but on a combination of mechanical, electronic and intelligent systems. These newer, rapidly emerging disciplines are borrowing from existing fields of engineering, applied mathematics, economics and even social sciences. For example, biomedical engineering arose from the intersection of biology, medicine and engineering. Similarly, mechatronics is a product of mechanical, electronics and computer science engineering. These intersections are important, considering the path-breaking work and research that occurs at such interactions. In fact, Richard Thaler from the University of Chicago received the Nobel Prize for Economics (2017) for his work based on the interaction between economics and psychology.

In the past, problems were static, well-defined, and relevant for a significant period of time. Educational institutions had the time to design programmes that trained students on these problems, and simulate those problems in controlled environments for students to learn. However, in today's world, since problems are rapidly shifting context and definition, the inherent lag in the education system is causing a large gap between industry requirements and the education provided. This has led to a situation where students graduating with a degree in engineering are not ready to deal with real problems in the industry, nor are they equipped to perform cutting-edge research.

A survey of the modes of education, both in the past and across other fields, provides an illuminating insight into ways to address this problem. Historically, it was the norm for artisans, craftsmen and other skilled workers to learn their trade as apprentices. They had access to real problems, which helped them develop the capability to solve a varied set of problems. But the scale at which engineering education is being provided today has become a barrier to the apprentice form of education. A look at other professions such as medicine, law and accounting also provides certain insights. In medical education, it is mandatory for medical colleges to have a hospital so that students get access to the real problem space. Similarly, in accounting and law, there is an over-indexing on internships and working at firms to ensure that students are learning by working on actual problems. This comes from the recognition that problem-solving is both an art and a science, and access to real problems is the only way to provide students an environment to bring both together and solve the situation at hand.

However, in the field of engineering, educational institutions have struggled to provide this kind of exposure. Even via internships, students working in the industry are not allowed to contribute directly to solving real problems, and thus, lack the necessary exposure to real-world problem-solving.

The engineers of tomorrow, especially Indians, require direct access to the changing problem space and preferably in real time, to develop their problem-solving skills. Our engineers play a key part in India's rise as a global hub for innovation, and to make that happen, they need to appreciate the fusion of multiple disciplines and use it to innovate at the intersections.

It is difficult for engineering educational institutions to invite problems to their ecosystems, simply because they currently lack a framework to enable this. Problems get invited to an ecosystem only when they see the ecosystem as a possible place for solutions. Today, if customer retention for an organization is a problem, the organization doesn't go to a university to solve it. It will engage either a consulting firm, or a business integrator, or perhaps a systems integrator or a design thinking company, or maybe even a product company. As of today, the places that invite problems happen to be in the industry and therefore, the fastest possible iterations or interactions between the solution space and the problem space must happen in the industry itself.

Implementation to Develop an Interdisciplinary Perspective

To address this problem, I recommend the following:

i) Collaborative delivery of undergraduate engineering education by the industry, through companies like Mu Sigma and academia, with the industry giving students access to the real problem space, and students learning by working on real problems.

ii) An interdisciplinary perspective developed amongst students, which enables them to grasp newer disciplines faster and innovate at the intersections.

I believe that for the programme to be most impactful, students much younger than the current workforce need to be involved—students in pre-college and pre-university. Today, there is not much 'learning' per se between the ages of 18–25, arguably the most important time in a student's life. This is primarily because they end up in ecosystems that have no means of providing access to present and the future problem areas.

This industry-academia programme will aim to develop an interdisciplinary perspective amongst students, and it will do so by providing exposure to a wide range of real problems across industries and multiple disciplines. The programme will not only educate students in those specific disciplines, but will enable them to learn newer disciplines quickly, and without direct teaching. This will also develop their ability to identify interconnections and potential for cross-pollination across disciplines, ultimately preparing them to be future innovators.

The curriculum needs to be designed in collaboration between industry and academia. This is to ensure that the subjects taught are relevant and applicable for problem-solving today. The following questions need to guide the design of the curriculum:

- What are the disciplines that are relevant to the industry today?
- How can students be exposed to increasingly interdisciplinary subjects, enabling them to gradually develop an interdisciplinary perspective?
- What are the fundamental concepts that students need to learn, and how can theoretical know-how be complemented with various applications of these concepts?
- How can students learn the art of problem-solving?
- How can guided learning be complemented and enhanced by problem-based learning?

The curriculum must include disciplines like mathematics and statistics which are fundamental and independently relevant. It must also include disciplines such as behavioural economics and decision theory which are, by nature, interdisciplinary. The curriculum also needs to be designed with the perspective that while some of these disciplines may be most relevant today, they may not necessarily remain so in the future.

Learning from both past modes of education and delivery of education in other fields apart from engineering, the programme needs to be designed to provide students maximum access to the continuously changing problem space. Students will need to learn and develop an interdisciplinary perspective by being exposed to real problems and working on them, while undergoing guided classroom learning across various disciplines in parallel. This structure should allow for minimal latency in learning fundamental concepts and their application in solving actual problems.

The programme will need to be delivered to students through a two-pronged approach:

i) Guided learning—ongoing taught courses
ii) Problem-based learning—working on solving real industry problems

Developing the Right Talent for the Future

The World Economic Forum (WEF) states[4] that how nations develop their human capital can be a more important determinant than virtually any other factor. Today, India is ranked a mere 103rd worldwide[5] on the Human Capital Index.

- India's deployment sub index (that covers skills application and accumulation of skills through work) is 118.
- India's development sub index (that reflects current efforts to educate, skill and upskill the student body and the working age population) is 65.
- India's know-how sub index (that captures the breadth and depth of specialized skills used at work) is 79.

The G20 continues to put the promotion of global human capital development high on its agenda, including the engagement of the private sector. India is the last ranked nation in the group.[6] Therefore, we must think about developing the right talent for the future in the right manner.

By executing this programme, India will have a workforce that:

1. Adapts to change effectively by learning through the lens of an interdisciplinary perspective, by developing the skills to learn new disciplines, technologies and concepts quickly, and by coping with an ever-changing, complex world.
2. Can break down ambiguous and complex problems as well as map their interconnected nature. They will be able to ask better questions, and through this process, identify holistic solutions.
3. Can demonstrate knowledge of ethics and its implications on a wide range of industries, problems and contexts.
4. Will be cognizant of the impact of solutions to problems on the society at large, as well as the need to develop sustainable solutions.

This combined with the government's efforts through programmes such as 'Skill India' and 'Make in India', will foster skill development of the Indian workforce and drive innovation throughout the country. India's rise in the 'Ease of Doing Business' rankings suggests that we are building an environment that encourages business and innovation. We need talent that can think in an interdisciplinary manner and has the ability to innovate at intersections. Developing such talent will accelerate our country's journey to becoming a hotbed of innovation.

◆

Dhiraj Rajaram is founder and CEO of Mu Sigma, the world's largest pure-play analytics company.

References

1. http://www.aei.org/publication/fortune-500-firms-in-1955-vs-2014-89-are-gone-and-were-all-better-off-because-of-that-dynamic-creative-destruction/, Perry Mark J., 18 August 2014.
2. https://www.facilities.aicte-india.org/dashboard/pages/dashboardaicte.php (2016–17).

3. Aspiring Minds National Employability report 2016, http://www.aspiringminds.com/sites/default/files/National per cent20Employability per cent20Report per cent20- per cent20Engineers per cent20Annual per cent20Report per cent202016.pdf
4. World Economic Forum, The Global Human Capital Report 2017, https://www.weforum.org/reports/the-global-human-capital-report-2017
5. World Economic Forum, The Global Human Capital Report 2017, https://www.weforum.org/reports/the-global-human-capital-report-2017
6. World Economic Forum, The Global Human Capital Report 2017, https://www.weforum.org/reports/the-global-human-capital-report-2017

Using Funding to Catalyze Education Reform

Ashish Dhawan

India's education system has seen tremendous success in ensuring that students are in school. Between 1990 and 2015, the country invested heavily on school access and enrolment, building seven lakh new schools and adding 45 lakh new teachers to the school system.[1] The government's commitment to education is also reflected in recent programmatic and legislative efforts. For example, the per-child allocation for elementary education has increased by 180 per cent[2] from ₹3,511 in 2010–11 to ₹6,350 in 2016–17. The Right to Free and Compulsory Education (RTE) Act has made education a fundamental right for all children in age group of 6 to 14 years. Consequently, India's gross enrolment ratio (GER) at elementary level rose from 78.6 percent in 1990 to 96.9 per cent in 2015.[3] Gender Parity Index (GPI), the number of girls enrolled per boy, in elementary school rose from 0.71 to 1.05 during the same period.[4]

Unfortunately, this success in ensuring that students are in school has not naturally led to the increase in their learning. Various national, international and third-party surveys point to the low, and in some cases, even declining learning levels in our country. The Annual State of Education Report (ASER) by the NGO Pratham shows that learning outcomes in rural India have declined between 2010–11 and 2016–17. The proportion of Class Five children in government schools who can read a Class Two-level text fell from 50.7 per cent to 41.6 per cent, and the proportion of children in Class Five who can do division exercises fell from 33.9 per cent to 21.1 per cent. According to the government's own National Achievement Survey data for Class Five there has been 6 per cent to 33 per cent decrease in learning levels between 2012 to 2015 for mathematics, language and environmental studies. This worrying decline could reduce the expected income of students by ₹1,827 per annum.[5] At the international level, India participated in the 2009 round of Programme for International Student Assessment (PISA), only to be placed second to last among 74 participating countries. It is clear that there has been a delink between education outlays and learning outcomes in the past few years. It is also clear that the input-centric strategy for school education is not the best way to dramatically improve outcomes.

It is encouraging to note the current government's focus on improving outcomes and ensuring that all children fulfil their potential through education. However, as school education is in the concurrent list, the centre has a limited role in implementation, and states/union territories (UTs) are primarily responsible for the quality of delivery. In this scenario, there is a need for the centre to catalyze the reforms in states/UTs by imaginatively using its funding and ensuring healthy competition between states in the spirit of cooperative and competitive federalism.

Result-based Funding: A Game Changer

Linking funding to performance is one of the critical structural reforms which can be a potential game changer. The idea is to link funding to implementation of key governance reforms critical to enable learning in the short term and learning outcomes in the long term. With greater devolution of finances to the states under the 14th Finance Commission and the increased focus on improving outcomes, this imaginative use of finance could catalyze education reform at the state-level. This would truly make states/UTs the laboratories for innovation and policy reforms, while the centre's role would be concentrated on providing technical assistance and holding them accountable to performance.

While linking funding to outcomes can indeed be a game changer, it is critical to articulate clear goals to ensure that it drives the right behaviour and policies. Given the current student learning levels, and system capacity to deliver learning, any result-based funding mechanism should focus on ensuring that all children attain certain foundational skills by the end of Class Three.

Foundational learning, i.e., the ability to read with comprehension and use the basic mathematical operations in real life are key gateway skills that help students access higher learning. Research shows that the learning gap widens if the students are not able to master foundational competencies by Class Three, resulting in a long tail of students who are unable to follow classroom instruction, thus falling further behind.[6] Since most of the learning happens in Classes One and Two, learning trajectories become flatter in higher grades for students who haven't mastered the basics. For example, ASER data shows that out of children who did not already master addition skills by Class Two only less than half gained the skill by Class Five (which is three full years of additional schooling).

Also, it is critical to ensure that *all students* in the system acquire foundational learning. Apart from the equity consideration, international research[7] suggests that as countries move from low to middling level of performance, they do so by 'pulling up the tail', i.e., by improving the performance of their weakest students.

To ensure focus on learning and to engender a spirit of competition, the centre can link a component of central assistance to states to improvement in learning outcomes, with an outsized focus on foundational learning outcomes. Further, district-level challenge grants could be disbursed to districts with strong plans for improving foundational learning.

The centre's new integrated scheme for school education, the Samagra Shiksha Abhiyan, which merges the three centrally sponsored schemes of Sarva Shiksha Abhiyan (SSA), Rashtriya Madhyamik

Shiksha Abhiyan (RMSA) and Teacher Education (TE), is a bold step in the right direction. It has greater focus on interventions related to improvement in quality of education, ensuring that funds related to quality 'will be allocated on two criteria: (a) core quality interventions, (such as school grants, student assessments, digital interventions etc.) and (b) flexible funds for innovative quality interventions, which in turn will be decided on the basis of performance (for example, based on NAS results).[8]

In similar vein, districts should be incentivized to develop 3–5-year plans to achieve improvement in foundational learning. This would help ameliorate the short-termism in implementation (where the plans are made and discussed annually) and would lead to healthy competition among the districts.

A potential example of how the centre can further revise the funding allocation to the states/UTs could be:

- Phase 1 (year 1–2): Link funding to governance reforms related to learning (20 per cent) and for providing challenge grants to districts on a competitive basis (10 per cent).
- Phase 2 (year 3–5): Link funding to improvement in student learning outcomes (20 per cent) and for providing challenge grants to districts on a competitive basis (10 per cent), with an outsized focus on foundational learning outcomes.

For both phases, the remaining 70 per cent can be split as:

- Fifty per cent of funds to be allocated on the basis of equality, i.e., on per-student basis.
- Twenty per cent of funds to be allocated on the basis of equity, i.e., more funding to be allocated to states/UTs which have traditionally been underdeveloped. This could be based on the proportion of educationally backward blocks (EBBs) in the state/UT or based on other similar criterion which explicitly focuses on disadvantages.

Result-based Funding: The Theory of Change

A close examination of school education budgets reveals two things. One, it becomes clear that states spend most of their budgets—approximately 64.7 per cent—on teacher salary, varying from 51.6 per cent in Bihar to over 80 per cent in Rajasthan, leaving very little fiscal space for quality improvements. Two, centrally sponsored schemes[9] form a significant proportion of states' education budgets (for example, share of SSA in total state education budgets in Bihar and Madhya Pradesh was 60 per cent and 41 per cent respectively in 2012–13). As one of the major sources for spending, central assistance can play a crucial role in shaping states' interventions and actions to improve student learning outcomes.

Unfortunately, the programmatic funding from the centre is primarily geared towards inputs. While this strategy works well to provide basic facilities and resources across states and UTs, it may not be most useful for improving quality. Although recent efforts after the integration of the centrally sponsored schemes have been focused on moving towards quality, there is still limited incentive for the states/UTs to spend on activities which might lead to maximum improvement in student learning.

Shifting the role of the centre from being deeply involved in state budgets to setting clear goals, measuring them periodically and rewarding the ones which show most improvement could turn states into laboratories of innovation. Such an environment will also maximize ownership in states over their quality intervention mix. This will result in more research into the cost-effective means to achieve outcomes and successful scaling of interventions which have worked in other context.

Design Process

The reform of linking funding to outcomes has some essential components which can broadly be divided into three categories:

    (a) defined prerequisites

(b) governance reforms
(c) challenge grants for districts

a. Defined Prerequisites

Getting reliable student learning data periodically is essential for designing an outcome-focused financing approach. Well-designed and administered assessment surveys are one of the strongest tools to introduce accountability into the education system. Over 60 countries conduct national surveys of learning, the results of which are widely used to drive accountability and to inform policymaking and intervention design, such as curriculum revamp, textbook and content development, teacher training and student remediation programmes. High-quality learning data is crucial to examine the health of education system and its performance against predefined learning outcomes; understand the strengths and gaps in student learning; and identify need-based interventions likely to have the maximum impact. While a series of attempts have been made to accomplish these goals through the National Achievement Survey (NAS) conducted by the National Council of Educational Research and Training (NCERT), the system of measurement could be further strengthened. A credible survey of learning outcomes will also go a long way in holding states accountable, and generate healthy competition amongst states and their political leadership to drive improvements in their respective student learning outcomes.

The survey of learning outcomes should be conducted biannually at district-level, assessing students of Class Three, Five, Eight and Ten across government, government-aided and private schools in language, English, mathematics, environmental science, science and social science. This survey should provide comparable results across years and classes, and should be administered by an external survey organization (at least at the state-level) to ensure complete reliability of results.

b. Governance reforms

The explicit focus on outcomes is the hallmark of performance linked funding. However, we expect 2–3 cycles of revamped NAS before the learning outcomes data is stabilized. In the meanwhile, it is critical to focus on key governance reforms which are key enablers for performance. Some of them include:

- Human resource management reforms: Over 4.9 million[10] teachers and a large number of administrators are engaged in supporting the public school system. However, the mechanisms to manage their recruitment, deployment, transfer, promotion and rationalization are woefully inadequate. This results in a scenario where a significant proportion of the state education department's time and mind space is spent resolving issues related to management, when they should be investing that to improve student learning. Centre and states must move to a system—policy and processes—that prioritizes transparency in recruitment and management. States like Karnataka have already built such systems.

  Another issue that deserves attention is of teacher accountability. Data[11] shows that private schools are delivering higher student learning outcomes than government schools, despite having teachers who are less qualified, paid lower salaries and have access to lower professional development opportunities. By few estimates, teacher absenteeism in India is 23.64 per cent;[12] in some states such as Jharkhand it is as high as 45.84 per cent. In addition to the lost instructional time, teacher absenteeism costs the exchequer over $1.5 billion per year (which is around 60 per cent of the entire revenue collected from the special education tax used to fund SSA in 2010). At the heart of this issue is a system that guarantees job security and that lacks any credible teacher performance evaluation system. The centre should push states to adopt teacher evaluation systems that hold teachers accountable for their performance, and also leverage technology such as biometric attendance systems to reduce teacher absenteeism.

- Merit-based selection of headmasters and middle management: In India, education leaders provide critical leverage to drive education reform. This demonstrates an urgent need to overhaul human resource management in education by introducing merit-based pathways for education leadership at all levels. A more selective and rigorous selection process will increase the likelihood of appointing the most suitable and qualified candidates.

  In Gujarat, the implementation of merit-based selection through the Head Teacher Aptitude Test (HTAT) for school leaders brought in a new cadre of head teachers with high academic qualifications. Head teachers recruited through this possessed an average of 11 years of teaching experience in various institutions and a majority (57 per cent) held postgraduate degrees. Similarly, 50 per cent of the positions for district/ block heads and Deputy Heads should be recruited through a rigorous assessment of administrative and academic aptitudes. The selection of coaches (B/CRCs) and facilitators (MTs, SRGs) should be done based on assessment of pedagogical skills and domain expertise.

- Examination Reform: International research shows that high-stakes assessments such as Class Ten and Class Twelve board examinations have a strong 'washback' effect on what teachers teach and students learn inside classrooms. Unfortunately, India's board examinations only test for recall or procedural skills (factual information). For example, over 60 per cent[13] questions in the Class Ten-level science and technology question paper of Gujarat Board tested procedural skills and only 7 per cent of questions checked for application of a few basic concepts. This results in a scenario where students (even high-performing ones) learn facts, without building any deep understanding of the underlying concepts. Over the next five years, the percentage of questions testing for analytical and reasoning skills should be gradually increased to about 65 per cent.

The above governance and institutional reforms are just indicative of the politically high-stakes decisions that individual states have limited incentives to take on their own. Hence, there is an urgent need to provide hard incentives such as funding while simultaneously providing states with the necessary technical support to make this transition.

c. Challenge Grants for Districts

For challenge grants, the process should be based on a clear outcome metric which is easily measured, drives alignment through the entire district, encourages transparency and promotes change from the start. We believe that while learning outcomes across the board are important, ensuring foundational learning is most critical and is also easily measured. A district-level plan with inputs from all district institutions (like District Institute of Education and Training, project offices of Centrally Sponsored Schemes, etc.) would go a long way in effective implementation. To achieve the outcome, districts should be free to call upon the resources of the state government or the expertise from the non-governmental sector.

Case Study: Race to the Top, USA

One country where a bold policy reform on similar lines was undertaken recently is the US. Just two months into his presidency, on 17 February 2009, then President Barack Obama launched Race to The Top (R2T), a $4.35 billion competitive grant program designed to encourage and reward states and districts to create the conditions for school education innovation and reform. The policy focused on driving reform in four core areas establishing high, challenging learning standards aligned to college and career readiness, developing and supporting effective school teachers and leaders, creating data systems to inform and enhance instruction and turning around the lowest performing schools.

Participating states bought together stakeholders at all levels— teachers, school leaders, teacher educators, district superintendents and state-level officials—to put forward plans to improve not a few isolated elements of their schools, but to design and operationalize a comprehensive reform agenda at a system level.

Out of 46 states in phase 1 and 12 states in phase 2, 12 were awarded grants ranging from $75 million to $700 million. Phase 1[14] winners Tennessee and Delaware were awarded $500 million and $120 million respectively, which amounted to 10 per cent and 5.7 per cent of the respective budgets of the two states for school education for a single year.

R2T was instrumental in catalyzing education policy reform across the country. Data[15] on policy enactments show, on average, states enacted 5.8x policies in the six-year period from 2009 to 2017, as compared to the previous eight years (2001 to 2008). With the previous trends, it would have taken multiple decades to accomplish what was accomplished in less than five years.

In addition to incentivizing states to undertake reforms in the focus areas mentioned above, the federal government assisted R2T States through the Reform Support Network (RSN). RSN connected states with technical experts in various fields, enabled cross-learning across states, and supported documentation of their reform efforts.

By increasing visibility for bold education, this programme, not just influenced policy in winning states, but also in states that participated and lost, and states that did not participate at all. The application process itself generated strong momentum behind policy reform.

Implementation Strategy

In phase 1, the 20 per cent funding linked to governance reforms can go to states/UTs who have passed bold reforms. Here the NITI Aayog's School Education Quality Index (SEQI) can play a major role. SEQI is an annual index that benchmarks states on three dimensions of outcomes—learning, access and equity—and key governance indicators. The index recognizes the crucial role of states and explicitly seeks to encourage positive competition and to propel them to innovate to improve outcomes and learn from each other. The index, with 36 per cent weight on outcomes, will bring in the much-needed focus on outcomes.

To start with, the funding could be linked to improvements in governance indicators of SEQI. This gives time for outcome data (which is primarily based on NAS) to stabilize. In the medium term, funding can move to improvements in learning outcome component of SEQI.

For the challenge grants, the programme could be implemented in a phased manner with competitive process among all the districts. Districts could be asked to submit a three-year plan to ensure all students by Class III have attained foundational literacy and numeracy, and the best 10 per cent among them could be selected. The districts, along with the state society for the new integrated scheme could get into a MoU with MHRD to ensure smooth fund flow and implementation. It would be important to ensure continuous monitoring and evaluation at the end of each year to ensure the progress is being made in the right direction.

Potential for Impact

The ultimate result of this policy reform would be to improve the learning trajectory of the entire nation as measured in national and international surveys. A positive externality would also be a body of evidence around practices and governance reforms which have helped improve the learning outcomes across multiple contexts in a cost-effective manner.

◆

Ashish Dhawan is founder and chairman of Central Square Foundation (CSF), a philanthropic foundation focused on systemic reform in school education. Ashish is also founder and chairman, Board of Trustees, Ashoka University.

Endnotes

1 Education Statistics at a Glance, MHRD, 2016 (NA values have been considered as zero).

2 Budget Briefs, Sarva Shiksha Abhiyan, Avani Kapur, Mridusmita Bordoloi, 2017.

3 Education Statistics at a Glance, MHRD, 2016.

4 Education Statistics at a Glance, MHRD, 2016.

5 World Bank Group, Value for Money from Public Education Expenditure on Elementary Education in India, World Bank, Washington, DC, 2016.

6 Prof. Karthik Muralidharan, Andhra Pradesh Randomized Evaluation Studies.

7 Luis Crouch, 'Raising the Floor on Learning Levels: Equitable Improvement Starts With the Tail'; 'Worldwide Inequality and Poverty in Cognitive Results', MHRD website: Draft Framework for Implementation of Samagra Shiksha Abhiyan.

8 'How Have States Designed Their School Education Budgets', CBGA and CRY, 2016.

9 Aiyar, Yamini; Ambrish Dongre; et al, 'Rules vs Responsiveness', Centre for Policy Research, 2015.

10 District Information System for Education (DISE), 2015–16.

11 Annual Status of Education Report (ASER), 2016.

12 Fiscal Cost of Weak Governance, Muralidharan, et al.

13 *Reforming Board Exams for Learning with Understanding*, Raghav Rohatgi & Pranav Kothari Educational Initiatives Pvt. Ltd., India.

14 Howell, William G., 'Results of President Obama's Race to the Top', Education Next, 2015.

15 Ibid.

SECTION 2

Transforming Rural India

Doubling Farmer Income: Case for Growth in Livestock Income

Adi Godrej

Last year, the prime minister, in his Independence Day speech, referred to farmers twelve times. The PM concluded by saying, 'Together, we will build such an India where farmers can sleep without worry. By 2022, they will earn double of what they are earning today.' The first time that the PM shared his dream of doubling farmers' income was in Bareilly, at a Kisan rally on 28 February 2016. Then, the finance minister's budget speech mentioned it on 29 February 2016.[1] Since then the question of how to double farmers' income has attracted the attention and efforts of all stakeholders in this space—farmers, policymakers, economists, agri-researchers and the industry.

Growth Trends in Farmer Income

Farm households earned ₹77,888 in the period from July 2012 to June 2013 or ₹6,491 per month during this period. During July 2002 to June 2003, the earning of the farm households, based on a similar survey by NSS, was ₹2,115 per month.[2] While in nominal terms, this implied trebling of farmer household income; in real terms, household income grew by 3.4 per cent CAGR over the period 2002–03 to 2012–13.

The survey also shows that about 53.37 per cent of farm

households earn income lower than the poverty line income. Bihar, Uttaranchal, Uttar Pradesh, Puducherry and Jharkhand had more than 60 per cent farm households earning less than the poverty line while Telangana, Sikkim, Gujarat, Lakshadweep, Jammu & Kashmir, Haryana, D&N Haveli, Meghalaya, Punjab, Kerala, Chandigarh and Delhi had less than 40 per cent farm households earning below the poverty line.[3]

Farmer's income has also remained low in relation to the income of those working in the non-farm sector (figure below). During the early 1980s, farm income per cultivator was 34 per cent of the income of a non-agriculture worker. After 1993–94, relative income of farmers worsened and reached one-fourth the income of non-agricultural workers. There was some improvement during 2004–05 to 2011–12 but no change over the 1983–84 level. Low levels of absolute income as well as the disparity between the income of a farmer and non-agricultural worker constitute an important reason for the emergence of agrarian distress in the country.[4]

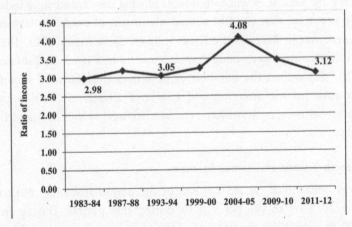

Figure 1. Ratio of Income Per Non-agriculture Worker to Income Per Cultivator[5]

Source: Doubling Farmer's Income, Ramesh Chand, NITI Policy Paper No. 1/2017, March 2017

Our internal analysis at Godrej Agrovet shows that inflation has driven nominal growth in farmer incomes over the last nearly fifteen years and going forward with inflation outlook being muted, the real income growth has to substantially jump to 6–8 per cent real income growth for farmers' income to double.

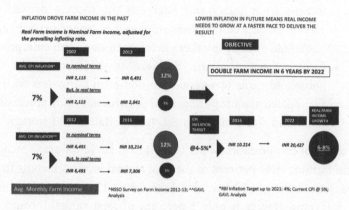

Figure 2. Drivers of Growth for Farmer Income

Components of Farmer Income

The government has defined four major components of the farmer's household income:

- Income from cultivation: is the income a household earns from cultivation of various crops (both seasonal and annual). The total value from cultivation is the sum of the value from sale of primary products and by-products. The costs incurred in cultivation includes seed costs, fertilizer costs, manure costs, pesticide costs, interest, costs of irrigation, cost incurred in hiring machinery, minor repairs, hired labour and animal labour. Hence, the total income from cultivation is arrived at by subtracting the total costs from the total value.
- Income from livestock: is the income a household earns from sale of various products like milk, eggs and live animals. Total value from this income source is calculated as the total value of milk, eggs, live animals, wool, fish, honey, hides, bones and manure. The costs incurred includes cost of animal 'seeds',

animal feeds, veterinary charges, interest, lease rent, labour charges and other expenses. The total costs are subtracted from total value to obtain net income from livestock.

- Income from wages and salary: is the income derived by various household members employed in labour outside their household—either in other's fields or in non-farm enterprises.
- Income from non-farm business: is the income that the household earns by engaging in non-farm businesses such as agri-related manufacturing, rural construction, food processing, water and waste management, transportation and storage.[6]

In terms of composition, as per the 2012–13 survey, average income from farming is 47 per cent of the total annual income, income from wages and salary is 32 per cent, livestock is 13 per cent and non-farm income average is only 8 per cent of total annual income. In the previous round (2002–03), these components were 46 per cent, 39 per cent, 4 per cent and 11 per cent respectively.[7] Thus, compared to the previous survey round, wages and salary income have shrunk and the largest expansion has happened in income from livestock. This is further corroborated by the breakdown of real farmer income growth of 3.4 per cent CAGR that corresponds to the following CAGR for farming income, livestock income, wage/salary income at 3.7 per cent, 14.3 per cent, 1.4 per cent respectively and non-farm business income growing negligibly.[8]

Looking at an aggregate level, analysis of state-wise compound annual growth rates for 14 major states in India for different components of farm household income and total farm household income over the period 2002–03 to 2012–13 shows that growth rates of total income in the decade have been highest in Haryana (8.3 per cent), Rajasthan (8.1 per cent) and Odisha (7.6 per cent), while it is lowest in the states of Assam (-0.3 per cent), Bihar (-0.8 per cent) and West Bengal (-1.3 per cent). Haryana's growth has largely come from incomes from cultivation (8.8 per cent) while that of Rajasthan and Odisha has come through growth in incomes from livestock (45.1

per cent and 36.1 per cent respectively). Incomes from livestock also show a high correlation with growth rates of total income (0.77). The three high-growing states in terms of livestock incomes are also the three high-growing states in terms of total income. On the low income states, Bihar has shown the lowest growth (-3.6 per cent) in livestock incomes.[9] Hence, policies that enable growth in income from livestock offer a potential option to grow real farmer household incomes.

Livestock Income—Benefits & Drivers

Livestock play important roles in farming systems in developing countries, helping provide food and income, draught power, fertilizer and soil conditioner, household energy and a means of disposing of otherwise unwanted crop residues.[10] They act as liquid assets that provide a hedge to inflation to farmer income, especially for small holding and landless farmers.

As per the NSS survey 2012–12, 69.42 per cent of farm households in India own less than one hectare of land and 86.58 per cent of farm households own less than two hectares of land.[11] Livestock is more crucial for lower landholding classes as it contributes 26 per cent of household income to the lowest landholding class and 7 per cent to the highest landholding class.[12] Research further indicates that livestock farming actually helps balance the income of the farmer. With most of the livestock business having better demand, production and remunerative prices in and around the Rabi season, farmers can look at more enhanced and balanced income in future. The profitability measured as GVO/cost is 1.94 in Kharif while it is 2.2 in Rabi.[13]

A USDA report (2012) on the effects of climate change on agriculture asserts that, 'Given the projected effects of climate change, some US agricultural systems will have to undergo more transformative changes to remain productive and profitable.' Adaptation measures such as diversifying crop rotations, integrating livestock with crop production systems, improving soil quality, minimizing off-farm flow of nutrients and pesticides, and other practices typically associated with sustainable agriculture are actions that may increase the capacity of the agricultural system to minimize the effects of climate change on productivity.[14] Thus, adding livestock to complement farming operation might be an effective way to hedge against weather extremes, while also improving and protecting soil health and cash flows.

The benefits from livestock farming are further augmented by the global and Indian headwinds on production and consumption of livestock-based food sources. As per the latest FAO data, around 7 kg of pulses are consumed worldwide per person per annum[15] while around 10.1 kg of meat is consumed worldwide per person per annum.[16] According to the OECD-FAO Agriculture Outlook 2017–26, in contrast with the previous decade, the overall growth in agricultural demand over the outlook period (2017–26) will be mainly driven by population growth. For livestock related commodities such as meat, fish and dairy, this increase in demand due to growth in population will be driven by population growth in developing countries, particularly India and Sub-Saharan Africa. In Sub-Saharan Africa, the population will increase from 974 million to 1.3 billion, an increase of 289 million; the population of India will grow from 1.3 billion and see an increase of almost 150 million. Together, both regions will account for 56 per cent of total population growth over the next decade, while India overtakes China as the world's most populous country.[17]

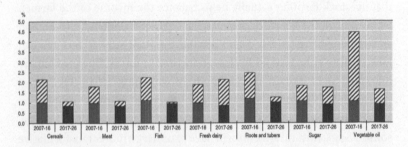

Figure 3. Annual Growth in Consumption for Key Commodity Groups, 2007–16 and 2017–26[18]

Source: Internal Godrej analysis

Additionally, as a major exception to this trend, growth in fresh dairy products will also be driven by increase in per capita demand. Projected growth rates for fresh dairy for the coming decade are higher than those experienced over the past ten years, driven by increasing per capita demand in developing countries, most notably India,[19] which is also expected to be a key source of animal protein in the coming decade.

Growing Livestock Income—Challenges and Enablers

Despite the importance of livestock, particularly to low-income farming households, the sector receives only about 12 per cent of the total public expenditure on agriculture and allied sectors and about 4–5 per cent of the total institutional credit flowing to agriculture and allied sectors. Only 6 per cent of the animal heads (excluding poultry) are provided insurance cover. Further, only about 5 per cent of the farming households in India access information on livestock. Organized slaughtering facilities are too inadequate.[20]

Additionally, the average yield of milk and meat in our animals is 20–60 per cent lower than the global average.[21] For example, India and the European Union (EU) both produced around 160 Mt in 2016; however, India achieved this level with an average yield of 1.3 t and 122 million heads, whereas the EU had an inventory of only 23 million heads but average yields of 7 t per head.[22] Deficiency of feed and fodder accounts for half of the total loss, followed by the problems of breeding and reproduction (21 per cent) and diseases (18 per cent).[23] Lack of access to formal markets and technical inputs often prevent farmers from further investing in livestock income.

While the government has covered significant ground in the areas of policy and investment towards breeding through the National Project for Cattle and Buffalo Breeding (NPCBB) and National Dairy Plan (NDP), and fodder and feed development through the Accelerated Fodder Development Program (AFDP), two areas require policy focus:

- Increasing fund utilization for funds allocated under existing livestock schemes.
- Increasing talent pipeline of veterinary doctors.

Bulk of the investment for livestock development comes from the state governments. The central government contributes about 10 per cent to the total investment. There is hardly any private sector investment in animal husbandry.[24] As per the Department of Animal Husbandry statistics, there was a shortfall of 31 per cent in animal husbandry and 23 per cent for dairy development in the expenditure to outlay. Thus, being a state subject, uniform implementation of funding and project management of livestock schemes is a key challenge. For the funding that is allocated, it is important to ensure that it is sufficiently and uniformly allocated across states for various livestock schemes.

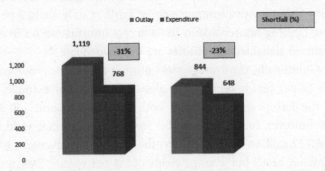

Figure 4. Funds Allocated and Utilized Under Livestock Schemes 2014–15 (INR Crore)
Source: Report Of The Working Group On Animal Husbandry & Dairying 12th Five Year Plan (2012-17)

It is suggested that an integrated approach similar to the National Skill Development Mission can be adopted to ensure the participation and coordination of various government departments, private organizations, NGOs and funding agencies. A central unified project monitoring mechanism must be created with clear targets by time frames and deliverables including fund utilization. Further, implementation time frames should be reduced to 18–24 months from the start of project to increase fund utilization. Schemes and programmes for livestock income development can be awarded for implementation in the competitive mode, rather than being solely under the purview of the state departments as the implementing agency.[25]

Another critical area requiring further focus is the availability of qualified and trained veterinary doctors to provide the necessary technical support and guidance to farmers to take up livestock as a source of income. Only 34,500 veterinarians are employed for field services against the requirement of 67,000. Similarly, against the requirement of 7,500 veterinary scientists for teaching and research, only 3,050 are available. Availability of para-vets and other supporting staff is only 52,000 against the requirement of 259,000. Shortage of technical manpower for teaching, research and extension and for field services thus further affects quality of manpower and services.[26]

Government institutes continue to be the primary source of qualified manpower in this highly specialized area. There are currently 48 government and seven private veterinary colleges in India with an average capacity of 60 students per college. For a country with one of the largest livestock populations in the world, this amounts to 3,300 veterinarians in a year. In particular, further growth in private education is constrained due to the stringent regulation by the Veterinary Council of India (VCI) of the Minimum Standards of Veterinary Education at National level. It stipulates, among others:

- A dedicated teaching veterinary clinical complex.
- An instructional livestock farm complex (min. 20 acres).
- Fully-equipped anatomy, physiology and biochemistry laboratories.
- At least 87 teachers at assistant, associate or full professor levels.

Currently, of the seven private veterinary colleges in India none has received the VCI recognition.[27] Fulfilling these minimum standards is difficult for private institutions and discourages private investment in livestock sector education. Additionally, training and development of para-vet staff that is involved in delivery of vaccination, artificial inseminations and other minor veterinary practices should also be encouraged, particularly in and around rural areas to further skill the youth. Hence, focused intervention to develop critical technical human resource with adequate infrastructure such as laboratories, colleges and polytechnics is essential for the growth of this sector.

Given the low growth and relative disparity of farmer incomes, the goal of doubling those by 2022 will require alternate options to be followed.

In addition to providing benefits of food and income, draught power, fertilizer and soil conditioner to the farmer, livestock-based food sources such as meat, dairy and fisheries is witnessing growth in consumption across India as well as globally. This is commensurate with the increase in population expected in India for the next few decades as well as per capita increase in consumption of animal protein buoyed by rising per capita income.

To enable the growth of this sector, policy focus is required around critical areas of central and integrated project and aid management as well as an impetus to human resource development in the highly specialized and technical area of veterinary and animal sciences. In my view, this should provide a significant fillip in the journey of doubling farmer incomes in coming years.

◆

Adi Godrej is the Chairman of the Godrej Group.

Endnotes

1. Gulati, Ashok, Hussain, Siraj, 'Doubling farmer's income by 2022: Here are the whopping numbers required', *Financial Express*, 28 August 2017.
2. 70th Round National Sample Survey, Ministry of Statistics & Programme Implementation, January–December 2013.
3. Farmers' Income in India: Evidence from Secondary Data, Thiagu Ranganathan, Report to Ministry of Agriculture.
4. Doubling Farmer's Income, Ramesh Chand, NITI Policy Paper No. 1/2017, March 2017.
5. Ibid.

6. Farmers' Income in India: Evidence from Secondary Data, Thiagu Ranganathan, Report to Ministry of Agriculture.
7. 70th Round National Sample Survey, Ministry of Statistics & Programme Implementation, January–December 2013.
8. Farmers' Income in India: Evidence from Secondary Data, Thiagu Ranganathan, Report to Ministry of Agriculture.
9. Ibid.
10. Livestock and Food Security, FAO Corporate Document Repository
11. 70th Round National Sample Survey, Ministry of Statistics & Programme Implementation, January–December 2013.
12. Farmers' Income in India: Evidence from Secondary Data, Thiagu Ranganathan, Report to Ministry of Agriculture.
13. Ibid.
14. Climate Change and Agriculture in the United States: Effects and Adaptation. USDA Technical Bulletin 1935, Walthall, C.L et al, 2012.
15. FAO Food Outlook, June 2016.
16. World Agriculture: Towards 2015/2030–an FAO Perspective, FAO Corporate Document Repository.
17. OECD-FAO Agriculture Outlook 2017–2026, OECD-FAO, 2017.
18. Ibid.
19. Ibid.
20. Report of the Working Group on Animal Husbandry & Dairying 12th Five Year Plan (2012–17).
21. Ibid.
22. OECD-FAO Agriculture Outlook 2017–2026, OECD-FAO, 2017.
23. Report Of The Working Group On Animal Husbandry & Dairying 12th Five Year Plan (2012–17).
24. Ibid.
25. Ibid.
26. Ibid.
27. Damodaran, Harish, '30 crore cattle and rising, but where are the country's vets?' *The Indian Express*, December 2014.

Sashakt Gaon, Samriddh Bharat: Transforming Rural India

Chanda Kochhar

India is an emerging economic powerhouse with the potential to sustain high growth over a long period. The government's policy initiatives and reforms are bringing about significant structural changes in the economy. In recent years, foreign investment has been liberalized, ease of doing business has been enhanced and far-reaching tax reforms have been introduced. Steps have been initiated to revamp the urban landscape. At the same time, there has been a strong focus on inclusive growth, with initiatives to improve financial inclusion, expand insurance and pension coverage, introduce efficiencies in social benefit transfers and bring needs like sanitation into sharp focus.

Achieving the objectives of national prosperity, eradication of poverty and deprivation and healthy living standards for our people requires viable livelihood opportunities, availability of social and physical infrastructure and access to markets—which are typically associated with urban areas. However, close to 70 per cent of Indians live in rural areas. Even after a decade from now, when an estimated 40 per cent of India is expected to be urbanized, we will still have approximately 900 million people living in rural areas. If India is to truly turn its demographics into an advantage, transforming the rural economy would be critical. This challenge could be broken down into two parts. First, urgent steps need to be taken to tackle low agriculture productivity and terms of trade for the agriculture sector. The other part, or rather the other side of the coin, is to find ways to productively absorb the surplus agriculture labour, through a range of livelihood related and capacity-building measures. The strategy for transforming rural India thus requires a multipronged approach, including improving the viability of agriculture, diversifying rural livelihood opportunities and building capacity among the rural population to capitalize on these opportunities. The focus has to be on creating holistic ecosystems of development that improve income levels of the rural population and boost overall growth, fully leveraging digital connectivity to link the hinterlands with the mainstream of the economy.

Revitalizing Agriculture

Despite the falling share of agriculture in India's GDP, from close to 30 per cent in the early 1990s to around 14 per cent at present, almost half of India's population still remains critically dependent on this sector. An estimated 57.8 per cent of rural households[1] in the country were agricultural households in 2013, with a large proportion concentrated in the north. About 35 per cent of agricultural households hold less than 0.4 hectare of land and another 35 per cent hold between 0.4 to 1.0 hectare of land.[2] In the countries that have achieved rapid economic transformations—whether the latest i.e. China, or Britain, the world's first industrial nation—agriculture revolutions have preceded industrialization. For instance, China recorded rapid agriculture growth between 1978 and 1984, when agriculture GDP grew at an average of more than 7 per cent, and income growth in rural areas rose even faster.[3] Agriculture productivity really took off in the 1980s, with one study noting that Chinese farmers could buy 80 per cent more industrial goods compared to what they could just ten years earlier. As a result, surplus farming incomes financed capital expenditure while excess farm labour moved out of fields, into the factories.

India lags global peers significantly in terms of agriculture productivity, be it in crops, or in other agriculture-allied activities such as livestock or fisheries. In the major crops, rice and wheat yields in India are 53.3 per cent and 57.2 per cent of the yield in China (based on 2016 figures). In horticulture crops, productivity is less than half of that of US for potatoes, and 68.8 per cent of that of Indonesia for bananas.

India can be optimistic about boosting agriculture productivity based on the fact that there is a large variation observed in yields across the country. High productive states such as Haryana and Punjab (the beneficiaries of the first Green Revolution) are vastly more productive compared to Madhya Pradesh, Maharashtra, Rajasthan, Odisha, Chhattisgarh and Karnataka. Thus, it is even more imperative to concentrate on low-yielding states when framing productivity improvement strategies.

Dimensions of Productivity Improvement

Productivity improvement in agriculture has many dimensions. These include investing in irrigation facilities to reduce weather dependency. Farmers can be educated about various options for high-quality inputs and crop varieties through digital means. Leveraging technology can substantially enhance access to both information and physical inputs. Development of physical infrastructure can ease access to markets for procuring inputs and selling produce. Digital technology and Aadhaar can be used to digitize land records and analyse landholdings as well as land use. Local communities and local self-governing bodies can be involved in building cooperative farming models using this data, to facilitate investment and achieve scale.

The minimum support price (MSP) regime could be reviewed and used as a tool for price support and food stock management, rather than income support to farmers. A new system of procurement of food stock could be envisaged which is guided by evolving consumption patterns and will kick in when prices are at or below MSPs in order to build buffer stocks; these stocks would be depleted whenever prices hit threshold above MSPs. In this way, procurement agencies would be trading in food crops with respective MSPs as the target price. This would however require coordination between central and state governments, decentralization of procurement operations and enhancement of storage capacities. The outsourcing of procurement and storage operations to the private sector may also be explored.

Creating Alternate Livelihood Opportunities

Pursuing a strategy of improving farm productivity and viability should be simultaneously accompanied with efforts towards generating opportunities for gainful employment beyond farming activities i.e. while increasing the surplus income from agriculture, the surplus labour engaged in agriculture would need to be given alternate opportunities. The typical growth path followed by other economies in Asia was to gradually transition from agriculture to low skilled manufacturing and finally to more skill intensive jobs. India leapfrogged this transformation, with exports geared towards high-skill intensive sectors such as engineering goods, petroleum products or software services.

The first alternate source of livelihood could be the agri-linked sectors themselves. As efficiency builds within agriculture sector, this will have a multiplier impact on other agriculture related activities like trade, food processing and the food service industry where opportunities will get created. India has significant levels of wastage of agricultural produce. Encouraging setting up of agri-ancillary industries in and near rural areas would provide twin advantages of providing employment and effectively using the agricultural output. Allowing large retailers to participate in the agri-value chain would encourage them to invest in building cold storage and processing facilities nearer to crop-producing areas. In addition the setting up of labour intensive industries requiring semi-skilled workforce, near predominantly rural areas, should be actively encouraged. As farm incomes grow, the surplus incomes will begin to finance capital and mechanized farming, while excess farm labour will move out of the fields to other forms of economic activity. India needs to have a planned approach for such a transition.

Enhancing the Participation of Women

A study on India's female labour force participation by the World Bank has shown that participation has dropped over the last decade.[4] Two factors are attributed to the decline. One is the extended years of schooling among females which keeps them away from the labour force. The other more interesting insight is that, with less than half of Indian men employed in agriculture, nearly two-thirds of working women are tied to farm-based activities. As rural areas develop, female participation drops as the number of women working in the services and industry sectors is low in India compared to other countries. Thus, as rural areas develop and begin to urbanize, women drop out of the labour force. Assuming a large number of these women are into subsistence farming, it is necessary to provide vocational training to women to be able to participate in economic activities in the manufacturing and services sectors.

A transformation of rural India thus requires empowering the women in these areas to be able to continue their participation in economic activities beyond agriculture. This will require putting in place gender-sensitive labour policies that promote female participation, vocational training for rural women to improve employability and creating village-level job opportunities in which women can also participate, to stem the dropout among women due to the changing character of rural India.

Building Capacity to Capitalize on Livelihood Opportunities

Our experience at ICICI Foundation confirms that skill development for sustainable livelihoods in the rural areas has to be a part of any solution for a rural transformation. This is necessary considering the low access to quality education and vocational training in these areas, which has hampered the employability of the rural workforce. As the rural economy transforms, it is necessary to support entrepreneurial thinking and providing opportunities for relevant training to be gainfully employed.

Skilling initiatives should have a specific focus on semi-urban centres near rural areas in order to augment the skill levels of rural labour. It is estimated that just around 2–4 per cent of our workforce is formally skilled. India should aim to get this proportion up to 25–40 per cent. It is thus imperative that skill gaps and limitations of skilling programmes are identified and then quickly addressed. In particular, imparting vocational skills in areas such as carpentry, masonry and electricals can go a long way in helping the rural youth attain sustainable livelihoods. Skilling operations need to be scaled up rapidly. For instance, in 2015–16, about two million people were enrolled for skilling under the Pradhan Mantri Kaushal Vikas Yojana.[5] But that enrolment needs to be at least ten times higher in coming years to fully leverage our demographic dividend. Further, the programmes should minimize dropouts and also aim for a high proportion of success in terms of employing the skilled. Skilling on a PPP-basis could also be encouraged, along with setting up of local small-scale units that enable the rural workers to act as suppliers to larger firms, enabling them to join the regional value chain. ICICI Bank and ICICI Foundation have undertaken significant initiatives in skill development in recent years. Our experience suggests that the approach to skill development should have the following key elements:

- Collaboration between government and private sector.
- Focus on identification of relevant skills.
- Two-pronged approach of training in skills required in developed urban markets as well as locally relevant skills in rural areas.
- Tie-ups with partners for both training and employment.
- Backward and forward linkages where skill training is focused on self-employment, including access to credit and linkages to markets.

- Focus on livelihood improvement i.e. the target should be to demonstrably increase the earning capacity through skill training.
- Outreach to local communities through multiple channels, encouraging participation in skill-training programmes.
- Special focus on women, whose participation can have a significant positive impact on household income.

Investing in Rural Infrastructure

Connecting the rural economy to markets and consumers, domestic as well as global, can play an important role in creating a structural shift and diversification in the rural economy. Investment in rural infrastructure can thus have a multiplier effect. Good telecom connectivity and an efficient transportation network have been proved to create significant direct and indirect benefits on economic productivity and economic growth. In addition to physical infrastructure and digital connectivity, education, health, water, sanitation and waste management are important components of rural infrastructure.

Significant efforts are underway for building rural infrastructure through roads, rail and digital connectivity. However, there are significant gaps in the availability of social infrastructure in rural areas that need to be addressed to enhance human capacities. In the area of education, access to primary stage school education facilities today is available within a distance of one kilometre in rural areas. Enrolment rates, including those of females, have increased substantially and are close to 100 per cent at the primary level. The student-teacher ratio has also been improving. However, learning outcomes at these schools are a challenge compared to urban areas. Further, higher education is characterized by low enrolment and high dropout rates.[6] In the area of health, there are significant gaps with a shortfall of 22 per cent in the availability of primary health centres and 30 per cent in availability of community health centres across the country as of March 2016.[7] A large part of medical expenses for low-income households are out-of-pocket expenses, unlike in most other countries where they are insured. Rural sanitation and availability of clean drinking water are also areas of concern.

Action has been initiated in many of these areas. The government's drive on cleanliness has helped in significantly improving the sanitation coverage in rural areas from 39 per cent in 2014 to 76 per cent in January 2018.[8] Housing is another area where the government has launched schemes to improve homeownership and build permanent dwellings. Focused, persistent and accelerated efforts are required till every Indian in the rural areas has access to basic health, education facilities, clean drinking water, sanitation and a shelter.

A transformation in the rural economic structure thus implies having a holistic approach to building infrastructure along with empowering the rural people to be able to avail of the benefits of the investments made. A regional approach to providing these facilities may also be explored, as the dynamics in the southern region may be very different from the requirements in the northern or eastern parts of the country. Private sector investments in tier 3 and below areas, particularly in those areas where education or health amenities are severely lacking may also help in bridging these gaps. Lessons from other countries that have also gone through this phase of developing rural infrastructure could also provide insights on the approach India needs to have to empower the rural economy.

Technology: A Transformative Force

Technology can be a significant force in transforming rural India, as the digital network expands to cover the entire country. It could be greatly beneficial in:

- Accessing information on real time basis relating to market prices for crops, farming techniques, weather, sowing patterns, input and output price trends, etc.
- Connecting to large markets, including through an online platform.

- Enabling a market for delivery of farm inputs to farmers at their doorstep.
- Creating a rental market for equipment and machinery. This can be hugely beneficial to small farmers who are unable to fund large fixed costs needed to access farm machinery.

There are already start-ups in the 'Farming as a Service' (FaaS) space modelled after the 'Software as a Service' (SaaS) paradigm. The appeal for small farmers is that such services can be availed on a rental or variable cost basis without entailing large fixed costs. Facilitating the spread of such companies will have positive externalities in the form of improved productivity, increased knowledge base and more employment opportunities. Rural youth can be trained to work for companies in the FaaS space. These firms should leverage on the official rural outreach channels already in place.

Technology could also be beneficial in the areas of education and health, through digital content creation to impart training and telemedicine for improving access to rural patients. Platforms could be created for local panchayats to monitor the functioning of local schools and hospitals. Further, technology brings transparency and increases the pressure on hospitals and teachers to perform better in these areas. Panchayats at the village level, with the help of the state governments, could also create a platform to showcase the key strengths of the local economy to attract investments.

From the government's perspective, technology can be leveraged to augment policy measures and strengthen the rural economy. A key area where technology is playing an important role, and which can be further accelerated, is in the delivery of financial services in rural India. The Jan Dhan-Aadhar-Mobile trinity, and the impetus given to digitization, creates the conditions to enhance financial inclusion. Financial inclusion is not limited to bank accounts or credit, but includes transaction facilities and insurance. Along with the creation of livelihood opportunities, financial services delivered using technology can go a long way in enabling growth and resilience in the rural economy.

A comprehensive approach is required that addresses multiple objectives of increasing agricultural incomes, creating alternative means of livelihood, building capacity among the rural population, especially women, and making the necessary hard and soft infrastructure available to support revitalization of the rural economy. A rural transformation is essential to achieve our goal of becoming a more prosperous country with endemic poverty firmly eradicated— *Sashakt Gaon, Samriddh Bharat.*

◆

Chanda Kochhar is the MD and CEO of ICICI Bank Limited, India's largest private sector bank by consolidated assets.

Endnotes

1. Source: NSS Report No. 576: Income, Expenditure, Productive Assets and Indebtedness of Agricultural Households in India, 2012–13.
2. NSS Report No. 569, Some Characteristics of Agricultural Households in India, 2013.
3. Sahoo Pravakar, Bhunia Abhirup, 'China's Manufacturing Success: Lessons for India', IEG Working Paper No. 344, 2014.
4. World Bank, India Development Update, Chapter: Unlocking Women's Potential, May 2017.
5. Press release of Ministry of Skill Development and Entrepreneurship, 'More than 1.17 crore people skilled under Ministry of Skill Development and Entrepreneurship programmes', 6 June 2017.
6. Ministry of Human Resource Development, All India Survey on Higher Education, 2015–16.
7. Press Information Bureau, Press release of Ministry of Health and Family Welfare, 28 July 2017, http://pib.nic.in/newsite/PrintRelease.aspx?relid=169215
8. Economic Survey 2017–18.

Promoting Solar Power as a Remunerative Crop

Tushaar Shah

In May 2017, the world's first Solar Pump Irrigators' Cooperative Enterprise (SPICE) completed its first year of operation in the village of Dhundi in central Gujarat. Solar pumps are not new in India, and their number has grown from less than 7,500 in 2010 to nearly 100,000 in 2015–16. Usually, these pumps continue to run whether the farmers need the power to irrigate or not, since surplus solar energy anyway goes waste. But the members of SPICE operate differently. Once the farmers are done with irrigation, they pool their surplus solar energy and sell it to the Madhya Gujarat Vij Company Limited (MGVCL), the local power distribution company (or DISCOM) under a 25-year power purchase agreement. In return, these farmers have surrendered in writing their right to apply for a subsidized grid power connection for 25 years.

The first group of farmers to join the cooperative were offered a feed-in tariff (FiT) of ₹4.63/kilowatt-hour (kWh) for the solar power sold to the DISCOM. In mid-2016, this was the lowest tariff any utility-scale solar generator had won in open bidding. To incentivize the farmers to conserve groundwater, the International Water Management Institute (IWMI) and CCAFS (CGIAR programme on Climate Change, Agriculture and Food Security), which piloted the Dhundi cooperative, offered farmers a green energy bonus of

₹1.25/kWh and a water conservation bonus of another ₹1.25/kWh, taking the total FiT to ₹7.13/kWh for the power sold.

Although solar pumps became operational in January 2016, the power purchase agreement came into force only in May. So, before May 2016, they used all the energy generated for pumping groundwater. But from June 2016 onwards, their energy use for pumping declined and their energy sales began to increase. This was consistent with IWMI's original premise: At a FiT of ₹7.13/kWh for solar energy sold, farmers would pump groundwater as if they were using the grid power supplied at ₹7.13/kWh.

Table 1
Operating Results of Dhundi Solar Cooperative January 2016–May 2017

Net income (Rs) from:	2015–16	2016–17
Crops	528670	497792
Sale of solar pump irrigation	133550	153850
Sale of surplus solar energy	6523	364534
Net household Income/year	668743	1016176

*Diesel pump irrigation sales by SPICE members ended in Rabi 2015
Source: DSUUSM 2017:6

Table 1 summarizes the initial results of Dhundi SPICE for the first 18 months with the installed capacity of 56.4 kWp of six solar pumps. 45,350 kWh (47 per cent) was used for irrigation and 52,150 kWh (53 per cent) was injected in/sold to the grid from the total generation of 97,500 kWh. The six member farmers earned ₹3.64 lakh from solar energy sales, which constituted 65 per cent of their net household income which increased by 52 per cent from 2015–16.[1]

Numerous Benefits to Farmers

Dhundi has plentiful groundwater, amply recharged by two surrounding minor canals of the Mahi irrigation system which wet parts of the village farmland. Yet groundwater irrigation has been expensive since all 49 owners of irrigation wells in Dhundi, except one, use 7.5 to 10 horsepower (hp) diesel engines to lift groundwater.[2] These diesel pumps deliver energy for pumping at an effective cost ranging from ₹18–₹25/kWh, whereas farmers in nearby grid-connected villages get subsidized electricity at ₹0.70/kWh. Little wonder Dhundi SPICE members find solar pump irrigation preferable not only to the costlier diesel pump irrigation, but also subsidized grid-electricity, which is supplied for seven to eight hours daily, with frequent interruptions and voltage fluctuations, often during the night (Shah and Verma 2008). Solar power, in contrast, is uninterrupted, predictable and available during daytime—free of cost.

Initially, farmers were worried about the land footprint of solar panels; but they are now experimenting with a range of high value shade-loving crops such as spring onion, spinach, carrot, garlic, beet and some medicinal plants that grow well under the elevated solar panels. Some are also growing paddy underneath the solar panels. The land footprint of Dhundi SPICE is thus insignificant.

Farmers visiting Dhundi SPICE marvel at the idea of 'growing' and selling solar energy as a cash crop that needs no seeds, fertilizer, pesticides, irrigation and back-breaking labour and has the DISCOM as a ready buyer at their farm-gate at an assured price. The income from the solar crop is not affected by droughts, floods, pests and diseases. Moreover, with the MGVCL's 25-year contract, they face neither price risk nor market risk.

However, the high capital investment in solar panels is a major deterrent. Initially, the farmers were neither sure whether solar panels could drive their pumps nor that MGVCL would pay for their surplus power. No wonder, the first six members grudgingly contributed only ₹5,000/kWp towards capital investment, the balance subsidized by the IWMI/CCAFS research grant. Now that both these doubts have been put to rest, three new farmers joining the SPICE have contributed ₹25,000/kWp, nearly 40 per cent of the total investment. This is not surprising. They view the solar pump not only as an irrigation asset but as a *kamadhenu* (cow fulfilling your wishes), delivering a 'climate-proof', risk-free and zero-cost income stream.

In Mujkuva, a village 30 km away from Dhundi, where tube well irrigation is done by using subsidized grid power, a dozen farmers have agreed to work with the National Dairy Development Board (NDDB)[3] and IWMI to organize a Dhundi-pattern SPICE by contributing ₹10,000 kWp for 10 hp pumps, ₹15,000/kWp for 15 hp pumps, and ₹20,000/kWp for 20 hp pumps.

Pro-poor Water Market

Dhundi SPICE has benefited not only solar farmers but also their neighbours. The arrival of solar pumps has transformed the area's water market in profound ways. Before the SPICE was formed, 49 diesel pump owners sold irrigation service to some 200 small farmers at ₹500/bigha of wheat crop, which roughly covered ₹280 towards diesel/kerosene cost and ₹220 towards maintenance cost, water seller's labour and profit. A five-kWp solar pump owner now irrigates a bigha of wheat crop in five hours, using 25 kWh of solar energy and charges buyers' only ₹250/bigha. At this rate, solar farmers earn ₹10/kWh, 40 per cent more than the FiT of ₹7.13/kWh for selling power to the MGVCL. For the water buyers, it is a bonanza as their irrigation cost has halved. It is no wonder that fifteen diesel pumps in the SPICE neighbourhood have shut down fully or partially. A consequence of the lower irrigation cost is that a larger area is being irrigated, leading to an increase in the aggregate groundwater draft. However, the adverse consequences would be much greater without a power buy-back guarantee, resulting in as much groundwater depletion as the use of free grid power has caused throughout western India.

Gains to DISCOM

SPaRC will liberate DISCOMs from the dead weight of farm power subsidies which are responsible for their precarious finances. Had the Dhundi SPICE members taken grid power connections for 56.4 kW instead of solar pumps, they would have been entitled to 162,000 units[4] of grid electricity annually at ₹0.70/unit as against the MGVCL's cost-to-serve of ₹4.50/unit.[5] Even if only two-thirds of this entitlement was used for irrigation, the MGVCL would have had to bear a subsidy burden of over ₹4 lakh per year.[6] Additionally, the MGVCL would have been required to invest ₹12 lakh[7] to connect these tubewells to the grid, at an amortized annual cost of ₹1.2 lakh.[8] Dhundi SPICE has saved the MGVCL all these costs.

The current power purchase agreement assigns to the DISCOM carbon credit for all solar power generated by the SPICE. Now that renewable purchase obligations (RPO) are being enhanced and enforced strictly, the market for renewable energy certificates (REC) has been revived (Nayar 2016). As a 'RPO-Obligated entity', the MGVCL has earned equivalent of ₹2.8 lakh[9] for 79,159 units per year of solar generation by Dhundi SPICE in its first year.

Overall, Dhundi SPICE will leave the MGVCL better off by ₹8 lakh/year[10] for 25 years with a present value of ₹73 lakh at 10 per cent percent discount rate. Even if the DISCOM shared a third of these annual gains with the Dhundi cooperative members, the latter would get additional FiT of ₹5.06/unit[11] over and above the DISCOM's average power purchase cost (APPC) of ₹3.5/kWh.[12] And even after paying such a remunerative FiT, the DISCOM will still be better off than supplying farmers grid power at ₹0.70/kWh.

Overall Benefits and Costs

The total capital investment in installing the solar pumps, micro-grid, cabling, switches, transformer and meters in Dhundi was ₹50.65 lakh, with SPICE members contributing ₹4.65 lakh and the CCAFS/IWMI contributing ₹46 lakh. Three parties—SPICE members, water buyers and the MGVCL—stood to gain from this investment. Figure 1 presents a partial budget of the decision to switch from diesel pump irrigation to solar powered pumps instead of grid-power connections in Dhundi.[13]

The benefits to SPICE members—which determine their willingness to invest capital—include increased irrigation of their fields, valued at the opportunity cost of ₹100/hour levied by diesel pump owners; net income from selling irrigation service; saving in diesel cost; and net revenue from the sale of surplus solar energy to the MGVCL. The water buyers benefit by an increase in the number of hours of irrigation, valued at the opportunity cost of ₹100/hour. The benefit to MGVCL is the implicit saving of farm power subsidy and the market value of RECs earned.

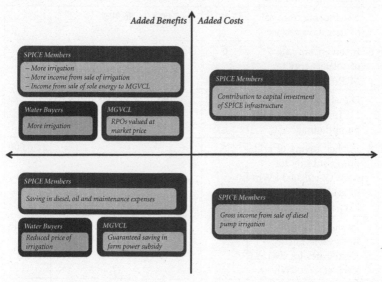

Figure 1. Partial Economic Budget of Transition from Diesel Pump Irrigation to Dhundi Spice Instead of Grid-Powered Tubewells[14]

Table 2
Financial and Economic Benefits of Dhundi SPICE:
Results from 1st Year of Operation (DSUUSM 2017)

		Before (Diesel Pumps)	After (Solar Pumps)	Gains to (₹)		
				SPICE members	Water buyers	MGVCL
1	Hours of irrigation spent on personal fields	1,032.5	1,696.5			

2	Market value of irrigation hours spent on personal fields	1,03,250	1,69,650	66,400		
3	Hours of irrigation sold	1,856.5	2,840			
4	Market value of irrigation hours sold	1,85,650	2,84,000		99350	
5	Net Income from sale of irrigation service	55,595[15]	1,42,000	86,405		
6	Income from sale of solar energy to MGVCL	0	3,64,500	3,64,500		
7	Diesel and oil costs (₹) [projected for solar pump hours]	1,73,340	2,72,190[16]	2,72,190		
8	Implicit saving of grid power subsidy for MGVCL: 28,000 kWh of grid power at ₹4.5/kWh					1,26,000
9	Implicit Value of Renewable Energy Certificates for 79,159 kWh at ₹3.5/kWh					2,77,056
	Total			7,89,495	99,350	4,03,056

Table 2 presents estimates of the benefits to the three parties. The SPICE members gained ₹7.9 lakh/year by generating 79,159 kWh of solar power (a weighted average revenue realization [WARR] of ₹10/kWh generated). Over 20 years of its economic life, the solar micro-grid will deliver an economic internal rate of return (IRR) of 23 per cent if benefits to all three parties are considered and 15 per cent if the benefit to SPICE members is considered. With a capital subsidy of ₹45/Wp, a generation factor of 4.5 kWh/kWp/day and a WARR of ₹6/kWh, Dhundi-pattern SPICE would be bankable with the economic IRR exceeding 21 per cent over a 20-year project cycle in addition to the extra benefits to water buyers.

Demand-side Groundwater Management

Managing groundwater demand is India's major resource governance challenge. Elsewhere in the world, 'persistent groundwater depletion is always self-terminating' (Vaux 2011) because rapidly rising energy cost of pumping makes groundwater irrigation progressively unprofitable as water levels fall. In India, however, perverse power subsidies incentivize the waste of energy and groundwater depletion through deep tube wells. Figure 2 shows that India's electric tubewells are concentrated in 10 states, which account for 90 per cent of the total number of agricultural grid connections in the country. All these offer free or subsidized farm power supply. No wonder, as Figure 3 shows, that four-fifths of India's groundwater overexploited blocks are concentrated in these ten states.

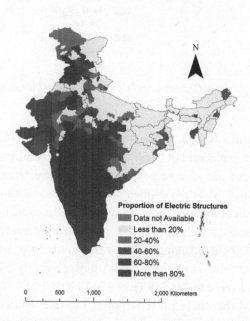

Figure 2. Energy Divide in India's Groundwater Economy (Shah et al 2016:14)

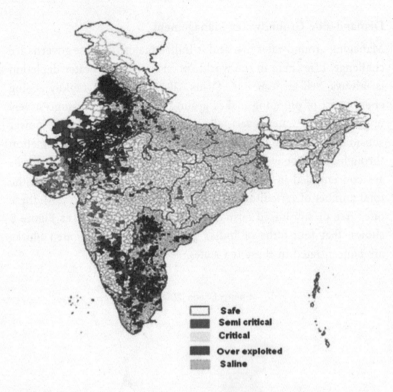

Safe
Semi critical
Critical
Over exploited
Saline

Figure 3. Geography of Groundwater Depletion in India (Planning Commission 2007:9)

State governments and NGOs have been trying hard to rein in groundwater depletion but to no avail, thanks to this perverse nexus. Worried about the adverse political fallout of the removal of farm power subsidies, state governments usually avoid tackling the issue. Power subsidies have accelerated groundwater depletion, raised energy use in irrigation, which in turn has made power subsidy impossible to abolish without invoking the farmers' wrath on a massive scale. Between 2000 and 2013, India's farm power subsidy bill increased from ₹27,083 crore to ₹66,989 crore (GoI 2001 2014). There appears no likelihood that these perverse power subsidies will end soon.

India's over 15 million electric tubewells consumed 168,611

million units of electricity worth ₹119,294 crore in 2014–15; against this, DISCOMs recovered ₹32,600 crore from farmers. This left a revenue gap of ₹86,694 crore (₹5.14/kWh), which was met by a mix of state government subsidy and cross-subsidy by non-farm consumers of DISCOMs (PFC 2016). SPaRC offers a painless and politically acceptable way to end these subsidies. As a bonus, solarizing tubewells can deliver the entire target of 100 gigawatts (GW) of solar capacity which the central government wants to achieve by 2022. Given India's massive agricultural load, Dhundi-pattern SPICEs, which get integrated at the tail-end of the grid, can contribute enormously in smart-grid management.

Presented properly, farmers would readily take to SPaRC under the Dhundi-type cooperatives. With a capital subsidy of ₹45/Wp in solar micro-grids and a guaranteed FiT of ₹5 per kWh, farmers would readily embrace the SPaRC option in which:

i.   They continue to have the option to use subsidized grid power.

ii. They also have more and better quality solar power.

iii. Once net-metered, they can also sell surplus solar power (net of grid power drawn).

iv. They can earn even more by conserving water and energy by adopting water-saving crops and efficient irrigation technologies. As a bonus, solarizing our electric tubewells will reduce India's annual greenhouse gas emissions by 4 to 5 per cent (Shah 2009), helping the country meet its committed Intended Nationally Determined Contributions (INDCs) in Paris treaty.

SPaRC Compared with other Models of Solar Pump Promotion

India's policy framework for promoting solar pumps should aim to:

i.   Incentivize farmers to conserve energy and groundwater to control over-exploitation.

ii. Reduce farm power subsidy burden on DISCOMs.

iii. Maximize farmer contribution to the capital cost of solarizing the groundwater irrigation economy.
iv. Contribute to doubling farmer incomes and to India's INDCs under Paris agreement.
v. Offer rapid scalability.

Several models of solar irrigation are being tried by NGOs and state governments. But there are five which have policy traction and need to be evaluated against the above stated objectives. This has been attempted in Figure 4 in which the number of dots suggests our qualitative assessment of to what extent a given model furthers a policy objective.

DISCOM-centred model: The current policy promotes solar pumps with attractive capital cost subsidy to farmers wait-listed for grid power connections by DISCOMs. Its supposed benefit saves subsidy burden on DISCOMs. In reality, it contributes to none of these six objectives, primarily because it adds to existing diesel or electric pumps rather than replacing them. Studies show that most solar pump owners use them as secondary or standby pumps to complement diesel/electric pumps. This policy will most likely accentuate groundwater depletion in western India and have little or no impact on farm power subsidies.

Farmer-centred SPaRC model: As Figure 5 suggests, SPaRC promotes the objectives which none of the other existing models claim to do. But the Dhundi model as implemented now is difficult to scale up as the capital cost subsidy extended by IWMI/CCAFS was high. Moreover, DISCOMs will resist a FiT of ₹7.13/kWh as the solar energy tariffs have plummeted. However, the model can be rapidly upscaled with a capital cost subsidy of ₹45/Wp and FiT of ₹5/kWh generating a WARR/kWh of ₹6 or more, offering IRR of 21 per cent over 20 years (see Table 2).

	1 DISCOM-centered Model	2 Farmer-centered SPaRC Model	3 Developer-centred Farmer-dedicated Solar Plant	4 Developer-centered Distributed Model I	5 Developer-centered Distributed Model II
Example	Present policies in all states	Dhundi & Mujkuva, Gujarat	PRAYAS model Maharashtra	Suryaraitha, Karnataka	Gujarat's draft policy
Objective 1: Will it incentivize farmers to conserve energy and groundwater?	●	●●●●●	●	●	●●●
Objective 2: Will it reduce farm power subsidy burden?	●●	●●●●●	●●●	●●●	●●●
Objective 3: Will it contribute to India's INDCs under Paris agreement	●●	●●●●●	●●●●●	●●●●●	●●●●●
Objective 4: Will it incentivize farmers to share capital investment in solarization?		●●●●●	●	●	●
Objective 5: Will it help in doubling farmer incomes?	●	●●●●●	●	●	●●●
Objective 6: Does it offer rapid scalability?	●●	●●●●	●●	●	●●●

Figure 4. Comparing Alternative Models for Promoting Solar Pumps in India

Developer-centred Farmer-dedicated Solar Plant

A tail-end solar plant model being promoted by the NGO Prayas is being piloted in Maharashtra, involving setting up of 1–2 MW size power plants on panchayat land near feeder ends. These plants, having standard power purchase agreements, will supply free-day time power to farmers with surplus/deficit being injected to/drawn from grid. These plants will be cheaper and more efficient, will not require any subsidy, will also help meet the DISCOM's RPO and will interest investors since it will save them the cost and hassle of acquiring land. But they will neither incentivize energy nor water conservation nor will they put any cash income in the hands of the farmers.

Developer-centred Distributed Model I: Another model promoted by the Bangalore DISCOM was piloted in Karnataka in 2016. In this model, 220 farmers surrendered their grid-power connections in lieu of solar pumps with 1.5 times more panels than the rated pump capacity. The farmers could use free solar power between 8 a.m. to 4 p.m. The surplus solar power was to be sold to the DISCOM at ₹9/kWh; but for the first 10 years, the rate of ₹8/kWh was to be applied to recover the capital cost, interest and developer profit. In effect, the farmers got free power for irrigation plus ₹1 per kWh for any power evacuated. Farmers have not yet been paid by the DISCOM and the only benefit for farmers now is free daytime power. Although the DISCOM meets the RPO obligation and developers save on the cost of land, the project provided no incentive for energy and water conservation nor did it offer an income flow to farmers.

Developer-centred Distributed Model II: A draft policy by the Gujarat government advocates Dhundi type solar cooperatives but grants developers capital cost subsidy at ₹41/Wp if they forgo accelerated depreciation benefit (or ₹34/Wp, if they do not) on three times more panels relative to the pump capacity. The panels will be owned by developers for a period of five years; but the farmers will get one-third of the power generated for free, while the developer sells his share to the grid at the agreed upon tariff. The farmers too can sell this power but at 85 per cent of the tariff, with the developer claiming the balance 15 per cent. The farmer gets free power, has some incentive to conserve water and power, and is spared the capital investment. The developer saves on the cost of land, benefits from the attractive capital subsidy offered, and remains the main residual claimant.

The Way Forward

The key infirmity in developer-centric models III, IV and V lies in the assumption that saving on land cost will be enough to attract developers to invest in distributed solar plants despite the ambiguous ownership and management conditions these models entail. In our assessment, the developers, besides the capital cost subsidy on offer under the JNNSM, will expect a high FiT (of ₹6–7/kWh or thereabouts, in our estimate) that will cover the cost of:

i. Providing free power to farmers.
ii. Chaotic operation and maintenance of distributed solar generation.
iii. Losing scalar economies of utility scale plants.
iv. Above all, high organizing, monitoring, vigilance and transaction cost of dealing with a multitude of farmers. This will be decisive because rampant power theft can turn the economics of these models awry.

Then there are issues specific to each model. In model III, two to four hectares needed for tail-of-the-feeder megawatt scale feeder plants will involve the additional costs of land as well as professional management, which may make upscaling difficult. In model V, the question is, why would the Ministry of New and Renewable Energy (MNRE) give a developer three times the subsidy a farmer is entitled to, and equally, what incentive would farmers have to cover three times more land with panels than they need to when they already get free or near-free grid power?

A central issue is that in all developer-centric models, the farmer is a passive recipient of free power in lieu of allowing panels to be laid on his fields. He has no stake in maximizing generation or in cleaning or safeguarding the panels or controlling theft. If the land cost is less than 5 per cent of the cost of a megawatt scale solar plant (Santhanam 2015), why would a developer have his panels scattered over several hundred fields in possession of farmers over whom he has no control? In models IV and V, neither farmers nor DISCOM lose from power theft. This will hit developer revenues, and he will find it difficult to control theft.

The SPaRC model suffers from none of these infirmities. It is the only model with a fully working pilot in Dhundi and another coming up in nearby Mujkuva village. It is farmer-centric. It has no duality of ownership and management: Farmers own solar panels, and their cooperative owns and manages the microgrid. Since farmers are full residual claimants, they will have a stake in efficient management of solar generation and its use. While all models only offer farmers free power, SPaRC also offers them a risk-free income stream. Since power theft will directly reduce their incomes, solar farmers will control theft. Being members of the same community, they are better placed to keep vigilance. The depreciation benefit to solar developers under the JNNUSM amounts to around 30 per cent of the capital cost (see Ronak and Parekh 2016).[17]

For SPICE to become bankable and scalable, all that is needed is a slightly higher capital cost subsidy of around ₹45/Wp to solar cooperatives and a guaranteed FiT of ₹5/kWh with an inflation-adjusted annual markup. Under such a regime, there is a distinct likelihood that solarizing our fifteen million grid connected electric tubewells through SPaRC model by itself can deliver 100 GW of our solar target, in the process transforming our groundwater economy and helping double farmer incomes.

◆

Tushaar Shah is a senior fellow at the International Water Management Institute (IWMI). The author would like to acknowledge the support of Neha Durga, Gyan Prakash Rai, Shilp Verma, and Rahul Rathod.

References

1. DSUUSM (2017): 'Dhundi Solar Energy Producers' Cooperative Society: First Bi-Annual Report', Dhundi Saur Urja Utpadak Sahakari Mandali (DSUUSM), iwmi-tata@cgiar.org
2. Gambhir, A, Dixit, S., 'A ray of hope for solar-powered agriculture', *The Hindu Business Line*, 8 July 2015.
3. Gujarat Energy Research and Management Institute (GERMI), Gandhinagar
4. Government of India (2001): Annual Report on Working of State Power Utilities and Electricity Departments (2000-01), Planning Commission, Power & Energy Divison, June 2001, New Delhi.

5. Annual Report on Working of State Power Utilities and Electricity Departments (2013–14), February Central Electricity Authority, Ministry of Power, New Delhi.

6. Nayar, R., 'Enforcing Renewable Purchase Obligations', *Economic & Political Weekly*, Vol. 51, No. 40, pp 21–23, 2016.

7. PFC (Power Finance Corporation Ltd) (2016): Report on 'The Performance of State Power Utilities for the years 2012–13 to 2014–15,' New Delhi.

8. Planning Commission (2007) 'Report of the Expert Group on Groundwater Ownership and Management', September, New Delhi: Yojana Bhawan, http://planningcommission.nic.in/reports/genrep/rep_grndwat.pdf

9. Ronak, M., Parekh, S., 'Accelerated Depreciation: A Major Benefit for Solar Power,' *Energetica India*, September–October, www.energetica-india.net/download.php?seccion=articles&archivo...pdf

10. Santhanam, Narasimhan, 'What are the Initial Investment and O&M Costs Required for a MW Solar Plant in India?' Solar Mango Newsletter, 20 September 2015, http://www.solarmango.com/ask/2015/09/20/what-are-the-initial-investment-and-om-costs-required-for-a-mw-solar-plant-in-india-what-kind-of-financial-returns-can-we-expect-from-it/

11. Shah, T., 'Climate Change and Groundwater: India's Opportunities for Mitigation and Adaptation,' *Environmental Research Letters Journal*, Vol. 4 No. 03 : 5005 (13pp), 2009, http://iopscience.iop.org/article/10.1088/1748-9326/4/3/035005/pdf

12. Shah, T., Verma, S., 'Co-management of Electricity and Groundwater: An Assessment of Gujarat's Jyotirgram Scheme,' *Economic & Political Weekly*, Vol. 43, No. 7, pp 59–66, 2008.

13. Shah, T.; Verma, S.; Durga, N.; Rajan, A.; Goswami, A.; Palrecha, A., '*Har Khet Ko Pani*: Rethinking Pradhan Mantri Krishi Sinchai Yojana', Anand: IWMI-Tata Water Policy Program, 2016, www.iwmi.cgiar.org/iwmi-tata/PDFs/iwmi_tata_pmksy_policy_paper_june_2016.pdf

14. IANS (2017): 'Solar powered solution for groundwater crisis,' *The Hans India*, 6 June, http://www.thehansindia.com/posts/index/Commoner/2017-06-06/Solar-powered-solution-for-groundwater-crisis-/304727, accessed 4 August 2017.

15. Vaux, H., 'Groundwater under stress: the importance of management,' *Environmental Earth Sciences*, Vol. 62, No. 1, pp 19–23, 2011.

Endnotes

1. Source: Computed from data provided in (DSUUSM 2017)
2. The main problem in Dhundi is that land records have not been updated for generations. As a result, every landholding has numerous registered owners including some who are long dead and daughters married off in faraway villages. Applying for an electricity connection requires a no objection certificate from all owners, which is extremely difficult and costly.
3. National Dairy Development Board has organized over 100,000 dairy cooperatives all over India since 1965.
4. 8 hours/day *360 days* 56.4 kW = 162,432 kWh
5. Given by Gujarat Energy Research and Management Institute and confirmed by MGVCL.
6. 162,000 units/year *0.66* (₹4.5–₹0.7) = ₹406,296
7. The average cost of providing new tubewell connections to Gujarat DISCOMs is around ₹2 lakh which rises to ₹3.5 lakh for High Voltage Distribution System (HVDS) connections (pers. Com. GERMI, Gandhinagar).
8. Assuming interest and depreciation cost of this investment at a conservative 10 per cent/year in perpetuity.
9. Renewable Energy Certificates currently trade at ₹3,500/MWh (see www.iexindia.com). This price may change in future depending on the demand-supply dynamics.
10. Subsidy on grid power saved (₹4 lakh) + amortized cost of connecting tubewells (₹1.2 lakh) + value of REC earned ₹2.8 lakh = ₹8 lakh
11. 0.33 (8 lakh)/52,150 units = ₹5.06/unit
12. This is currently around ₹3.50/unit (Source: MGVCL).
13. 'Partial Budgeting: A Tool to Analyze Farm Business Changes,' Iowa State University, Extension and Outreach, https://www.extension.iastate.edu/agdm/wholefarm/html/c1-50.html
14. Developed by authors using information from DSUUSM 2017.
15. Assumed that ₹30/hour is the net income after fuel and maintenance cost.
16. Estimated diesel use to provide 4536.5 irrigation hours valued at ₹60/litre.
17. If the developer claims 100 per cent depreciation in year one, he will earn tax benefit of ₹40.8 lakh on a capital cost of ₹120 lakh. The 2016 Union budget curtailed this benefit somewhat; but the benefit remains nearly the same.

Overcoming Liquidity Constraints to Manage Farmer Risk

Shubhashis Gangopadhyay

Prior to the Pradhan Mantri Fasal Bima Yojna (PMFBY), only 23 per cent of Indian farmers availed of crop insurance. Under the PMFBY, the government expects this figure to rise to 50 per cent. To achieve this, the government will subsidize the actuarial premium so that farmers do not have to pay, as premium, more than 2 per cent of the total sum insured (SI).[1] According to the latest Agriculture Census of India (2010), 85 per cent of farmers have less than two hectares of land and are in the small and marginal category. By 2030, the Agriculture Minister believes that this number will become 91 per cent.[2] Thus, even if PMFBY meets its target, significant numbers of small and marginal farmers will remain uninsured. This is a serious concern as weather shocks, especially in rain-fed agriculture, are a big problem for Indian farmers, regardless of the size of their landholdings.

Adverse shocks do not only have disastrous implications for vulnerable farming households when they happen. The threat of such adverse shocks in the absence of insurance distorts crop and farming technology choices that affect soil quality leading to long-term impacts on farming incomes. Farmers, however, have not been insuring themselves even when premium rates have been subsidized. Market driven premium rates cannot be less than the probability of adverse shocks. Thus, if the weather fails once in five years, implying a 20 per cent probability of a negative shock in any year, the market premium has to be at least 20 per cent. This lower bound on the market premium is attained only when the insurance market is competitive and the probability of an adverse shock faced by a farmer is independent of what is happening to other farmers. Any relaxation of these assumptions will imply an even higher premium rate.

To understand this, consider the premium paid on things that we routinely insure, e.g., a car. Most of the things we insure have premiums that are less than 2 per cent of the sum insured. That is because the probability of loss on these items is less than 2 per cent. Indeed, insurance markets work when loss is a low probability event. But in the case of weather, we would need a premium of at least 20 per cent for sustainable, or no subsidy, insurance to work. This, however, is a problem because such high premiums require farmers to have enough liquidity to buy insurance.

To put matters in perspective, let us do some simple calculations. The 2011–12 poverty line, according to the Rangarajan Committee's 2014 report, was ₹32 per day in rural areas.[3] Multiplying by 30, this implies a monthly expenditure of ₹960 to stay above the poverty line. This translates into ₹11,520 (960 x 12) per year. For a family of four, the annual household expenditure must, therefore, be at least ₹46,080 (4 x 11,520). We expect insurance markets to function in a way that enables the farmer to keep his, or her, household away from becoming poor because of a weather shock. With a 20 per cent probability of crop failure, this would imply a minimum market premium of ₹9,216 for a total coverage, or SI, of ₹46,080. That is a lot of money to be paid upfront as premium and it assumes that a farming household has that amount of liquidity before it has received any income!

Alternative Financial Instruments

The low uptake of market crop insurance is a worldwide phenomenon. An important reason for this is the lack of liquidity that farmers of all sizes, small to large, and in all countries, developing and developed face at the time of paying premiums. Insurance premiums have to be paid at the beginning of the season, when farmers have the greatest need for liquid funds to finance their expenditures on seeds, fertilizers and hired labour. This is highlighted in a report of the US Department of Agriculture,[4] which states that 'with savings, relatively wealthier farmers appear to spend less on insurance and self-insure through savings, while limited-resource farmers with low farm income use savings to increase insurance coverage.' Given that our small and marginal farmers have little or no savings, liquidity becomes a binding constraint that discourages them to buy insurance. In other words, more than the premium *rate*, it is the premium *amount* and its timing that results in low insurance uptake.

The obvious question to ask is whether there exists a financial instrument, other than insurance, that achieves the same objective that insurance does, but overcomes the liquidity constraint faced by the farmer. If a farmer wants to buy insurance coverage of ₹100,000 and the premium to be paid for that is ₹5,000, then by the beginning of the sowing season, the farmer buys insurance by paying the premium upfront. In the event of a loss at the end of the season, the insurer pays the farmer ₹100,000 and if there is no loss, the insurer pays nothing. So, in insurance, first the farmer pays (the premium) and then the company pays (coverage bought) if the weather is bad.

Now, suppose we were to make the farmer pay *after* the weather shock is resolved, i.e., defer the payment of the premium. Then, if there is no adverse weather, the farmer pays the insurance company deferred premium; if there is a negative weather shock, the insurance company pays the farmer the coverage bought minus the premium. Continuing with our example, in bad weather, the company pays the farmer ₹95,000 (deducting the hitherto unpaid premium) and when there is no loss, the farmer pays the insurer ₹5,000. In other words, with this new instrument the farmer is called upon to make the payment only when he has enough cash inflow, i.e., when there is no income loss. An instrument that effectively ensures this deferred payment of the premium was developed in Gangopadhyay (2004)[5] to address the risks faced by the small Indian plantation growers.[6] A major aspect of this alternative instrument is that it eases the liquidity constraint faced by the farmer.

A modified version of the instrument suggested by the author[7] was tried out in Ethiopia as a randomized control trial with more than 8,600 farmers in three districts. While the control group was offered the standard insurance product, the deferred payment alternative (called the IOU) was offered to various treatment groups. The properties of the IOU, except for the delayed payment of the premium, are exactly the same as that of a standard insurance product. The delayed premium is higher than the standard premium by the amount of the risk-free interest rate to make the two premiums inter-temporally equivalent. While the insurance uptake was only around 6 per cent, more than 60 per cent of the relevant treatment group took up the IOU instrument. The trial was carried out by the author with a team of researchers from the Netherlands and Ethiopia and the study was funded by 3ie and DFID. In addition to researchers, the team included the private insurance company that sold the insurance and took in the IOUs.

The findings of this study are particularly relevant for farming households that cannot smoothen income throughout the year. While the usual policy approach is to subsidize crop insurance, for the farmers themselves this is an irony since insurance requires payment of premium when the farmer's disposable income is at its lowest to receive compensation after the harvest when disposable income and food are usually higher than when planting!

Addressing Challenges

There are two hurdles that need to be addressed when premium payments are deferred: (a) This is a new instrument and so requires awareness training and (b) the fact that premium payments are deferred leads to major trust issues. Trust is an important factor because while farmers may line up to claim when weather is bad, they may abscond (to avoid paying the premium) when the weather is good. So, it is essential to introduce an intermediary between the farmers and the insurance company. This intermediary, or institution, will be credible to the insurance company and, at the same time, enjoy the confidence of the farmers. In the Ethiopian experiment, the 'Iddir' was used as the relevant institution. They are informal social institutions that can be found almost throughout Ethiopia. Originally, Iddirs were created to help their members organize burial ceremonies. Nowadays, they also provide mutual aid and financial assistance when members face a variety of shocks. The Ethiopian experiment used Iddirs because, in the Oromia region where the experiment was carried out, they were credible institutions to both the insurance company and farmers.

India has a rich experience with microfinance institutions (MFIs) as well as self-help groups (SHGs). Further, when it comes to commercial crops, we also have grower associations. In other words, there are enough organizations that can act as the intermediary between the farmers and the insurer. So, how exactly will it work?

Farmers 'write' IOUs that promise to pay a certain amount if the weather is good and nothing if the weather is bad. These are picked up by the MFI and 'sold' to people or organizations that are willing to buy these IOUs. These IOUs are contingent claims and, hence, have value. It can be shown that the IOU is equivalent to an 'all-or-nothing' option, a financial instrument that can be very easily priced. The revenue earned from the sale of these IOUs, or options, generates the money that covers the farmers in the event of loss.

Suppose the farmer earns ₹100 in good weather and nothing if the weather fails. Suppose also that the farmer buys an insurance coverage of ₹100 at a premium of ₹10 in a perfectly competitive insurance market where loss probabilities are independent. This assumes that the probability of loss is 10 per cent (the perfectly competitive premium rate is equal to the probability of loss and here the premium rate is 10 per cent). In good weather, the farmer makes an income of ₹100, gets nothing from insurance, but has (already) paid the premium of 10; in bad weather, the farmer earns 0, gets ₹100 from the insurance coverage bought but, again, has already paid premium of ₹10. Loosely put, the farmer gets (100 – 10) in good weather and (0 – 10 + 100) in bad weather. In both cases, the farmer gets ₹90.

Now consider what is being proposed here. The *farmer* promises to pay the company ₹100 if the weather is good and nothing if the weather is bad. (Under the insurance mechanism, the company pays the farmer if the weather is bad and nothing if the weather is good.) Observe that this is a claim contingent on the weather being good. The IOU thus becomes a financial asset that will sell at prices at or below ₹90. This is because the person buying the IOU expects to get 100, the promised value on the IOU if the weather is good 90 per cent of the times and nothing 10 per cent of the times. In other words, the expected value of the IOU to the buyer is 90 and, hence, he, or she, will buy at any price less than or equal to 90. But now what happens to the farmer? In good weather, the farmer earns 100, but has to honour the promise made to give 100 against the IOU if the weather is good. But, remember the farmer has already 'sold' the IOU for 90! So, in good weather, the farmer gets (90 + 100 – 100). But in bad weather, the farmer does not earn any income, and neither has to make any payments on IOUs sold. So the farmer gets to hang on to the 90 that he received when the IOUs were sold! Thus, the insurance outcome and the IOU outcome is exactly the same to the farmer. The big difference, however, is that the insurance requires the farmer to have ₹10 to pay the premium, while for the IOU, the farmer requires no liquidity to begin with. The IOU calls upon the farmer to make payment only when he has enough liquidity (when good weather and, hence, good harvest happens).

How significant is the 'default' by farmers—farmers refusing to pay the deferred premium, or honour the IOU, when the weather is good? In the Ethiopian experiment, such default was very small. Indeed, in one version of the experiment, the deferred payment was implemented through a joint liability contract but without any role of the village Iddir. There was little difference in the default rates and in both cases they were very small. We could thus implement the instrument through MFIs or self-help groups and the national agricultural insurance company.

The advantage of the IOU is that agricultural risk management strategy no longer needs to be specific to the crop thus reducing, to a large extent, the distorted technology choices and moral hazard resulting from subsidized insurance. It also enables aggregating farming risk nationwide by integrating IOUs generated by farmers growing different crops and in different regions. In the insurance set-up, the premiums paid by farmers who suffer no loss are used to pay farmers that suffer loss. In other words, the insurance game is played between the insurance company and all those who are exposed to the risk (the farmers). With an IOU mechanism, the game is played among the farmers, the intermediary and those who want to buy the farmer IOUs. The latter choose to expose themselves to the risk in much the same way as a person buying a company share chooses to expose himself to the risks borne by the company.

◆

Shubhashis Gangopadhyay is Research Director, IDF; Professor of Emerging Market Finance, University of Groningen, Netherlands and Visiting Professor, Gothenburg University, Sweden.

Endnotes

1   Government of India, *Operational Guidelines: Pradhan Mantri Fasal Bima Yojana,* Ministry of Agriculture, Cooperation and Farmers Welfare, http://agri-insurance.gov.in/Pmfby.aspx (as on August 27, 2017)

2   http://economictimes.indiatimes.com/news/economy/agriculture/91-land-holding-would-belong-to-small-farmers-by-2030-radha-mohan-singh/articleshow/50978336.cms, 27 August 2017)

3   http://www.hindustantimes.com/business/demystifying-india-s-poverty-line-here-s-everything-you-need-to-know/story-43vy1sQ7LrCZuezTakDnkM.html, 27 August 2017)

4   Farrin, Katie; Miranda, Mario J.; O'Donoghue, Erik, 'How Do Time and Money Affect Agriculture Insurance Uptake? A New Approach to Farm Risk Management Analysis', *Economic Research Report,* No. 212, USDA, 2016.

5   Gangopadhyay, Shubhashis, 'An Alternative to Crop Insurance', *Economic and Political Weekly*, 39(4), October 30, H.T. Parikh Finance Column, 2004.

6   This was submitted as a report by this author to the PSFT Task Force in 2007 where the author was an adviser.

7   Farrin, Katie; Miranda, Mario J.; O'Donoghue, Erik, 'How Do Time and Money Affect Agriculture Insurance Uptake? A New Approach to Farm Risk Management Analysis' *Economic Research Report*, No. 212, USDA, 2016.

SECTION 3

Towards Inclusive Growth and Prosperity

Digital Onboarding and the Future of Finance in India

Adhil Shetty

Digital technologies—and how we use them in our personal lives, work and society—continue to change the face of businesses worldwide. The financial services industry, in particular, continues to undergo dramatic digital disruption. Retail and small business banking customers now expect instant, seamless experiences across channels. Customers no longer just compare the product offerings from competing brands, but also compare their banking experiences with e-commerce players like the Amazons and Ubers of the world. Customers are increasing the use of digital channels, and digital usage now accounts for the majority of banking interactions in India.

In the coming years, as technology (4G, LTE) improves and smartphones become ubiquitous, cell phone usage will become the epicentre of digital banking. More than half of all mobile devices sold today are smartphones; and this figure is expected to rise to 80 per cent by 2020. The Internet has become the most favoured channel for customers and many of them are migrating to mobile banking. A decrease in internet costs and proliferation of smartphones has opened the door to digital onboarding. As customers migrate to digital channels in greater numbers, it has become crucial for banks to meet their increasing expectations. Conventional, paper-based processes are too slow to compete with modern, digitized businesses, and banks will have to work to digitize all aspects of business—most importantly, the customer onboarding process. In future, customers are more likely to select a bank with a good digital banking platform. Mobile banking will be the cornerstone of the digital strategy moving forward. As smartphones become most customers' first touch point, banks need to digitize entire processes, from customer-facing to customer onboarding, loan approval, underwriting and loan closing processes to meet customer expectations and resolve manual processing issues.

In an ever-changing digital environment, banks are required to meet regulatory requirements, while also delivering the enhanced customer experience that consumers demand across a digital platform. Regulatory reform must be up to speed with digital innovation in order to allow more customers to be onboarded paperlessly and instantly. This is also the way forward for increasing the reach of formal finance. Hundreds of millions of Indians today do not have bank accounts, but they do have cell phones and Aadhaar. Using the power of the two, they can access basic financial tools such as savings accounts before graduating to buying insurance, taking loans and investing in mutual funds. Digital onboarding is not just more efficient in terms of processing time and costs, it also allows banks and financial institutions to reach deeper geographies in the country where branches and ATMs can't easily be set up.

Design Process

Customer onboarding is one of the most arduous and time-consuming functions burdening banks. On average, banks still need one to two weeks, and in some cases a month, depending on the complexity of the case, to bring a new customer on board. This appears to be a mammoth task compared to digitized onboarding, where documents may be shared instantly. However, it is surprising that many nationalized and private sector banks do not have this facility or do not accept the same due to their interpretation of the regulations and/or internal policies, which can be frustrating for customers.

Typically, while considering a customer's identity, onboarding systems at financial institutions do not give due weightage to documents collected through digital channels. The additional time that is required for manual workarounds, and the paperwork related with the onboarding process, are other reasons for the customer's frustration. Banks need to give due weightage to digital onboarding (non-face-to-face onboarding) process that will help deliver a seamless experience to the customers, and is not focused just on data capture.

Many high-value relationships evolve from low-value transactions, such as opening an account. Institutions need to establish excellence at the outset. Banks and other financial service providers have been using Aadhaar OTP based e-KYC to partially digitize the customer onboarding process. However, Aadhaar e-signatures have not been utilized for account openings. Regulatory compliance is and always will be a major challenge for financial institutions, particularly when it comes to customer onboarding. New regulations and enforcement are occurring at an unprecedented rate and continue to impact onboarding times and customer experience. Banks need the ability to update rules rapidly, and the Aadhaar ecosystem has the potential to enable that.

Physical onboarding demands staff attention, feet on street and its manual nature means that it is error-prone and its costs are relatively high. The overarching reason for banks that face regulatory scrutiny to retain traditional face-to-face onboarding is the need to identify the person opening the account and check his or her documentation. In most instances, a photo ID is all that is needed for successful authentication. Additionally, the customer also has to physically sign documents in front of the bank employee, adding another layer of authentication. This process is perceived as lowering the incidence of identity theft and reducing the opportunities of fraud.

However, the great benefit of digital customer onboarding is the automation of compliance. ID checks happen in real time, meaning that the thousands of man-hours per month spent on manual compliance checks can be saved. This process integrates digital data collection related to the applicant in real time directly from the source to make sure that approvals are fast, omniscient, and up-to-date. It fits seamlessly with risk management and fraud detection programmes because there is no time-lapse between the customer providing the information and that information going into the decision-making system of the banks and financial institutions. Digital customer onboarding assures the integrity of client data. It is more secured; it simplifies the process of meeting new regulatory changes, and also reduces the cost of compliance checks.

The Reserve Bank of India (RBI) has allowed the acceptance of Aadhaar OTP-based digital identity in the process of entering into an account-based relationship, though with certain limits. The advantage Aadhaar has over other traditional identity proofs in India is the OTP-based authentication that can be established in real time. This has led to disruption of customer onboarding process in terms of efficiency, authenticity and turnaround time. In India, Aadhaar has already created a single digital market and is being integrated with other customer identifiers like PAN, mobile number, etc. To say that in the coming future customers will need Aadhaar for any kind of payment-related services is not far-fetched.

Aadhaar-based digital identity meets the regulatory standards required for identifications by the RBI. The PMLA and KYC directions prescribe a risk-based approach, meaning that regulated entities should assess the risk involved in the account-based relationship and the procedures they apply for onboarding. The current KYC direction partially allows digital onboarding, and requires Enhanced Due Diligence procedures (EDD) for natural persons who are not physically present at a branch. The directive offers specific and adequate solutions to mitigate the risk associated with digital onboarding, and requires:

1. Establishment of an identity based on additional documents: This can be taken care of by enablement of a document upload feature.
2. Certification of documents: This can be achieved by certifying

any document through Aadhaar e-signature.

3. A first payment from an account with another regulated entity: REs can use their online/net-banking facility to one time debit (OTD) a certain amount from the non-face-to-face customer's KYC-compliant account with another RE to onboard such customer seamlessly in a simple, convenient and paperless manner.

4. Improving customer experience begins with a fully digital onboarding experience: At BankBazaar, we believe the goal for banks (and credit card providers) should be that customers can apply, access an account (digitally), and start spending through it, all on the same day. This is possible if customers' onboarding becomes completely digital and paperless. The most direct way financial service providers can improve onboarding is by ensuring the process remains fully digital. It is all about speed, lesser manual work, fewer errors, tighter compliance and meeting expectations for a modern experience.

5. The Aadhaar workflow eliminates errors (OTP e-KYC and e-Sign): All data points (customer identification and verification) and e-signature are captured correctly directly from the source without any human intervention, during a single transaction session. Manual processes result in errors, such as missing signatures and empty data fields on paper forms. Manual documentation process are time-consuming and expensive to correct. Also, fixing errors is 3–4 times the cost of an error-free digital process, simply because of all the extra time and effort involved in going back to the customer for reworks.

6. Aadhaar e-signatures expedite the process, compressing it from days or weeks to a single session: Mobile-first customers now have an alternative to paper. When people sign on a mobile device, the signing experience becomes easier and more convenient, personal and accessible than on desktops

or laptops. Giving customers the ability to e-Sign using their personal smartphone removes barriers and gives them the freedom to choose how they will transact with banks.

The Aadhaar ID can be downloaded on smartphones or other devices and allows consumers to complete a variety of operations including opening bank accounts and even filing tax declarations. The good news is that technology is not only enabling factual, practical implementation of services that could be acquired only in traditional face-to-face settings, but also satisfies any associated legal compliance requirements.

Implementation Strategy

Complex legacy systems and technologies prevent banks from adopting complete digital onboarding. The entire experience falls flat as soon as the interaction with legacy systems begins. A major barrier to transforming the customer onboarding process and designing customer-centric processes is this conventional mindset. Paperless finance helps to digitally onboard consumers looking to purchase a financial product without their presence. Consumers, no matter where they are in India, should be able to access loans, cards, deposits from any financial institution on their mobile phone without a single shred of paper or the need for a physical meeting. The biggest stumbling block is friction in the offline process i.e. physical KYC and wet-signature. This journey from paper-centric to a frictionless finance will depend on the following support from the regulators:

a.   Acceptance of e-Signature: The use of Aadhaar based e-Sign has not gained sufficient momentum in moving towards paperless digital transactions in spite of the Information Technology Act, Indian Evidence Act and the Negotiable Instruments Act recognizing its validity. Early adopters leverage e-Sign to get customers to sign loan and card applications and loan agreements, but many financial institutions are yet to adopt e-Sign though the Information

Technology Act and Evidence Act allow for it. Banks should use e-Sign to get customer to electronically sign applications and agreements. Also, an express clarification from the RBI in this regard will assist in adoption of the legally valid e-Sign within the banking domain.

b. OTP-based e-KYC onboarding: The e-KYC via OTP caps under the 8 December 2016 RBI amendment should allow for increased limits that handle the average customer requirements on the Internet today. The initial response to the circular on Aadhaar e-KYC via OTP has been muted from banks because of the limited value of the transaction that is permissible. The average loan size through the online digital mode is approximately ₹3 lakh which is higher than the allowable maximum of ₹60,000. The regulator may consider enhancing the limits for credit accounts based on second factor checks including PAN validity alongside e-KYC via OTP. There also needs to be clarity permitting the usage of OTP-based e-KYC process for credit cards.

c. C-KYC: If the current form of CKYC process is allowed to set in, it might require banks to get customers to physically complete a new CKYC form and physically sign the same. This would derail the paperless system and undo the good and successful work done towards paperless and presence-less onboarding of customers. The problem can be solved if the CKYC form, which is to be filled by the customers, can be digitized so that banks can update the CKYC database based on data collected as part of regular bank e-KYC via OTP process without the need to collect a new paper-based form for CKYC. In this regard, the support of the Ministry of Finance is required to digitize the CKYC process based on existing e-KYC processes and give the much deserved weightage to Aadhaar-based OTP e-KYC process.

d. E-NACH: The last leg of the loan disbursal process involves setting up the repayment instructions for the loan. The

NPCI has released a standard operating procedure (SOP) for E-NACH debit E-Mandates using e-Sign. Today, there are only eleven banks live with NPCI E-NACH SOP. It is important that all banks adopt this SOP so that the E-NACH mandate will be available to all loan applicants without having to resort to multiple workflows. It is requested that the RBI encourage all banks adopt NPCI's E-NACH SOP to set up e-Mandates via e-Sign.

e. Addition of issuers on the DigiLocker: DigiLocker today enables a secure, customer consent-based sharing of documents from issuer to bank. A push is required from Ministry of Electronics and Information Technology for the addition of more issuers on the DigiLocker platform, enabling users to share documents like income tax returns, TDS records, indirect tax challans and banking transactions. The addition of more issuers on DigiLocker will create a trusted paperless ecosystem enabling individuals and small businesses to share their data paperlessly for availing credit from the formal financial system.

f. RBI Master Direction of KYC to be aligned with PMLA (Maintenance of Records) Second Amendment Rules, 2017: The RBI may deliberate on reviewing its KYC guidelines/ directions to bring them in line with the PMLA requirement. It should categorize Aadhaar OTP-based e-KYC process coupled with PAN verification as complete 'Customer Due Diligence' equivalent to Aadhaar biometric authentication. RBI may also consider removing the limits imposed by its 8 December 2016 notification on account-based relationship opened via Aadhaar OTP-based e-KYC process.

Impact Assessment

Today, India has the technology and the underwriting processes to deliver paperless access to financial products. If financial institutions and regulators come together to solve the obstacles mentioned above, paperless finance will be a mass reality in the near future. The enablers will result in driving down credit and operating costs of the formal financial sector, thereby facilitating credit at better terms to retail individuals and small businesses. The absence of a significant banking infrastructure in rural India means that the Aadhaar OTP identification and e-Sign will have far-reaching advantages once the banks decide to incorporate digitalization as a customer onboarding strategy.

With technology and customer readiness, we are at the cusp of paperless onboarding of consumers through mobile phones that will democratize finance in India.

As rightly pointed out by Amitabh Kant, CEO of NITI Aayog, 'Paperless, cashless, and seamless transactions are a big revolutionary movement forward.'

◆

Adhil Shetty is the co-founder of BankBazaar.com and also serves as its CEO.

Inclusive Finance:
The Way Forward

Chandra Shekhar Ghosh

Oh God, yet another piece on financial inclusion!

At first glance, I am sure readers of this essay would react this way considering the number of articles that have been written on the subject by regulators and financial sector commentators in the aftermath of the 2008 financial crisis. This is a practitioner's point of view, laced with some suggestions on how to make inclusion in the finance space meaningful.

Understanding Financial Inclusion

Former RBI Governor Dr Y.V. Reddy coined the term 'financial inclusion' while working on the draft of the annual monetary policy statement for the fiscal year 2006–07 (statement was issued on 18 April 2006), along with then deputy governor, Usha Thorat. They came across many policy actions addressing the issue of 'financial exclusion' and, in fact, Dr Reddy had thought of using this term initially and announcing measures to overcome it. While finalizing the draft, it dawned on him that the central bank had been trying to encourage commercial banks and other financial intermediaries to reach out to more and more people and hence the right term for these activities should be 'financial inclusion' and not exclusion.

The term may have been coined in 2006, but the task of reaching out to more and more people by the Indian banking system had started in 1960s with an emphasis on giving loans to the neglected sectors of the economy and weaker sections of the population.

In the 1970s, the RBI also formed norms for priority sector lending, whereby banks were asked to channel 40 per cent of their loans to agriculture, small industries and the weaker sections of the society. The priority loan stipulation continues till date even though the constituents of the borrowers and the profile of such loans have changed. There have been experiments also with regional rural banks, local area banks and the self-help group-bank linkage programme, among others, to spread the banking service in the hinterland.

To summarize the views of two important committees (one on financial inclusion and another, on financial sector reforms) chaired by two former RBI governors—Dr C. Rangarajan and Dr Raghuram Rajan, respectively—financial inclusion is the process of ensuring access to financial services and timely and adequate credit, by the weaker sections and low-income groups of society at an affordable price. Broadly, it refers to universal access not only to banking products, but also other financial services such as insurance and equity products.

In essence, financial inclusion ensures delivery of financial services, including bank accounts for savings and transactional purposes; low-cost credit for productive, personal and other purposes; financial advisory services; and mutual fund and insurance products to this segment of people who otherwise do not have access to the high-street banks.

What Comes First?

There have been several debates on what should come first—economic and social inclusion or financial inclusion? Can we achieve financial inclusion without economic inclusion? Financial inclusion draws low-income groups within the formal banking sector and, by doing so, it frees them from the exploitation of usurious moneylenders. This means the cost of money taken on loans comes down, which enables them to build assets, support children's education and the family's health, and also creates savings habit.

Microfinance entities outside the ambit of the banking system also entered the arena offering small loans and even competing with the self-help group-bank linkage programmes in at least one state. Banks are required to channel 40 per cent of their loans to the priority sector but for logistic reasons not all banks are able to do so directly. So, they lend the money to the microfinance entities, which in turn, lend them to their borrowers. This is considered banks' exposure to priority loans.

In spreading financial services, the microfinance industry has played a critical role. Indeed, the cost of loans taken from a microfinance entity is higher than bank loans, but one must remember that microfinance entities do business in those pockets where banks fear to tread because of high transaction costs and probability of higher defaults as the loans are not backed by collaterals. For small borrowers, access to finance is more important than the cost of funds. Also, local moneylenders are far more expensive than microfinance institutions.

The First Big Step

The monetary policy of April 2006 signalled a new phase in the RBI's efforts to spread financial inclusion in a structured way. Since banks do not find branch expansion in rural India commercially viable for various reasons—ranging from low volume of business to high transaction costs and unwillingness of employees to relocate from urban centres and metros for lack of right infrastructure in terms of health and education—the framework of Banking Correspondents (BCs) was designed to enhance the access of banking services.

The RBI also encouraged banks to adopt a planned approach to financial inclusion through board-approved Financial Inclusion Plans (FIPs) the first two phases of which were implemented over 2010–13 and 2013–16.

The business model included a new type of account, called the Basic Savings Bank Deposit (BSBD) accounts, besides the issuance of

RuPay Cards—a debit card for use within India. The BSBD accounts offer certain facilities such as no requirement for minimum balance, deposit and withdrawal of cash at the bank branch and ATMs, receipt/credit of money through electronic payment channels and facility of providing ATM card.

The Know Your Customer (KYC) norms were relaxed and simplified to facilitate easy opening of bank accounts, especially for small accounts with balances not exceeding ₹50,000 and aggregate credits in the accounts not exceeding ₹1 lakh a year.

Besides, the RBI also relaxed the branch authorization policy to address the issue of uneven spread of bank branches. Indian banks are now allowed to freely open branches in tier 2 to tier 6 centres with population of less than one lakh as long as they keep the regulator informed about the branches. They do not need any permission from the RBI to open branches in northeastern states and Sikkim.

As a result of these efforts, the number of banking outlets in villages went up from 67,694 in March 2010 to 586,307 in March 2016, largely boosted by the BCs. The number of urban locations covered through BCs has also surged from 447 in March 2010 to 102,552 in March 2016.

Certain other data also show the improvement in banking coverage. Between 2006 and 2015, the number of savings bank accounts in rural India rose at a compounded annual growth rate (CAGR) of 15.8 per cent and in semi-urban pockets at 16.6 per cent—more than the all-India average (15.6 per cent). However, in terms of branch expansion, rural and semi-urban India lagged behind urban and metropolitan India. Between 2006 and 2015, the branch network in rural and semi-urban pockets rose from 45,673 to 82,794 versus 23,904 to 43,901 in urban and metro centres.

Even before the completion of the second phase of the FIPs, India witnessed the world's biggest-ever financial inclusion drive in the form of Pradhan Mantri Jan-Dhan Yojana (PMJDY), in August 2014, by the Bharatiya Janata Party (BJP)-led National Democratic Alliance (NDA) government. Its objective is to ensure access to various financial services such as availability of basic savings bank account, need-based credit, remittances facility, insurance and pension to the excluded sections. The plan also envisages channelling all government benefits (from centre/states/local bodies) to the beneficiaries' accounts and pushing the direct benefits transfer (DBT) scheme of the union government.

As on 20 September 2017, the PMJDY scheme opened 30.26 crore accounts—out of this 18.05 crore are in rural and semi-urban pockets and 12.21 crore in urban India. The balance in these accounts was to the tune of ₹66,606.01 crore. The scheme has also issued 22.81 crore RuPay cards.

The aggressive push by the PMJDY has changed the landscape dramatically. Basic savings bank deposit accounts have gone up from 7.3 crore in March 2010 to 46.9 crore on 31 March 2016. The total number of transactions done by the BCs, which were around 2.6 crore during 2010–11, has increased to 82.68 crore as on 31 March 2016.

The third phase of FIP for 2016–19 focuses the progress minutely at the district level. The banks have been mandated to open Financial Literacy Centres (FLCs) and Rural Self Employment Training Institutes and Centres for Financial Literacy (CFL) at the block level. The FLCs and all rural branches of scheduled commercial banks are encouraged to spread financial literacy by conducting outdoor financial literacy camps at least once a month. At the moment, close to 1500 FLCs are functional across India and camps are regularly held for five different target groups—farmers, small entrepreneurs, SHGs, school students and senior citizens. Meanwhile, training institutes set up at various districts offer short-term training and long-term handholding and create credit linkages for trainees.

The DBT—for which the Jan Dhan accounts are used as vehicles—has the potential to change the culture of banking in rural India. When such entitlements under various state- and centre-sponsored schemes directly flow into bank accounts, account holders feel encouraged to save. This paves the way for initial investments by an individual and flow of bank credit.

Opening Up the Sector

The RBI has, though differentiated banking licences, aggressively opened up the banking sector to foster competition and spread banking services. From Independence till July 2015, India got twelve new banks (all of them have not survived), but since August 2015, we have got two new universal banks, ten small finance banks and eleven payments banks (a few payments banks have surrendered their licences).

The payments banks can accept demand deposits up to ₹1 lakh per individual customer, issue ATM and debit cards, offer payments and remittance services through various channels, and distribute mutual fund units and insurance products. Besides, they can act as the BC of another bank.

The small finance banks, on the other hand, are required to extend 75 per cent of their loans to sectors eligible for classification as priority sector lending. While 40 per cent of such loans should be allocated to different sub-sectors of priority loans, they can allocate the balance 35 per cent to one or more sub-sectors where they have competitive advantages. The maximum loan size and investment limit exposure to a single and group borrower of such banks is capped at 10 per cent and 15 per cent of capital, respectively, and at least 50 per cent of their loan portfolios should constitute loans and advances of up to ₹25 lakh. Clearly, the focus is on small borrowers.

To intensify competition, the RBI has also put the licence for universal banking on tap. This means, there is no special window for seeking a new bank licence.

The banking regulator is also planning to open the turf for new kinds of banks such as wholesale banks and depository banks. Besides, foreign banks operating in India are being encouraged for local incorporation and one of them, Singapore's DBS Bank Ltd, has already got the regulator's nod for setting up its Indian subsidiary.

We Have Come a Long Away

The 59th National Sample Survey in 2003 found that 51.4 per cent of farmer households were financially excluded from both formal/ informal sources and overall, while 73 per cent of farmer households had no access to formal sources of credit. Across regions, financial exclusion was more acute in central, eastern and northeastern regions, and all three together accounted for 64 per cent of all financially excluded farmer households in the country. There was no dramatic change in the 60th National Sample Survey in 2013. The Government of India Population Census 2011 showed that only 58.7 per cent of households were availing banking services in the country.

In 2011, an RBI working paper worked out an index on financial inclusion (IFI), based on three variables—penetration (number of adults having bank account), availability of banking services (number of bank branches per 1000 population) and usage (measured as outstanding credit and deposit). The results indicated that Kerala, Maharashtra and Karnataka achieved high financial inclusion, while Tamil Nadu, Punjab, Andhra Pradesh, Himachal Pradesh, Sikkim and Haryana were identified as a group of medium financial inclusion.

The results of the 2011 World Bank 'Financial Access Survey' showed that financial exclusion, measured in terms of bank branch density, ATM density, bank credit to GDP and bank deposits to GDP, was quite low in India compared to most developing countries in the world. For instance, in India, the number of bank branches per 1,000 km was 30.43; number of ATMs 25.43 and number of bank branches per 0.1 million population and number ATMs were 10.64 and 8.9 respectively. Bank deposits were 68.43 per cent of GDP and credit was 51.75 per cent. The comparable figures in China were 1428.98, 2975.05, 23.81, 49.51, 434 per cent and 288 per cent respectively.

The Way Forward

The spectacular success notwithstanding, there are several challenges, including low volume of transactions in basic bank accounts, inactive BC outlets, inaccessibility and weak Internet connectivity, among others.

Going forward, we must first appreciate that the cost of credit for small borrowers cannot be compared with corporate loans and even retail loans in urban India. There have been experiments with 'no-frills' and 'zero-balance' accounts. They are savings instruments and results are not that encouraging. Credit is a different thing that must factor in other aspects. Even a small borrower with access to bank credit must furnish documents, travel to a branch and thereby spend time and money (and probably lose half a day's wage). And, after all, this there is no guarantee that the person would get the credit. So ideally, the loan should be disbursed at her home or in the close vicinity. The cost of such a loan will always be higher as the financial intermediary will factor in the delivery cost, besides the lack of securities.

High-street banks will always find it difficult to disburse such loans because of their relatively high operational cost and cost of wages and salary. Their employees are recruited though all India examinations and officers have business school background. Most of them are not equipped to understand the psyche of a rural borrower. Besides, lack of good healthcare and educational facilities will deter them from working in rural India. Those who agree to work will not compromise on their salary and perks. Further, public sector banks follow an industry-wide wage pact and they cannot pay an employee in rural India less than another who works in a metro.

Former RBI Governor Dr Reddy once said that ordinary people in India want a safe place to keep their cash, especially poor women who have to keep their earnings out of the reach of their drunken husbands. Ninety per cent of India's population is employed in the unorganized sector with seasonal or uncertain income flows. This includes migrant workers who need a remittance policy. They will get into the banking fold only when they trust the bank. Typically, a villager has to either walk miles to the nearest bank branch or wait for an itinerant banking correspondent to come by to either keep money or to withdraw. They will trust a bank when they see a structure, a signboard and the same set of people working their every day. The industry must form an exclusive rural cadre for spreading financial services. We need thousands and thousands of small banking outlets, managed by two to three employees to create trust.

Most of such branches, however, will take years to break even. Till such time, the government should support us by offering subsidies in terms of interest subvention and tax holidays. The IT companies had enjoyed such support when it was a sunrise industry.

Small and marginal farmers, sharecroppers, micro and small industries and the millions of workers in unorganized sectors want bank credit, but most of them depend on informal sources to meet their credit needs. The challenge is to make them creditworthy. One way to do this is to focus on skill development, which Bandhan Bank has done for more than decade since it was set up as an NGO (and later transformed in to a non-banking finance company).

Mere access to financial services will not change the lives of the poor. If we want them to become entrepreneurs and generate sustainable income and lift their families out of poverty, we must help them acquire skills to stitch clothes, raise goats or sell vegetables, market those products and also manage their money. In other words, we need to adopt a credit-plus approach.

Finally, we need to look at the financial literacy drive in a new light. There have been sustained efforts to make rural folks financially literate, but the results have not been encouraging. They continue to lose money to chit funds and shadow banks. We need to make them understand a shadow bank does not have an ATM; it does not offer debit cards and chequebooks.

We need to teach them why savings are a must for everyone to take care of their daughter's education, son's wedding, spouse's health and old age.

We need to spend on the financial literacy drive. This programme is now included in the list of activities eligible to be accepted as corporate social responsibility (CSR). The CSR Rules, which came into force on 1 April 2014 under the new Company's Act, direct all companies with a net worth of ₹500 crore or revenue of ₹1,000 crore or net profit of ₹5 crore to spend 2 per cent of their average profit in the past three years on social development. The board of any company can undertake such activity approved by its CSR committee. According to a report of CRISIL Foundation—the philanthropic arm of credit-rating company CRISIL Ltd—CSR spending of 1,505 companies out of the 4,887 BSE-listed firms showed an increase of 22 per cent to ₹8,300 crore in the financial year 2016–17, with the bulk of the funds going to education, skill development, healthcare and sanitation initiatives. The spending on financial literacy continues to be low. More and more companies should come forward to spend in this area, which will give a big boost to our efforts for financial inclusion.

◆

Chandra Shekhar Ghosh is the founder, MD and CEO of Bandhan Bank Ltd.

Evolution of Fiscal Policy
and Debt in India

N.K. Singh & Prachi Mishra

Fiscal coherence, much less rectitude, was not a popular theme of the twentieth century. Many erstwhile underdeveloped but populous countries had successfully secured independence and were crawling out of the shadows of the long colonial era. For a country like India, the immediate compulsions of post-Independence was food security and adequacy of reserves post-liquidation of the sterling balances to finance essential imports, particularly food. The management of the food economy and aid from external donors occupied centre policy space. Fiscal strategy was hardly a dominant concern. It had multiple compulsions like:

First and foremost, its high incidence of poverty, severe infrastructure deficiencies, both physical and social and consequently an almost exclusive reliance on enhanced public outlay. The debate between macroeconomic stability versus fiscal profligacy, remained muted. The choice between growth versus inflation was invariably tilted in favour of growth. There was limited realization that this was a false hiatus and only sound macroeconomic policies could foster long-term growth.

Second, the compulsions of a parliamentary democracy with periodic accountability through free and fair elections. This meant not only rising expectations for public goods but very often populism financed through higher fiscal deficit. Subsidies, including cross subsidies in multiple forms, vitiated sound economic policies. Electoral politics often resulted in competitive populism irrespective of its medium economic consequences. Public utilities and public sector undertakings including banks were its worst victims.

Third, given the nascent private sector development, the obligations of the state necessitated high public outlays. Private sector investments often piggyback on rising public outlays and excessive regulations in multiple ways curbed private entrepreneurship. There was excessive protection through high tariff and non-tariff barriers which further dented competitiveness and productivity.

Finally, in the fragmented world in which globalization had yet to commence, it enabled countries to pursue policies which were independent, autonomous and could be autarkic. Planned economic development through five-year plans which controlled allocation of resources only compounded the necessity of higher public outlays.

Subsequent developments, however, altered policy contours in multiple ways.

- In an increasingly interdependent world, sound macroeconomic policies are central to attracting private capital flows.
- Jobless growth and accelerating job creation is a key priority. With new technological changes which are increasingly labour displacing, productivity improvements are linked with technological innovations. The challenge is not only job creation but quality jobs which do not impair the competitiveness of the economy.
- The increasing role of private investment in enhancing productivity providing capital and improving managerial practices necessitate an acceptable balance between finances available for both public outlays and private investment.
- Both monetary and fiscal policies need to be congruent and

balance the virtues of growth with macroeconomic stability. Combining the dynamics of growth with fiscal prudence is the new norm. It is increasingly recognized that unhappy episodes of economic crisis including Balance of Payments (BoP) distress were the outcome of fiscal profligacy and loose monetary policies, resulting in bouts of inflation which hurt the poor disproportionately. The threshold of inflation tolerance in India is shallow given the absence of robust social security systems.

• The challenge is to sustain a rate of growth closer to double digit in a stable macroeconomic framework. Enabling a regulatory framework conducive to private investments is now an inescapable necessity. Equally, since global competition is about competitiveness in the global value added chain a sound regime can attract external capital flow to boost domestic savings, as predicated on a macroeconomic framework.

The evolution of India's fiscal policy must be seen in the aforesaid background, the background of changing electoral expectations even while the role of the state is being readapted for an increasingly interdependent world.

Evolution of India's fiscal deficit

Periods of macroeconomic instability in India have invariably been predated by fiscal profligacy. In the 1980s, the combined fiscal deficit of the general government (states and centre combined) increased from a low 5.6 per cent in early 1980s to 8.6 per cent in 1984–85 and breached 9 per cent of GDP in the ensuing years. An indisputable proximate cause of the 1991 Balance of Payments crisis was the unsustainable fiscal deficit in the years preceding the crisis. Following the crisis, fiscal corrections were made coupled with other sector-specific structural reforms. A combination of these macro policies and other reforms stabilized the economy. It deregulated the private sector, and with progressive reduction in financial sector repression, it enhanced competitive efficiency and our economic performance.

Since the mid-1990s, government finances in India once again went on a path of steady decline. The deterioration was the result of several factors: Reform induced losses in revenue (customs and excise), poor tax performance due to narrow tax base, low tax buoyancy; but also government's inability to contain spending. Both the centre and states contributed to this deterioration (Figure 1). The implementation of the 5th Pay Commission recommendations widened the deficits especially at the state-level. In FY02, at 9.6 per cent, India had a record deficit based on its own history but also compared to rest of the world. Persistent primary deficits also led to an accumulation of debt. Gross debt reached close to 85 per cent of GDP around mid-2000s.

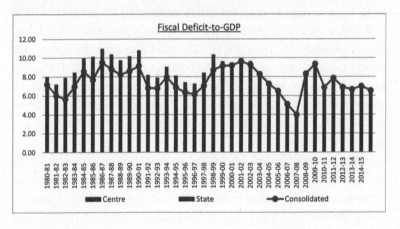

Figure 1.
Sources: DBIE, RBI.

Against this background, a Fiscal Responsibility and Budget Management Act (FRBMA) was enacted in August 2003. The FRBM Act proposed that the central and state deficit would each be progressively reduced to reach 3 per cent of GDP. The fiscal deficit target of 6 per cent was argued as being consistent with household financial savings. It was calculated that a total of roughly 12 per cent of GDP of household savings and external borrowing—comprised household financial savings of 10 per cent of GDP and a current account deficit of 2 per cent of GDP—would be allocated equally between public and the private sector. This would lead to a combined fiscal deficit of the centre and the states of 6 per cent of GDP, and at the same time also ensure an investment by private corporates (and public enterprises) of 6 per cent of GDP. The 6 per cent general government deficit was divided equally between the centre and the states.

After the enactment of the FRBMA, there was a clear improvement in the fiscal position of the government. The general government deficit declined from a peak of 9.6 per cent in FY02 to 4 per cent in FY08. In fact, the central government deficit declined to 2.5 per cent of GDP in FY08, a year in advance from when the 3 per cent deficit target was to be achieved. The debt to GDP ratio also declined during this period from 83 per cent in FY03 to 71 per cent in FY08. The entire fiscal adjustment during this period came from enhanced revenues, while there was no adjustment on the expenditure side. In fact, there was an increase in quasi-fiscal expenditures, issuance of subsidy related bonds, etc.

The process of fiscal consolidation, was, however, reversed after the global financial crisis. After recovering quickly from the global financial crisis, the Indian economy slowed down markedly (growing at 6.2 per cent and 5 per cent in 2011–12 and 2012–13 respectively) due to a combination of both external and domestic factors. A demand was boosted by the monetary and fiscal stimulus following the crisis. The stimulus was not only large, but lasted perhaps too long. This, coupled with supply-side constraints, led to higher inflation and a powerful monetary response that slowed down consumption. The annual growth of private final consumption expenditure declined considerably to 4 per cent in 2012–13, from 8 per cent in the previous year. Corporate and infrastructure investment also slowed as a result of policy bottlenecks and tighter monetary stance, with corporate sector investment declining by 2.8 percentage points of GDP in 2011–12. Faltering global growth due to the Euro crisis and uncertainty over the resolution of fiscal problems in the US; and a weak monsoon, at least in its early phase, were further hits to a slowing economy.

The growth slowdown implied that revenues could not keep pace with spending, putting pressure on the fiscal deficit targets. Household financial savings also fell sharply to 8 per cent of GDP in 2011–12 from 10.4 per cent in the previous year. With both government and private savings shrinking significantly with only a moderate fall in overall investment, the current account deficit (CAD)—the investment that cannot be financed by domestic savings but has to be financed from abroad—widened to 4.2 per cent of GDP in 2011–12, and to 4.6 per cent of GDP in the first half of 2012–13. A high fiscal deficit, falling investment, falling savings, a high current account deficit, and high consumer price inflation suggested the urgent need for macroeconomic stabilization.

The general government deficit reached 9.3 per cent in FY2010. The central government deficit was at a historical high. Part of this was due to crisis-related measures, the slowdown in activity, and the resulting low tax revenues, discussed above. However, the sharp rise in fiscal deficit can also be attributed to measures unrelated to the crisis, which were planned in any case. For example, the implementation of the 6th Pay Commission recommendations, and the expansion of the Mahatma Gandhi National Rural Employment Guarantee Act (MNREGA) in the run-up to the upcoming elections, contributed to the sharp rise in fiscal deficit. Moreover, in the absence of any expenditure reforms, the increase in global commodity prices in the first half of 2008 led to very high subsidy bills. These developments undermined the credibility of the government's commitment to fiscal discipline. Importantly, these developments established that revenue gains by themselves could not single-handedly bear the burden of fiscal adjustment and sustainability of India's fiscal policy.

Since FY09, there has been some improvement in the fiscal balances, but not to levels we saw before the crisis. The combined fiscal deficit is estimated to decline to [7.5 per cent] of GDP in FY16, but still much higher than the pre-crisis lows of 4 per cent in FY08.

Evolution of India's Public Debt

Public debt in India has been in the range of 48 per cent and 83 per cent of GDP between FY81 and FY16. The lowest point of 48 per cent of GDP was achieved back in FY81, however, it increased since then to reach a peak of 83 per cent of GDP in FY03. Since mid-2000s, public debt has indeed been on a declining trend, and is estimated to reach close to 70 per cent in FY17 (49.4 per cent and 21 per cent for the centre and states respectively). The total liabilities of the centre include 'debt' and other liabilities, broadly representing public account liabilities, and are currently estimated at ₹7,438,481 crore, or 49.4 per cent of GDP (see Annex 5 [i] of Receipts Budget FY17). The total liabilities of the central government include the securities issued by the centre under the Market Stabilization Scheme (MSS) that are used by the RBI for liquidity management operations, and the part of liabilities of the centre under the National Small Savings Fund (NSSF) that are invested in special securities issued by the states. These are of a sizeable magnitude, and they together account for 2.6 per cent of GDP. There are three key arguments for including these in the centre's liabilities. First, irrespective of how these liabilities are used by the centre—to lend to the states, or to be used by the RBI—these are, in effect, the centre's liabilities. Second, the total liabilities are what appear in key official documents such as the Finance Accounts and the Budget, and can be easily communicated and cross-checked with official documents. Third, the Comptroller and Auditor General, the supreme audit institution in India, does not give any credence to these adjustments, and treats them as centre's liabilities. The figure for the state government includes the debt of state power utilities taken over the state governments under the UDAY scheme, but excludes the states' share of NSSF liabilities to avoid double counting as they are already included in the centre's debt figure. Notably, many of the implicit and rising contingent liabilities of the government, which pose a threat to government finances, and also to the banking system, are not included in the official figures (see Box 2).

As discussed above, India underwent substantial fiscal consolidation after the introduction of the FRBMA in 2003 till FY08. During this consolidation phase, the debt ratio was reduced from 83 per cent in FY03 to 71 per cent of GDP in FY08. Despite a fiscal expansion since FY08, where the gross fiscal deficit increased from 4 per cent in FY08 to around 7 per cent in FY15, debt/GDP ratio continued to decline. This is primarily because during the entire

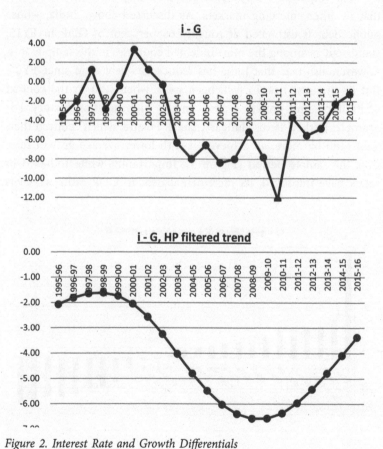

Figure 2. Interest Rate and Growth Differentials
Notes: *i* is the yield on 10 year G-Sec, G is the growth in Nominal GDP.
Sources: Bloomberg, CSO.

period, it is, in fact, a favourable interest rate growth differential arising from high growth rates and relatively low interest rates that has facilitated the consolidation of debt (Figure 2). However, a negative interest growth differential cannot be a long-run equilibrium, and will not persist over time. For example, the trend has already begun to slope upwards, which may make it difficult to sustain India's debt in the long run.

It is important to compare the evolution of India's debt with that in other emerging markets. As discussed above, India, whose public debt is estimated at roughly 68 per cent of GDP in FY15, stands out as among the most indebted countries in the sample. It is, however, also true that India has reduced its debt ratio since FY06. But its progress has, in fact, been weak when seen in the context of its impressive growth record, and its high inflation history. For example, Turkey, Peru, Hungary, Israel, Poland, which reduced their debt ratio by more, all achieved it with lower average growth rates over the sample period (Figure 3). Importantly, while India's debt ratios have improved, its incremental debt to GDP ratio, which is

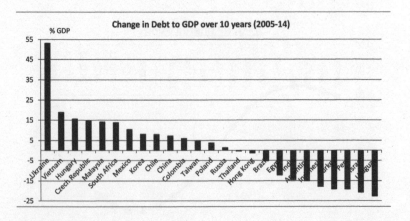

Figure 3

Source: General Government Debt from World Economic Outlook, IMF.

equal to its fiscal deficit, remains one of the highest among emerging markets (Figure 4).

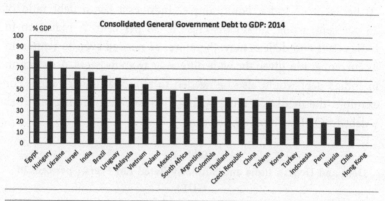

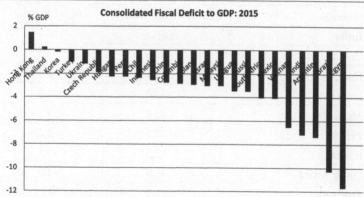

Figure 4

Source: General Government Debt from the World Economic Outlook, IMF. Fiscal Deficit from Global Fiscal Monitor, IMF.

Credit Rating Agencies

The stock of public debt and fiscal deficit are also important determinants of sovereign ratings in the models of credit rating agencies (e.g. S&P, Fitch, and Moody's). They appear as an important input in the 'Fiscal Assessment' block of their models. Table 1 shows that in comparison to other countries with similar ratings, India reported much higher debt and deficits. On average, EMs with similar ratings reported a debt/GDP ratio of 40, compared to close to 70 per cent of India. For example, Indonesia has a debt ratio of 25 per cent, while Turkey's is close to 38 per cent. A reduction in India's debt and deficits may, therefore, be needed even to remain in its current grade, given the wide difference from its peers. A reduction in India's debt would also be needed to attract a higher rating. For example, the median country with a Fitch sovereign rating of A has a debt to GDP ratio of 45 per cent.

Table 1
Debt and Deficit: India and Similarly Rated EM Peers (per cent of GDP)

Country	Average Debt	Fiscal Balance
India	**67.3**	**−7.2**
Colombia	37.6	−2.8
Hungary	78.5	−2.2
Indonesia	24.0	−2.5
Mexico	44.9	−4.1
Peru	22.1	−2.2
Russia	12.5	−3.5
South Africa	41.0	−4.0
Thailand	41.4	0.3
Turkey	37.5	−1.0
Uruguay	59.3	−3.5
Similary rated EM Peers* −		
Average	**39.9**	**−2.6**

Source: Debt from World Economic Outlook of the IMF; Deficit from Fiscal Monitor of the IMF.* If ranking similar to India as assigned by any of the three rating agencies, S&P, Fitch, and Moody's. Debt is averaged over 2010–14; whereas fiscal deficit is reported for 2015.

State Government Finances

Given India's vibrant federal structure, increased devolution of resources from the centre to the states under the 14th Finance Commission, and the fact that total state expenditures (as a percent of GSDP) is now even greater than the centre, state finances have become a crucial lynchpin in India's fiscal framework. Many state governments have adopted state-level fiscal laws and sought to adhere to a 3 per cent fiscal deficit target for states under the first FRBM. However, according to the recently released report on state finances by the RBI, the combined deficit of seventeen states reached 3.6 per cent of GDP in FY16 from 2.6 per cent in FY15—much higher than the 3 per cent envisaged under the first FRBM, and a whopping increase of one full percentage point over the previous year. As a result, the consolidated fiscal deficit for the general government (centre and states combined) is estimated to increase from 6.7 per cent in FY15 to 7.5 per cent in FY16, as fiscal consolidation by the centre is more than offset by expansion by the states. This is partly explained by the state power distribution companies' (DISCOM) debt, 75 per cent of which will be explicitly accounted for in states' balance sheets, and will be treated as capital spending by states in India's fiscal accounts (see Box 1 for details). But even excluding the DISCOM liabilities, the consolidated fiscal deficit of India has remained close to 7 per cent of GDP. In fact, while India performs well relative to emerging market peers on macroeconomic indicators like growth, inflation and current account balance, India's high general government fiscal deficit stands out, compared to an average of 2.6 per cent for EM peers with similar ratings.

The quality of compliance by the states has sharply deteriorated over the last few years due to an increase in liabilities such as the debt of the power utilities which are to be explicitly taken over by the state governments under the UDAY scheme, irregularities in food credit accounts of state governments with commercial banks, off-balance-sheet expenditures, and accounting engineering practices to evade the stated target.

Are States' Debt 'sustainable'?

Economists have established that debt is defined as 'sustainable' if debt/GDP ratio is on a stable or declining path. This is a necessary condition for solvency of any government's finances. While debt ratios for the central government are projected to decline under different plausible assumptions, the behaviour of the states turns out to be strikingly different. The debt ratio for states' under status quo or even the present FRBM scenarios is actually predicted to increase! This is mainly due to the fact that primary deficit (total deficit excluding the interest payments), which is one of the driving variables in the debt dynamics, is much higher for the states compared to the centre. The centre's primary deficit comprises only 0.7 per cent of GDP while according to the RBI report, the combined primary deficit of states was reported at 2 per cent of GDP. The central government's overall fiscal deficit remains higher than that for the states, but is directed mainly towards making interest payments on existing borrowings; unlike the states which spend relatively less on interest payments. If the states' primary deficit remains at 2 per cent of GDP, we can show that under plausible assumptions states' debt would increase from close to 20 per cent to 35 per cent of GDP over the next ten years. In fact, a significant consolidation would be required even for the states to keep their debt ratio stable, let alone have them decline.

Importantly, given increased foreign holdings of Indian government bonds, a further worsening of state finances can also lead to a loss in India's credibility among foreign institutional investors (FIIs), which can reduce the demand for Indian securities, particularly state government securities in which FIIs have been allowed since the last few years, reduce their price, and increase state government bond yields. The rise in government bond yields for state government securities would lead to an increase in the interest burden on new debt, and also for the old debt that is repriced. Such a scenario can also make the states' debt path explosive. Indeed the yields on state government debt have increased, remains higher than central government securities, and the spread vis-à-vis the central has shown an increasing trend.

On the whole, it is imperative that states partner the central government to reduce the consolidated debt ratios, which at 70 per cent of GDP, remains much higher than an average of 40 per cent for similarly rated peers.

Composition of the Deficit

While the primary deficit for the states is higher compared to the centre, the states' revenue deficit (in common parlance deficit excluding 'capital' expenses; or more accurately borrowing for recurrent spending, which have to be incurred year after year) is much lower. Revenue deficit for states was reported at 2.5 per cent of GDP for the centre, whereas only 0.2 per cent for the states. Therefore, while the centre tends to borrow largely for recurrent spending, e.g. wages and salaries, states borrow more for capital expenditures e.g. infrastructure. This is despite the fact that recurrent spending essential to delivering public services that complement growth (such as health and education) are, in fact, the principal responsibilities of the states. This has some implications for growth as fiscal multipliers for capital spending tend to be higher than those for recurrent spending. Overall, however, this is more of a compositional issue, and matters less for solvency or debt sustainability of the government.

Significant Differences Across States in Fiscal Prudence

Although composite state finances are useful to analyse the fiscal stance for the general government, it masks variation across states. In fact, states like Tamil Nadu, Gujarat and Maharashtra report lower fiscal deficits as a fraction of their incomes, and at the same time make more intensive tax efforts, whereas states like Bihar, Jharkhand and Uttar Pradesh, collect lower taxes, and are also less fiscally prudent.

But Markets Are Not Rewarding Fiscally Prudent States

The puzzling fact is that despite significant variation across states in the degree of fiscal prudence, we find almost zero correlation between state government yields (measured as spread over the central government securities) and fiscal deficits. It remains a puzzle why the spread across states remain small, or unrelated to the states' fiscal prudence. Perhaps it is the implicit guarantee by the sovereign. The implicit sovereign guarantee, however, cannot explain why state bonds consistently trade above central government Gsecs, and the spread may, in fact, suggest the additional credit risk associated with state bonds. Or perhaps, the latter spread could reflect the liquidity risk.

What is the Prognosis for State Finances, Going Forward?

Borrowing by states is increasing sharply, and is likely to increase further, due to interest payments on UDAY bonds, and importantly, also due to announcements of farm loan waivers by states like Punjab, Tamil Nadu, Maharashtra and Uttar Pradesh, and more recently demands by farmers in Madhya Pradesh. Farm loan waivers remains a key risk for banks, and in turn for the states' fiscal position, and therefore for the general government position.

What Can Be Done in the Short Term?

What matters for the health of the Indian macroeconomy and debt sustainability is the general government fiscal position. If there are fiscal sustainability issues at the centre or the states, markets will react, and it will have spillovers for both the centre and the states, irrespective of the source of the problem. Neither the centre nor the states can be insulated in times of crises. While deviations from the prescribed fiscal path for the centre require securing parliamentary consent and approval, there is no clear enforcement mechanism to ensure fiscal discipline in the state finances, making the role of 'bond market vigilantes' even more pertinent.

What role can the centre play in these circumstances to minimize spillovers from fiscal slippages at the state level? Due diligence conducted by the centre of the states' fiscal accounts would be a first step. More generally, institutional reforms in general government's fiscal management, e.g. issue of detailed policy guidelines on the procedure for central government consent to state borrowings under Article 293 of the Constitution of India, could serve as a proactive guidance to the state governments.

How can regulatory measures make the state bond yields responsive to market signals? The investor base has already been expanded to include foreign participation in state government securities, which will help, but further steps e.g. gradually increasing the limits, to increase responsiveness of state finances to market signals, may be needed.

Ultimately, in any parliamentary system, it must be assumed that the sovereign acts responsibly. All rules and regulations are designed to only assist the sovereign in reaching decisions, which promote growth and welfare. Importantly, the very fact, that the central government commissioned a review of its fiscal framework, suggests an increased awareness and consciousness of the sovereign about fiscal responsibility. The same consciousness must percolate to the states as well.

Box 1
Issues in the Power Sector

Electricity production: Generation capacity has increased significantly over the last few years—by 50 per cent between FY08 and FY15.

Consumers' demand: Despite a record generation capacity, the final demand of consumers continues to remain unsatisfied. Based on the limited data we could gather from several sources, outages in metropolitan cities such as Delhi increased by more than 40 per cent between FY15 and FY16. This is because intermediaries like the state power distribution companies (DISCOMs) create a 'wedge' between the supply by generation companies and final consumers' demand. This mismatch between the supply and demand occurs partly due to the weak financial health of state power utilities. For example, the outstanding debt (excluding DISCOM bonds) of the DISCOMs of Rajasthan, Haryana, Uttar Pradesh and Tamil Nadu was around ₹213,446 crore as on 30 September 2015.

Financial health of state power utilities: The UDAY scheme aims to improve the financial health of power utilities, but it solves only the debt 'stock' problem whereas the 'flo' problem continues to exist as described below.

- Stock problem addressed by UDAY: Under the UDAY scheme, 75 per cent of the 'stock' of debt outstanding as on 30 September 2015 is envisaged to be taken over by the state governments over a two-year period.
- Flow problem remains: 25 per cent of the debt outstanding as on 30 September 2015 will, however, remain in the books of the DISCOMs. The debt that will continue to be in the banks' books will be charged an interest of 0.1 per cent over the base rate.

Box 2
Contingent Liabilities of the Central Government

This box discusses two of the implicit and rising contingent liabilities of the government, which pose a threat to government finances, but also to the banking system.

A. Food Credit

Facts

State governments maintain food credit accounts with commercial banks. The credit is used by certain for centralized procurement of cereals on behalf of the Food Corporation of India (FCI).

There are long delays in servicing these accounts, particularly in the case of some states. These arise mainly due to several disputes between the state governments and the FCI, and resulting delays in the FCI finalizing and effecting reimbursement of procurement expenses to the state concerned. In principle, these accounts should have long back been classified as Non-Performing Assets (NPAs).

As a result of the above delays, there are significant and rising 'irregularities' in the food credit accounts. These irregularities arise because the outstanding food credit often exceeds the amounts that can be drawn based on the procurement value of the grain stocks. The irregularity in the food credit account (defined as the difference between the outstanding credit and the drawing power available in the account) was high for certain states and comprised a large fraction of the total outstanding credit. This is a chronic and continuing irregularity. Such irregularities will remain a constant feature unless the food credit mechanism used by the FCI for centralized procurement through states is centralized with the FCI.

Way forward

Food credit to centralized procurement states could be routed only through the FCI, duly guaranteed by the Government of India. This would streamline the process, improve the efficiency, and minimize disputes between the procuring states and the FCI that lead to persisting irregularity in the food credit account of the concerned states. In addition, the present irregularity should be accurately determined after a comprehensive special audit of grain stocks, and adjusted by the GoI/FCI at the earliest.

B. Government Sponsored Credit Guarantee Schemes

The Government of India has launched many credit guarantee schemes, viz., Credit Guarantee Fund Trust for Micro and Small

Enterprises (CGTMSE), Credit Risk Guarantee Fund Scheme for Low Income Housing, etc., to aid higher credit flow from formal credit channels to certain targeted beneficiaries. While these credit guarantee schemes have helped the intended beneficiaries in getting credit at more favourable terms, it is important that these schemes are run in a prudent and transparent manner.

These credit guarantee schemes are heavily under-capitalized in relation to the aggregate amount of guarantees outstanding under the respective schemes. Loan losses are mounting in CGTMSE suggesting that the guarantees have reduced the quality of loans banks have made, and reduced the willingness of the bank to monitor and collect, or borrowers to repay. Further, very little information is available on the operations of these schemes for an independent evaluation of their operations. In the absence of regular and adequate disclosures on their operations and solvency, these schemes may pose unexpected and huge challenges to the government finances, especially if the government has to meet any sudden and large deficit on account of their operations.

While GoI has explicitly assured to fund these schemes in case of deficit in their corpus fund, it would be important to make sure that the schemes are run well so that loan losses are minimized, and are kept adequately funded on an ongoing basis, based on certain prudential norms.

C. Bank Recapitalization

The recapitalization of the government has come in the wake of sluggish economic growth of which an important proximate reason was Twin-Balance Sheet problem.

Twin Balance Sheet problem is a twofold problem for Indian economy which deals with:

Overleveraged companies: Debt accumulation on companies is very high and thus they are unable to pay interest payments on loans.

Bad-loan-encumbered-banks: Non Performing Assets (NPA) of the banks is 9 per cent for the total banking system of India. It is as high as 12.1 per cent for Public Sector Banks. As companies fail to pay back principal or interest, banks are also in trouble.

Greater transparency and recurring of the impaired assets of banks suggested a massive need to recapitalize the banks not only to meet the revised Basel norm standards but more so enable a healthy balance sheet. Besides, the implementation of the new Insolvency and Bankruptcy Code, 2016, would inevitably necessitate banks taking, sometimes, deep haircuts.

It was in the context of the aforesaid, the government has announced the proposal to recapitalize PSBs with a view to support credit growth and job creation.

A ₹211,000 crore capital infusion into the banking sector will come over the next two years. It will come in three parts. The government itself will directly pay banks ₹18,139 crore by buying their shares. It will also encourage banks to raise ₹58,000 crore from the market. The bulk of the amount—₹135,000 crore—is expected to come from recapitalization bonds.

The present decision further builds upon the Indradhanush Plan for recapitalizing and revamping PSBs as announced by the government.

The unprecedented recapitalization is expected to have a positive impact in the near-term, contributing to augmented economic activity and growth of the economy.

What is the Impact on the Government's Fiscal Health?

The direct budgetary impact of the recapitalization bonds is around ₹10,000 crore annually. More importantly, there is the issue of whether and to what extent the debt-GDP ratio would deteriorate to the detriment of India's credit upgrading prospects.

In the report of the recent FRBM committee, it was visualized that central government debt should decline to 40 per cent from 49.4 per cent by FY 23 and the balance 20 per cent would be the prudent ceiling for states. Further recalculation would suggest that instead of reaching the preferred 40 per cent, it could be pushed back by a year or so to FY 24, considering that 49.4 per cent could be closer to 50 per cent debt to GDP. The report has assumed a nominal GDP growth of 11.5 per cent and interest rate of 7.3 per cent on central government debt.

Considering that the recapitalization bonds will make an effective dent on the Twin-Balance Sheet problem and that investment in physical infrastructure would have its own multiplier effect on growth, these variables are to change in a positive direction. Even this negative effect could be diluted over a period of time.

Even as recapitalization helps resolve the 'stock' problem, we need to be cognizant of the 'flow problem' so that we are not in the same boat a decade from now. The legacy of what is called 'telephone banking' directed lending through government intervention must end. Domain expertise in public sector banks, improved quality of managerial decisions, project preparation and appraisal by following best international practice are integral to this process.

India is in a very different place than it was in 2003, when it adopted the first FRBM Law. India is increasingly getting financially integrated with the world economy. Capital flows have increased dramatically over the last five decades (gross capital flows increased 81 times since 1970); but the real take-off happened since the early 2000s. In particular, portfolio flows have increased sharply. Although there still exist separate investment caps on sub accounts of foreign institutional investors (FIIs), foreign holdings in government and corporate bonds currently stand at US$ 22.5 billion and US$ 23.7 billion respectively (compared to, for example, US$ 8.5 billion and US$ 15 billion in 2011). Increased international financial integration has coincided with domestic financial sector reforms. Policy induced frictions, e.g. on account of the Statutory Liquidity

Ratio (SLR), imposed on banks to hold a minimum fraction of their deposits in the form of government bonds, have also come down from 30 per cent in the late 1990s to 21.5 per cent recently. In fact, the de facto SLR requirement is even lower at 11.5 per cent. This is because 11 per cent of the total investment in SLR securities can be included in the Liquidity Coverage Ratio (LCR), envisaged as a form of prudential regulation under Basel III, and are therefore no longer captive. This has direct and important implications for the fiscal framework, as the extent of automatic financing of high fiscal deficits by banks through financial repression has reduced, and is likely to decline further in the future, and intensify the challenges on the fiscal front going forward. Finally, increasing recourse to market borrowings have made both the appetite and the cost of borrowing a significant economic variable in India. Fiscal profligacy enhances the cost of debt. Investors' confidence, attitude of credit rating agencies, and market forces are all having an increasingly powerful influence on a country's macro management.

At the same time, the global backdrop has also changed substantially. The prolonged global slowdown, characterized by some economists as a secular stagnation—developments in China, uncertainties in the Eurozone, demographic imbalances in several countries (like the aging population of Japan, significant debt burdens, low inflation, and the pursuit of unconventional monetary policy by many central banks under pressure to restore growth and achieve their inflation targets—have made the international environment increasingly challenging. More recently, the new US administration, the anticipation of expansionary fiscal policies and reflation, continued tightening of monetary policy by the Federal Reserve, and the perception of increased protectionism in the US going forward, have all made the global environment highly uncertain. These external challenges also come at a time when India has become increasingly globalized. Trade as percentage of GDP has increased significantly even in the last decade, necessitating policymaking to become far more cognizant of global events.

There is no doubt that domestic fiscal policies must reckon with an increasingly challenging domestic situation, as well as an uncertain and volatile exogenous environment.

◆

N.K. Singh is a politician, economist and former Indian Administrative Service officer. He is also a senior member of the Bhartiya Jantaa Party (BJP).

Prachi Mishra is a Columbia University-trained economist, now a specialist adviser in the Reserve Bank of India.

A Holistic Approach to Financing
Our Urban Future

Naina Lal Kidwai

There is already a major transformation taking place around us. Although we remain one of the last major economies in the world yet to urbanize, that is changing fast. Some estimates suggest that 30 Indians move from a rural to an urban area every minute. By 2050, India's urban population will nearly double to 814 million from around 410 million in 2015.

Our cities hold the key to our future prosperity. Our 100 largest cities already account for 43 per cent of India's GDP whilst accommodating just 16 per cent of the population. Over the next 15 years, our cities will also account for 75 per cent of India's national income and will be home to the majority of new jobs created. In fact, research from the New Climate Economy showed that better, smarter urban growth could be an economic opportunity for India worth up to an additional 6 per cent of GDP by mid-century, with significant savings at the household level.

Ahead of us is the opportunity to ensure a better urban development pathway: Cities where people can thrive, breathe, move safely and easily, and be productive. This pathway requires investing substantially and smartly in urban infrastructure at a scale far greater than we have managed thus far. It is estimated, for instance, that as much as 80 per cent of the urban infrastructure that will be needed in India in 2050 has yet to be built.

Getting the right kind of infrastructure in place—that which ensures more compact, coordinated and connected urban development—will be key to ensuring that we avoid locking in unsustainable urbanization and instead help lift millions out of poverty. Recent research has shown that our current poorly planned, sprawling, unconnected pattern of urbanization could impose an estimated cost of ₹2–12 lakh crores (US$330 billion to US$1.8 trillion) by 2050. This includes increased costs of providing public infrastructure and services, transportation costs, traffic casualties, traffic congestion, air pollution and health risks. The costs could be much higher when factoring in increased road and parking capital requirements which could be upwards of ₹4 lakh crores (US$600 billion) per annum by 2050, plus other costs such as the value of displaced agricultural farmland. The costs of providing public infrastructure and services are also likely to be 10–30 per cent higher in more sprawled, automobile-dependent neighbourhoods compared with more compact, connected locations.

The urban infrastructure investment gap in India is estimated to be around ₹6.4 lakh crores (US$1 trillion) in 2011 prices, from 2012–31, although this number may be even higher. Meeting this investment need will require India to raise, carefully steer and blend new finance, from both the public and the private sectors, towards compact, connected and coordinated urban development. The government of India should take this opportunity to look at the various tools available to enable investments in sustainable infrastructure and urban development and drive reforms that can provide an enabling environment for private capital to flow in at the scale required. Limited public finance needs to be carefully used in ways that will leverage private investment.

Our Cities Today

Building the cities of the future necessitates a hard look at the cities of today. We need to do better on many fronts—such as air pollution, congestion, and sanitation—if we are to better reap the benefits of urban development. Our cities pose unique challenges that require tailored responses. While we cannot simply lift solutions that may have worked in other countries and apply them to India, we can certainly draw relevant insights, particularly in ways they may have unlocked financing for sustainable urban infrastructure.

Prime among the challenges we face is alarming levels of air pollution: 14 of the world's 30 most polluted cities are in India. Outdoor air pollution in Indian cities is estimated to cause around 1.1 million premature deaths per year. In Delhi, for example, the local air pollution was so severe in 2017 that doctors prescribed patients with serious respiratory problems to simply move out of the city.

High levels of air pollution are often linked to urban transport with up to 75 per cent of urban air pollutants coming from fuel combustion in motorized vehicles. Our roads are quite literally deadly with the highest number of fatalities in the world: 150,785 traffic deaths officially reported in 2016 alone. In addition to the human cost, congestion also places an economic burden on commuters. In Delhi, traffic congestion costs averaged ₹4.91 per kilometre for cars and ₹9.83 per kilometre for buses during peak periods.

Quick fixes often inspired by efforts in other cities, such as odd-even traffic restrictions that worked for Beijing ahead of the 2008 Olympics, rarely offer a lasting solution. Rather, a comprehensive package of urban development should include policies on congestion charging and regulated parking fees, while enhancing public transit options in order to make them overall a more attractive alternative for city dwellers.

An especially unique challenge for our cities is that they are extremely dense. Homes in Mumbai have only about 30 square feet per person, less than a quarter of what's available in urban China. Sprawl in India means something quite different than in regions such as the US. It is better understood as a low density of built-up floor space per unit of land area, combined with severe overcrowding per unit of built-up area. Addressing sprawl in India therefore will require a greater emphasis on 'appropriate' or 'good' density combined with adequate provision of accessible and well-connected infrastructure and services.

Urban Finance Reform: A Boost to Existing Urban Policies

A number of government initiatives are already focusing on improving the quality of urban development. Smart Cities is an urban renewal and retrofitting programme to develop 100 cities with a focus on core infrastructure services such as water, sanitation and solid waste management, efficient urban mobility and public transportation, affordable housing for the poor, power supply, robust IT connectivity, governance, safety and security, health and education, and sustainable urban environment. The mission of AMRUT is to ensure that every household has access to water and sewage connections, to increase green and open spaces and to encourage public or non-motorized transport options, particularly with support from the private sector. Swachh Bharat's main objective is to reduce or eliminate open defecation through the construction of individual, cluster and community toilets. Finally, PMAY-U seeks to provide affordable housing to the urban poor.

Of particular note in the current challenge is the role played by Urban Local Bodies (ULBs), the third institutional tier of urban government, after the central and state authorities. ULBs often lack the necessary combination of technical capacity and fiscal autonomy required for urban finance reform, but could be key to delivering infrastructure services, planning, regulation, welfare, health and safety. Improving their governance, capacity and expanding their remit to manage urban finance would provide a strong complement to these flagship urban initiatives and help to deliver sustainable urban development.

A holistic urban finance policy package supported by strong institutional leadership and a productive enabling environment that enhances local capacity and improves governance can support the goals of these initiatives and help unleash our full urban potential.

Raising Finance

There are broadly three sources of potential finance for urban development. First, own-source revenue, such as tax revenues (property tax yields the majority of ULB income, but there are others, such as for lighting, vehicles, advertisement, etc. which vary greatly across the country); and non-tax revenues (for instance, user charges for services such as water). Research has shown that reformed property tax mechanisms could increase revenues by as much as 71 per cent, but many ULBs lack the capacity to administer and collect both taxes and other revenues effectively and efficiently.

Second, grants from state governments to ULBs (including, for instance, funding available through AMRUT or Swachh Bharat to improve basic infrastructure or solid waste management, as well as fixed and performance-based grant allocations, and potential GST-derived revenue) are substantial sources of revenue. However, only 9 states received 100 per cent of the basic grant recommended by the Fourteenth Finance Commission, whilst 9 states received 50 per cent or less in 2015–16.

Third, debt financing, where wide variations across the country exist because ULBs lack the sound financial footing to borrow, and even where borrowing is possible, restrictions or approvals required by states often prevent it. Notable exceptions are large, financially powerful cities such as Ahmedabad and Bangalore, and the pooled financing mechanisms being deployed by smaller ULBs in Tamil Nadu and Karnataka.

To increase the ability of ULBs to raise finance, we might consider ways to build their capacity to collect own-source revenues and to demonstrate municipal creditworthiness in order to attract private investment.

- **Improve the efficiency of property tax collection** such as by creating Property Tax Boards that would establish state-wide methods for property valuation and assessment (as has been proposed by the 13th Finance Commission) and keep the collection of tax as well as decisions about spending at the ULB level. We should also explore innovative solutions for registering properties, including through GIS systems, perhaps using the Smart Cities style competition approach so cities that demonstrate improvements in certain areas may receive financial support for more expensive tools.

- **Make service delivery financially sustainable**, for instance, by unbundling user charges and subsidies. This approach would enable ULBs to set charges for users at a level that would sustainably finance utility investments over the long term, whilst separately supporting the poor urban groups that otherwise cannot afford to access such services.

- **Make fiscal decentralization more efficient and empower ULBs to develop capacities**. The GST could provide a unique opportunity to provide some of the financing needed and support ULBs—the 25–30 per cent share recommended by the Ministry of Urban Development (MoUD) could be used to fund their infrastructure requirements as well as develop the capacity of ULBs, and would be a valuable compensation for the revenues they give up as part of the GST's creation.

- **Improving ULBs' creditworthiness to enable access to debt financing**, including by creating a good enabling environment. This could mean, for instance, expanding the credit ratings developed by the MoUD under Smart Cities and AMRUT, currently covering 94 out of 500 cities, and developing MoF guidelines for ULBs on the issuance of tax-free bonds. States can undertake similar supporting efforts as a complement to these central efforts.

Steering Finance

Meeting our urban infrastructure investment needs will require us to steer large-scale finance effectively into compact, coordinated and connected urban development. Some steering measures already exist, such as the Energy Conservation Building Code, which encourages investment in energy-efficient building approaches and is already being implemented in 22 states; and the Indian Corporate Average Fuel Consumption Standard which seeks to encourage investment in more efficient vehicles and the tax on coal, which steers finance towards sustainable investment via the Clean Energy Fund.

To ensure finance is appropriately steered into sustainable urban development, we should explore the potential of mechanisms that capture increased urban land values to finance sustainable infrastructure.

- **Refreshing regulations and incentives**, whereby those that encourage 'sprawl' are removed or amended (such as minimum parking requirements, set-back requirements, and maximum building heights) and replaced with policies that encourage dense, sustainable developments (such as access to public transport, minimum sanitation requirements to reduce pollution, and encouraging density by establishing maximum floor space). Other policy levers, such as parking fees and congestion charges, can also encourage the use of public transport and reduce the congestion that, as above, hampers our overall development.

- **Expanding the Land Value Capture Financing policy** (implemented so far only at the central level from April 2017) to the state and ULB level to capture the increases in land value created by their investments in transport and infrastructure. Businesses already recognize the value of developed urban land— that explains its high cost—and governments can capitalize on this, but to be really successful, such measures should be complemented with clear master plans that steer development towards more compact urban form, along with social safeguards that demonstrate structured, long-term urban growth.

- **Using competition to incentivize sustainable urban infrastructure investment.** Smart Cities demonstrated that competition was a powerful motivator for ULBs to act. An annual ranking of cities based on key sustainability measures (similar to the Swachh Sarvekshan survey that ranks over 70 cities based upon their cleanliness, expanded to cover air pollution, energy efficiency, congestion and public transport provision) could act as an incentive for cities to invest their own resources in sustainable urban infrastructure.

- **Engaging with other national or international funds.** One of the key recommendations of the recent UNEP-FICCI report on sustainable finance in India which I chaired was to better leverage international funds, like the Green Climate Fund (GCF). The GCF or the US$500m UK-India Infrastructure fund can effectively provide cheaper loans for sustainable urban infrastructure with the central government playing a key role by helping support sustainable projects.

Blending Finance

During my time at HSBC, we started to engage fully with issues of sustainability. Acting on multiple fronts—green investments, reducing our own carbon footprint, seeking out sustainable business opportunities and investing in communities—helped make our business more sustainable while also making a perceptible difference to communities in which we operate. Banks can ensure we do not fund companies that do not comply with norms set by Indian regulatory authorities and can therefore push companies to comply. IBA issued guidelines on responsible banking in 2015 which is a good start for ensuring that all banks include sustainability in their lending decisions.

The private sector has a major role to play in meeting our urban development needs. The 12th five-year plan envisaged almost 50 per cent of the total investment coming from the private sector. PPPs were also outlined as key objectives in JNNURM. In 2011, over half of all investment in PPP projects in developing countries occurred in India. But despite the increase in private investment in infrastructure, PPPs in India have a number of drawbacks. Contract enforcement and lengthy litigation processes—as much as 30 per cent more time than the average in South Asia—pose major challenges that deter private sector investment.

As a result, private sector actors who do invest can often renegotiate terms midway and gain additional advantages at the expense of the public good. Issues around land acquisition have also stalled PPPs and any measures to address this must take into account the needs of vulnerable urban communities. Investors are also wary of some urban infrastructure projects where the returns are harder to demonstrate because of public good attributes (water, as noted above, a clear example of this), and where the regulatory landscape is crowded with multiple government agencies overlapping.

In order to blend finance at the scale required, we may wish to build investor confidence in PPPs by addressing the effectiveness of contract enforcement.

- **Address the challenges around contract enforcement and dispute resolution**, including through effective, quick and low-cost alternative resolution mechanisms such as forming an independent body or mechanism that can facilitate mediation between disputing parties and without further burdening the court system. Special courts, specifically set up to deal with contract enforcement, can also speed up resolutions with PPPs and make them more attractive to investors.
- **Other measures, including pooled financing mechanisms**, may also be explored to meet the needs of smaller projects with state governments or donor institutions playing a role in guaranteeing risk or enhancing creditworthiness. Replicating the Tamil Nadu Water and Sanitation Pooled Fund—a successful pooled finance mechanism that enabled ULBs to access almost inaccessible private finance—could be a good complement to the bigger blended model offered by PPPs.

Turning Ambition into Action

These recommendations are well-suited to attract the financing we need for India's urban transition and to transform the urban financing landscape. As a country with an established financial system and governance framework, as well as globally competitive urban centres, we are well-positioned to both leverage advanced financial instruments that draw upon the resources of a strong private sector, and to better utilize the capabilities of strong and mature public institutions.

At the same time, we need to be aware of how financing urban infrastructure will impact the poorest and most vulnerable—to make sure that investments are well-governed and equitable. For instance, if user charges for key services go up (which they should to ensure long-term investments in maintaining the infrastructure), they should be accompanied by strong and inclusive social protection measures. In terms of land acquisition, governments should work with current owners and occupants to find mutually satisfactory arrangements. Low-income and other marginalized urban residents should not be displaced unnecessarily or without adequate compensation to create formal commercial space or high-income residences.

How India finances its urban expansion today could be of great interest to other countries seeking to do the same in the future. Some of the measures to evaluate success relate specifically to ULBs— for instance, the sum and proportion of own-source revenue they generate, their creditworthiness, and total lending to them and how those loans perform. We should also assess capital flows into sustainable urban infrastructure, as well as how these are funded. These measures can complement assessments of more traditional urban and environmental indicators, such as access rates to housing, infrastructure and services, or air pollution and emissions, etc.

A more holistic approach to financing our urban future is available to us, and is essential if we are to realize our full economic potential.

◆

Naina Lal Kidwai is chairman of the India Advisory Board of Advent Private Equity and Past President FICCI and Chair, Sustainability, Energy and Water Council.

India's Rise as a Global Financial Superpower

Rashesh Shah

The Indian economy is at an important juncture in its evolution. The confluence of a number of fundamental changes, including structural reforms like Goods and Services Tax (GST), Insolvency and Bankruptcy Code (IBC) and Real Estate Regulatory Authority (RERA), growing retail participation in capital markets and the digitization of the economy, coupled with India's strong GDP growth, has created a potent mix for the next phase of scale-up driven by the power of compounding.

Typically, compounding relies on three factors—size, rate and time. India stands out on all these counts—we are one of the largest economies in the world with a Gross Domestic Product (GDP) exceeding $2 trillion and a growth rate which is among the fastest in the world. At the same time, this strong rate of growth will continue for a sizable period of time with the government undertaking a slew of reforms. Together, these three levers will drive India's growth creating India's 'Golden Age of Compounding'.

Golden Age of Compounding

According to a quote that is often attributed to Albert Einstein, 'Compound interest is the eighth wonder of the world.' The Indian economy is set to witness and benefit from the power of compounding. With the triumvirate of size, rate and time clicking together, we expect the Indian economy to touch $5 trillion by 2025.[1] At that point of time, we could be adding $1 trillion to the economy every 18 months! That is akin to saying we would be adding one India of 2007 (when India's GDP touched $1 trillion) every 18 months to our economy. By 2040, India could potentially be one of the three largest economies in the world with a GDP of $20 trillion.[2]

A large part of this progression would be driven by a few factors which are already in play—households' shift from savings to investment, democratization of credit and reforms like GST, IBC, etc.

Financialization of Savings

Real estate and gold were the traditional asset classes where Indians used to plough their savings over the years. However, the asset mix has started changing with domestic flows into the equity market rising incrementally over the last couple of years. While there have been surges in domestic flows into equity earlier, this time the change is structural in nature due to a variety of factors. Sustained investment for an extended duration of time, significantly better performance of equity as an asset class compared to classes like real estate and gold, lower equity ownership of Indian households compared to global peers, low share of savings in the typical household asset profile and increased awareness, access and belief in India's equity market opportunity are some of these factors.

This structural change is clearly reflected in the numbers from the Mutual Fund (MF) Industry as well. From around ₹6 trillion in March 2012, the MF Industry's Assets Under Management (AUM) has seen a fourfold increase in a span of six years to around ₹23 trillion in March 2018. Monthly SIP flows are now around ₹5,000 crore—an annual inflow of more than ₹60,000 crore.[3] From a long-term perspective, MFs in India still have a lot of potential. The MF industry's total AUM/GDP in the US is in excess of 100 per cent, nearly 80 per cent in France and above 50 per cent in Brazil, while in India it is still around 15 per cent. The scope for growth is obviously very high.

The growing awareness and interest in financial markets, along with a proven regulatory framework, will have a related positive impact on investor interest in other financial assets like insurance and bond markets. With growing acceptance in the power of investing, retail investors will be open to exploring newer and more innovative avenues of investment. At the same time, regulators and organizations are making a concerted effort in educating the investor on financial investments where under-penetration provides ample room for growth and expansion.

Democratization of Credit

The financialization of savings is only one part of India's growth story. An equally important facet deals with the democratization of credit allocation in the economy. Earlier, a significant portion of banking credit was largely extended to top 100 business houses. However, today the gap is being successfully bridged with credit being offered to the under-funded retail segment, both business and personal.

Furthermore, with the sizeable leveraging ability of households, the Indian household is ready to borrow more. Today, the government balance sheet is already being leveraged for considerable capex investments and corporate balance sheets are also leveraged but with substantial expansion expected in a couple of years. In this scenario, Indian households are the only segment with borrowing capacity currently. There is a significant untapped opportunity available in the retail lending space to help seed and support local business microsystems. SME lending is, in fact, a form of retail lending where the personal and the business balance sheets of the self-employed entrepreneurs commingle.

This demand for higher credit by households has been further supplemented by a variety of efforts of the government towards universal financial inclusion. The introduction of Aadhaar coupled with the JAM trinity has helped bring a huge part of the population under the financial net. With the continued strengthening in Credit Information Bureau (CIBIL), improved credit underwriting mechanisms and the use of a wider variety of data points to assess the creditworthiness of both individuals and small businesses, access to credit is expected to increase significantly for the credit-deficient sections of society and lead to a broad-basing of credit allocation in the economy.

There has also been a significant broad-basing in credit givers to the Indian corporate. Bond markets particularly have come up in a big way in the last couple of years as a viable capital avenue for corporates. Several reforms have been undertaken for this shift to happen—however, there are still some reforms which could potentially alter the credit landscape in the country and accelerate India's compounding effect. If done in a timely and concerted manner, there is a good chance that we will hit the $5 trillion mark even before 2025.

Bond Markets in India

Bond markets in India have been steadily growing in influence and importance over the last decade as a large number of corporates have leveraged the uniquely efficient credit allocation mechanism of the Indian capital markets. Equity capital markets and increasingly debt capital markets have relied on the wide expanse of information available publicly to efficiently allocate capital to corporate entities. This kind of efficiency has not yet completely percolated to the credit allocation being done by financial institutions and is one of the major reasons why debt capital markets could be one of the drivers of corporate credit uptake in the Indian economy over the next few years. With limited credit bandwidth amongst the banking sector owing to the stressed assets challenge, it is extremely important that corporates have a viable alternate mechanism to get credit.

The popularity of the bond market took off slowly but has improved considerably over the last few years. From 2006 to 2014, issuances in the bond market only increased from ₹0.8 lakh crore to ₹2.7 lakh crore, a CAGR of 16 per cent. However, by the end of 2018 this had risen to nearly ₹6.4 lakh crore with a four-year CAGR of 24 per cent.[4] The usage of bonds by corporates for financing is also on the rise. With private investment expected to start rising soon, the demand for bonds as an avenue for raising capital will only increase.

The strong uptake in the last couple of years has not only been driven by external factors like positive macroeconomic environment, need for long-term funding for financing infrastructure projects and lending constraints in the banking sector, but also due to an enhanced focus from both the regulator and the government, culminating in a slew of reforms. This has created a conducive ecosystem for the scale-up in bond markets reflected in the nearly 22 per cent year-on-year jump in the secondary market volumes in FY18.[5]

While these are commendable metrics and indicative of a sound launching platform, a few crucial reforms, if implemented in a timely manner, can take India on an accelerated trajectory towards achieving the vision of a vibrant bond market that ensures that funds flow towards productive investments and market forces exert competitive pressures on lending to the private sector. Not only will this help create the bond market as a strong support mechanism to the banking credit system, it will also help India's GDP growth move to an elevated trajectory.

Reforms to Achieve the Vision of a Vibrant Bond Market

There are four broad buckets which can subsume the different reforms that we need to undertake:

1. **Liquidity**: This is an oft repeated word when it comes to corporate bond reforms and rightly so. Average daily traded volume of ₹7,000 crores does not do justice to the corporate bond market with an outstanding of ₹27 lakh crores.

   The primary reason why the corporate bond segment on the exchanges has not found favour is because it is limited to a small section of the corporate bond universe. The real need of the market is an electronic repo platform resident on the exchanges and the RBI has indeed included this as part of the corporate bond reforms released in 2016. The exchanges are ready with the mechanics for the same and the system will go live shortly. It is essential that the usage of this platform and user feedback is continuously tracked to ensure usage across a wide spectrum of market participants.

At the same time, the regulator needs to incentivize market-making to promote secondary market volumes. Primary dealer model for market-making of corporate bonds is yet to make its impact felt. Regulations for credit enhancement of corporate bonds by NBFCs can be relaxed to give further impetus to the corporate bond market as they will then be able provide necessary liquidity for the market to take off. Steps should be taken to encourage large NBFCs (with a certain minimum net worth) to play an active role as market makers and they may be facilitated by extending dedicated credit limits (possibly at repo rates). The regulator may put in place appropriate performance metrics to review such arrangements on an annual basis.

2. **Investor Diversification**: Public issuances form only a small fraction of the total bond issuances. This skew needs to be corrected to attract greater retail participation. It could be done by a cap on proportion of private placement in overall debt raised by each issuer. On the lines of equity capital raising via Offer For Sale (OFS) mechanism, bonds may also be offered via a real-time book-building platform for public debt issues with exchange being the bidding platform.

   Beyond retail investor participation, we should also consider lifting restrictions on investments and trading by provident funds (PFs) and insurance firms. Given the large pool of capital being managed by PFs and insurance firms, they may be allowed some flexibility in portfolio allocation towards private sector corporate debt from the current norms which are slightly restrictive. The Union Budget this year has taken cognizance of this fact and proposed that the government and concerned regulators will take necessary action to permit bonds with rating up to A (as against the current AA threshold) as eligible for investment.

3. **Transparency**: A big reason why investors still continue to shy away from the bond market is the perception of information asymmetry amongst the various market participants, more so in comparison to the efficiency in the equity markets. The creation of a centralized database which can consolidate all information that is currently available on multiple platforms and make it available to the investors can help in allaying this perception. This can be accentuated by a uniform credit rating framework with designated agencies accountable for standardized unbiased rating methodologies. An all-India level corporate credit risk metric system across risk profiles can serve as a reliable guide to investors about the investment climate and the risk-reward. In parallel, a stable and predictable tax structure which is competitive with other emerging markets will help India attract stable, long-term capital which is needed for its sustained growth over coming decades.

4. **Foreign Portfolio Investors (FPIs) related reforms**: While the mechanism to secure FPI licences has been significantly liberalized over the years, there are some teething problems faced by large asset managers with multiple accounts. Presently, each account needs to follow the registration process which makes it very cumbersome, so an online platform to facilitate single-window registration for multiple accounts is a suggested solution.

   Liquidity continues to be a big challenge particularly for the rupee-denominated offshore bonds. To ensure continued issuances, this needs to be corrected. Domestic entities are presently not permitted to hold these bonds and relaxation on this front might aid effective market-making and liquidity. On similar lines, fungibility/repatriation of such bonds should be allowed akin to ADRs/GDRs, whereby an investor may sell the bonds to a domestic investor via conversion of the offshore units to onshore units.

Also for FPIs withholding tax is a dampener and for issuers, it is an additional cost as they also need to bear the illiquidity premium asked by FPI, thereby making the overall issuance expensive by 50–80 bps over onshore.

Lastly, the new regulations governing FPI investment norms and the FPI KYC requirements can potentially be restrictive and must be considered after taking inputs from all stakeholders to arrive at a holistic solution.

While these reforms might seem immense, these are small steps which can agglomerate into a massive impetus to India's bond market. The timing is opportune with the intense investor interest being seen in Indian markets today. Combined with the absence of adequate sources of cost-efficient capital for corporate, these small steps could help propel bond markets in India at par with the equity markets or maybe even higher.

Looking Beyond

With such a wide variety of factors seemingly falling in place, there is significant cause for optimism for India. Fundamental structural changes are reshaping the economy and cyclicals are starting to become stronger. With the global economy also starting to recover, the cumulative effect should drive the economy to new heights.

Amidst all this, it is important to develop bifocal vision to truly understand the India story—one which can cut through the short-term volatility and challenges and look at the long-term trend, which has always been upwards. Because near-term volatility is inherently visible and long-term growth usually invisible, a truly all-encompassing bifocal vision helps assess the economy in a comprehensive manner. In this situation, the mantra should always be to play the long-term positive trend and manage the short-term uncertain volatility, rather than the other way round, which people often tend to do. If the short-term is managed well and the long-term played to its optimum, it is a great time to be a part of India's growth story and to reap the growth dividend along with the economy.

India has all the ingredients required to become a global financial hub of the future. What is required is to create an enabling and conducive economic environment that can utilize India's core strengths to create a distinctive competitive advantage. This has to be achieved through a variety of government and regulatory reforms, many of which are already underway. With this combination of reforms and the India hinterland growth, we are well on our way to becoming a global financial superpower.

◆

Rashesh Shah is chairman and CEO of the Edelweiss Group.

Endnotes

1 Edelweiss Research
2 Ibid
3 AMFI, Edelweiss Research
4 Prime Database, Edelweiss Research
5 SEBI, RBI, Edelweiss Research

MISSION 2032:
Towards an All-Electric Nation

Mahesh Babu

In 2017, the Government of India announced an ambitious mission of making India an all-electric nation by 2032. The announcement was preceded by a groundbreaking report released by NITI Aayog titled 'India Leaps ahead: Transformative Mobility Solutions for All'.

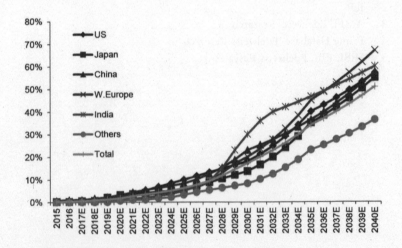

Fig 1. Regional EV ratio vs total sales forecasts (Hyper-adoption)
Source: IHS. Goldman Sachs Global Investment Research.

This announcement changed the global narrative for electric mobility.

Suddenly, the second most populous country in the world housing more than a billion people was talking about a complete overhaul of their transportation. This had a massive impact on reports and forecasts of the Electric Vehicle (EV) Industry. The graph below from a Goldman Sachs report shows that between 2030 and 2035, India would lead the world in EV ratio vs total forecasted sales.

The same report also shows that India is likely to become the second largest EV market in the world by 2030 with three million odd EVs being sold.

To give some context on the magnitude of this change, in the year 2016–17, India sold only 2000 4W EVs and Mahindra was the only OEM supplying EVs in the country.

As I lead India's pioneering EV brand, the opportunity to make a difference through electric mobility, both in personal vehicle ownership and public transport infrastructure, is becoming clearer with every passing week. Mahindra has been committed to electric mobility since 2010 with the belief that sustainable mobility is the future.

When people ask, 'There are so few EVs in India, how would my single purchase make a difference?', I tell them that since 2013, our customers have collectively achieved a landmark figure of over 50 million emission free kilometres through our e2o and e2o Plus products on Indian roads. This has lead us to collectively negating 2,500,000 kgs of CO_2 in the atmosphere, which is equivalent to planting 250,000 full grown trees. What also gives us great pride is that we have avoided 5,000,000 litres of fossil fuel in the process.[1] That is the collective power of electric vehicles!

Why Electrify India?

Urbanization will be the defining feature of India's growth in the coming years. It is estimated that Indian metros will witness a population increase of one crore every year for the next five years.[2] This will have a massive impact on urban transport system—both public and private. Industrial and vehicular emissions are a pressing concern to India, which is home to half the world's twenty most polluted cities.[3]

The energy required to run these urban centres and the industrial backbone of India's economic growth has resulted in a staggering 214 million tonnes of crude oil imports last year. This is a serious threat to the country's energy security in an increasing volatile global geopolitical scenario. An opportunity to change our energy mix has risen with India becoming a power surplus country for the first time in its history in 2017, on the back of aggressive renewable energy investments in solar and despite the average utilization of thermal installed power capacity at 60 per cent.

The automotive industry in India contributes ~7 per cent and along with the ~2 per cent from automobile components industry has made India the sixth largest producer in the world. Combine this with the rapid growth of the IT-BPM sector (which is the largest private sector employer—delivering 3.7 million jobs in the country) and India is well-positioned to transition to a manufacturing hub for EVs.

Electric drivetrain and battery technology has also come a long way since the initial limitations that resulted in the long reign of Internal Combustion (IC) Engines in automotive applications. With the Paris Climate accord and global drive to reduce CO_2 emissions, this is changing. The chart below shows that in the coming years, investment in IC Engines to comply with emission norms would increase and, at the same time, EV costs will fall. By 2022, there would be a period when both would likely to be equal and thereafter, EVs would get more cost-effective.

Megatrends in technology also point towards a change in the traditional vehicle ownership models on the back of strong smartphone adoption, rise in popularity of Shared Mobility models and Internet of Things (IoT) enabling Connected Cars.

India is amongst the lowest in terms of per capita penetration of motor vehicles—currently only 18 cars per 1,000 people. As a result, unlike other countries, India has a very strong focus on mass

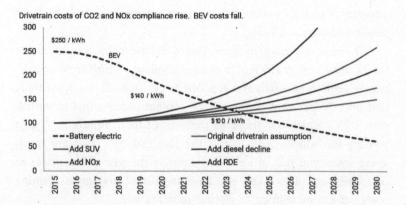

Fig. 2. The costs of getting internal combustion engines to comply with CO_2 and particulate emissions standards keep rising.

Note: NOx = Nitrogen oxide emissions; RDE = real-world driving emissions testing. The chart assumes no major changes to battery cost calculations.

Source: Morgan Stanley Research estimates

mobility. This includes buses that ply between fixed routes within the city or even stage carriers that ply for shorter distances within the city or intercity routes. With the metro projects planned in almost all tier 1 and proposed 'smart cities' in India and the e-commerce driven upswing in delivery logistics, the requirements for last mile connectivity are also increasing rapidly.

In this context, unlike the rest of the globe, EVs will have to address the mass mobility segment first before any type of high performance vehicles to really make an impact.

To ensure we and our future generations live in 'habitable cities' strict measures to control congestion and pollution become more vital than ever—and a shift to electric mobility will be a large part of the solution.

Electric Advantage

Our customers see value in the unmatched ecological and economical advantages that EVs offer, making them extremely suitable for both public and personal usage.

The basic advantage in converting to electric mobility is that an EV is ~3x more energy efficient than an equivalent IC Engine vehicle. IC engine vehicles generally run at about 28 per cent efficiency, meaning that over 70 per cent of the energy content of their fuel is wasted, versus EVs which put about 85 per cent of their input energy into turning the wheels. Add to this the fact that fuel costs are much lower when you talk of electricity rates vs the ever-rising prices of petroleum and diesel, and you have significant savings in running costs per km by shifting to electric mobility.

A typical EV may also have only approximately 18 moving parts compared to 2000 in an equivalent ICE vehicle.[4] As the number of components are fewer, the vehicle is much easier to maintain over the years, which again contributes to reducing running costs.

EVs might have a higher acquisition cost, but the benefit in terms of low running costs offers greater economic advantage in terms of Total Cost of Ownership (TCO) when compared with ICE vehicles (which have a lower acquisition costs but significantly higher running cost in comparison). However, customers often find it difficult to think in terms of TCO and balk at the higher upfront price. This is similar to the situation that existed a few years ago between LED and Incandescent bulbs and will require a similar intervention to drive awareness and adoption.

Ecologically, the most powerful benefit of EVs is, of course, that they have zero tailpipe emissions. That implies an immediate positive impact on the local air quality in urban centres after a shift to electric mobility. This is not only in terms of CO_2 emissions but also includes other gaseous by-products of vehicular emissions like CO, unburnt HC, NO_x compounds and Particulate Matter.

Even if you include all of the CO_2 emissions from power generation at the current mix in India (what is called a well-to-wheel emissions calculation) EVs are far superior. This is set to improve even further as the Central Electricity authority is targeting a 30 per cent reduction in CO_2 emission from power generation in India by 2026–27 through an increase in contribution from renewable energy sources.

Moreover, from a technology standpoint, with the mega trend of IoT (Internet of Things), EVs are a great foundation for the connected car technology, since all EVs at their core are electronic devices.

Challenges to Change

To make electric mobility accessible to a large chunk of the country's population, EVs have to be supported by a 360-degree ecosystem of supply chain, manufacturing, charging infrastructure and demand generation.

Localization of EV manufacturing and EV related components are vital to bring the costs down and grid independent charging stations both within the city and intercity corridors will build confidence among citizens that the shift to electric isn't restrictive. As one of the largest nations of two-wheelers and three-wheelers, we have a unique opportunity to leverage this shift to electric mobility to our advantage. Adapting suitable policies will help us take the leap to electric mobility.

For fence sitters, the top reason for not moving to an EV is the premium the technology demands at present. India is a value-conscious market. We Indians want more bang for our buck—either rationally or hedonistically. While electrics offer both, the prospective customers are not convinced to pay the premium. Even in commercial applications, at current product prices there are only a few takers—the visionaries and the early adopters.

Targeted interventions are required from multiple stakeholders in the automotive space to create an ecosystem that supports EVs.

Lack of charging infrastructure is a major challenge that deters mass adoption. This was compounded by restrictive policy around the resale of electricity as per the Electricity Act 2003. Until about three to four years ago, we even found it very difficult to convince reputed banks to offer auto loans to our customers for EVs as it was a new technology.

However, we have also observed a dramatic shift in the industry, supported by the Indian Government in the last three years. This has led the industry to move from a four-wheeler single car market to multiple segments, including electric vans, buses and electric three-wheelers. While the FAME incentive introduced in April 2015 gave a new lease of life to the industry across sourcing, manufacturing and demand generation, the increasing involvement of the Indian government ever since to make electrics more accessible to common citizens is commendable.

The announcement of the Bharat Charging Standards and the Power Ministry also confirming their stance to treat charging of EVs as a 'service business' as opposed to 'resale of electricity', has cleared the road to investment and rapid development of charging infrastructure.

The launch of the electric Ola pilot in Nagpur in May 2017 with Mahindra e2oPlus helped thousands of people experience electric mobility with the touch of an app. After successfully running more than 25 lakh e-kms, it is also providing valuable feedback on what interventions will be required to replicate the initiative across the country.

With the world's largest government-organized tender of 10,000 electric cars, Energy Efficiency Services Limited (EESL) made international news establishing the intent of the Government of India to make the shift to electric vehicles. This is a beginning in providing support to the industry through increased awareness, demand generation, enabling economies of scale and thereby making EVs more affordable to the masses similar to the 'UJALA' initiative for LEDs.

However, there is still a lot of work to be done to realize the vision of converting India to electric mobility. The involvement of industry, academia and the potential customers is required over and above the Government of India to champion the cause of building a supportive ecosystem for EVs.

Make in India Opportunity

The prime reason for EVs to carry a price premium is because there is low economy of scale within India. Apart from Mahindra, there are only few who believe in EVs. The most vital component of the EVs, the Li Ion battery cell, is imported. Policies mentioned below can help get more OEMs and entrepreneurs to invest in localizing R&D, prototyping and manufacturing of EVs and EV-related components, thereby enabling increased collaboration:

1. Encourage local cell and battery manufacturing through tax breaks.
2. Dedicated EV SEZs to encourage technology development.
3. In the short term, tax breaks or rebates on earnings from EV industry will encourage investment from industry.
4. Lower duties on import of manufacturing equipment and machinery for EV industry until it reaches maturity.
5. Greater focus on technology incubation projects in EV domains at premier educational institutes.

Electric technology is at an adoption stage even in developed countries. Looking at India's vision to become all-electric, if we invest now in R&D, manufacturing and the ecosystem of EV technologies, there is a high possibility that India can become a globally attractive destination for manufacturing EVs, EV components and EV software by 2032, thereby boosting many industries under the 'Make in India' initiative. Automobile, automobile components, electrical machinery, electronic systems, IT and business process management, renewable energy, road and highways—all these would be impacted positively by localizing production and component manufacturing for EVs.

A New Industry—Charging Infrastructure

The emergence of EVs has changed the industrial landscape, especially in terms of the equation between the automotive and energy sectors. As the automotive industry evolves to providing mobility solutions and the major oil companies redefine themselves as energy providers there is a need to work closely and integrate strategy in the face of new technologies and models like Charging Infrastructure.

While studies show that only approximately 20 per cent of EV owners charge their cars in public charging stations/outside their homes, with OEMs offering longer range EVs in future, owners would like to take their cars farther. Thus improving charging infrastructure is inevitable.[5] Both regular and fast-charging network is required preferably powered with renewable energy sources. Battery swapping technology for certain applications can also be explored. Organized private players should be supported by the Indian government to roll out charging infrastructure both within city and on intercity corridors. Some ways of supporting this change can be:

1. Lowered energy rates for EV charging stations can be initiated for a few years.
2. Smart cities can be planned with dedicated EV support systems for charging/swapping.
3. New, large apartment complexes/hospitals/hotels, schools or government offices can be planned with EV charging points.
4. Special tax exemption can be considered for EV owners who offer their home/office charging facilities to other EV owners.

Driving EV Adoption

At present, we have to lure people towards EV technology. This can be driven with strategic interventions from the Government of India, industry and on the customer front—for both public and private EV applications. The FAME scheme was a good start, and is evolving quickly to optimize support for the burgeoning EV industry. Some other suggestions include:

1. Higher investments initially in fleet segments for large scale adoption, with focus on mass mobility segments.
2. Higher incentives in initial years that gradually taper off.
3. Mandate a certain percentage of EV usage for public transport/metro feeder to build momentum.
4. Special number plates for EVs with no permit/road tax and toll charges for the next few years.
5. Priority lending (with lower rates) for EV's from banks (like

home loans) in the short term.

6. Free charging and parking facility in corporate/malls/ government offices/airports and metro stations for the next few years.

7. Exemption from congestion restrictions for commercial EVs in urban centres.

8. Higher benefit for EVs in the proposed CAFE norms.

9. Rationalize inverted duty structure to reduce after market rates for spares.

10. State government targets for EV adoption.

The Future of Mobility—Clean, Connected and Convenient

Mobility and transportation as we know it is being disrupted after decades of being the cornerstone of economic development. At this turning point, we have a choice to make that will determine if history will view India as a leader in the modern automotive revolution.

The future of mobility is electric, fuelled by renewable energy for a cleaner planet. It is connected, allowing us to control, hail and monitor vehicles from the smartphones in the palm of our hands. It is convenient, giving flexibility and customized mobility experiences to all stakeholders in a supportive ecosystem.

As the world moves to electric mobility for the next generation, India must be ready to lead, like it has been doing for Information Technology over the past several years. The electric revolution starts with you!

◆

Mahesh Babu is currently CEO at Mahindra Electric Mobility Ltd., a pioneer in the Electric Vehicle space and part of $17.8 billion global federation of companies under the Mahindra Brand.

Under his leadership, Mahindra Electric has launched four new models in the past year, including the award-winning e2o Plus. He has been instrumental in shaping path breaking initiatives in the electric mobility space.

Endnotes

1. Considering real world mileage in city for similar IC Engine automatic hatchbacks to be 10 litres/km, to cover 50 million km, these ICE vehicles would require 5,000,000 litres of fuel.
2. http://www.thehindu.com/features/homes-and-gardens/indias-challenge-of-disordered-urbanisation/article8285145.ece
3. http://www.hindustantimes.com/delhi-news/four-out-of-top-five-polluted-cities-are-in-india-delhi-not-among-them/story-Gn2htcLbESB3BpeYJ4mY8K.html
4. https://valueinnovations.com/tony-seba-predicts-the-internal-combustion-engine-will-be-obsolete-by-2030-why-what-are-the-implications/
5. https://energy.gov/eere/electricvehicles/charging-home

#SusFin—The India Propeller

Rana Kapoor

The Indian economy continues to act as an outlier, consistently establishing itself as one of the fastest growing nations in the world, poised to grow at 7.3 percent in 2018–19.[1] Fuelled by the government's acceleration of the reform agenda, ambitious policy initiatives such as 'Make in India', overall macroeconomic stability, and the continually improving competitive environment, India has been able to consistently outperform the world, and usher in phases of renewed growth and positivity. Such remarkable economic performance has enabled India to emerge as the fastest-growing economy amongst the G20.[2]

The economic buoyancy has also helped India address some of its sizable developmental challenges. Sustained growth over the last three decades has helped reduce poverty across the spectrum. In less than 10 years (2004–11), about 140 million people have been taken out of poverty,[3] as the annual per capita income of India's poorest has seen a steady rise.[4] Improving incomes and better access to healthcare have helped cut the Infant Mortality Rate from 57 in 2005–06 to 41 in 2015–16,[5] and increased life expectancy by more than 10 years in two decades.[6] But as the country firmly sets its sights on transitioning from a low-income to a middle-income economy, some large challenges still remain—the performance on human development needs to undergo a marked improvement, and the country's population needs diversified livelihood options, moving away from the climate-dependent agricultural sector. With approximately one million Indians joining the workforce every month,[7] optimizing the demographic dividend not only requires new-age skills and employment opportunities, but also calls for reorienting the country's economic trajectory towards a future of sustainable growth.

New Paradigms

This recalibration of the economic compass towards a more equitable, inclusive and sustainable future calls for the envisioning of new paradigms that redefine the metric of economic growth and development. Emphasis must shift from mere productivity to efficiency, profitability to sustainability, economic growth to sustainable and inclusive growth, and from expanding footholds to minimizing carbon footprints. The government's visionary leadership has already seen India take pole position on several of these issues, including voluntarily undertaking Hanumanian climate commitments of reducing emissions intensity of its GDP by 33–35 per cent by 2030, reducing India's reliance on fossil fuels and increasing the share of renewables in its energy mix to 40 per cent, by 2030.[8]

These ambitious Nationally Determined Contributions (NDCs) are estimated to cost India \$2.5 trillion by 2030.[9] Additionally, implementation of India's Sustainable Development Goals (SDGs) is estimated to require a financial outlay of \$8.9 trillion, by 2030.[10] Juxtaposing the mammoth scale of such funding requirements against India's total budgetary expenditure of approximately \$327.6 billion for 2017–18,[11] highlights a significant financial gap.

Over the next five years, India faces the biggest financing challenges given the magnitude of its developmental needs. Mobilizing capital towards a green and inclusive economy is imperative and, therefore, India stands on the anvil of opportunities that would turn it into the primary investment destination for SDGs and climate action. Inducing a disruptive evolution of the current financial architecture and instituting a robust policy framework, will be extremely critical to make a successful transition to an inclusive, low-carbon and sustainable model of development.

Marshalling an integrated and collaborative approach between the policy and financial pillars of the economy, the country must immediately act on five key areas to propel India as a front runner in sustainable finance—#SusFin.

Define Sustainability Taxonomy

It is critical to have a well-defined sustainability taxonomy that describes and catalogues the different components of sustainability and aligns them to national socio-economic and climate goals. A clear classification of assets and sectors that fall under the ambit of sustainable finance would serve as a starting point towards the deployment and tracking of finances towards sustainability.

It is evident that certain sectors, sub-sectors and initiatives have principles of sustainability built-in, such as renewable energy, water, food, affordable housing, to name a few. Identifying and enlisting all the sectors and initiatives under a single umbrella would eliminate ambiguity and create common ground for all key stakeholders.

The booming Chinese Green Bond market provides ample evidence of the enabling effect of instituting a well-defined taxonomy for sustainable finance. The launch of the Green Financial Bond Directive along with the well-defined green project catalogue in December 2015 in China,[12] led to exponential growth in green bond issuances in the country. There were issuances of about $36.2 billion in 2016,[13] followed by $37.1 billion in 2017—a marked jump from $1 billion in 2015.

Sustainability taxonomy would have manifold benefits for the financial sector in particular, and contribute to the realization of India's supremacy in spearheading sustainable finance, by setting the pace for critical outcomes such as:

- Providing a structure to the complex, overlapping network of financial flows towards sustainable development
- Providing a basic and common sustainability fabric for the country, aligning the nations' priorities with the private sector
- Enabling identification of emerging potential markets and investment opportunities in sustainability
- Measuring and adjusting the misalignment between financial markets and sustainability

Drive Nexus-based Efficiencies

The launch of the 17 global goals for sustainable development marked a global consensus on embracing sustainability and inclusivity as critical components of future economic growth. These SDGs are highly interlinked with complex and dynamic interactions and interdependencies that have a cascading impact on each other, in a direct or indirect manner. These interlinkages also preclude the achievement of any single goal in a silo, making it imperative to treat these dynamic interactions as opportunities to build synergies, increase efficiency, and effect multiple goals simultaneously.

One key to address these interlinkages among goals is to leverage the nexus between food, energy and water security with land as a key resource. Treating FEWL (Food, Energy, Water and Land) as interconnected gears of a single machine would drastically expedite the achievement of several of the SDGs—Zero Hunger (SDG 2), Clean water and sanitation (SDG 6), Affordable and Clean Energy (SDG 7), Climate Action (SDG 13), and Life on land (SDG 15), amongst others.

Ignoring the nexus between resources can in fact result in reversing the achievement of key goals, as evidenced by the negative impacts of the power subsidy reform for agriculture (Figure 1). While the reform in subsidies have enabled cheaper irrigation, contributing to higher agriculture yields, and improved food security (and thus SDG 2—Zero Hunger), it has inadvertently resulted in the overuse of ground water, leading to drastic declines in the water table[12] (and in turn reduced availability of Clean Water—SDG 6). This increased water stress is now raising serious questions on the sustainability of agricultural activities, and paradoxically threatening the achievement of SDG 2—Zero Hunger, coming a full circle.

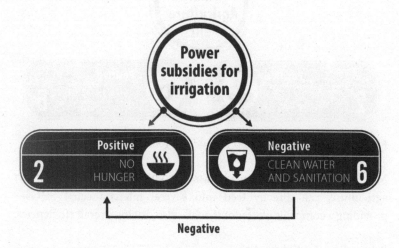

Figure 1. Positive and negative impact of power subsidies for irrigation on different goals

On the other hand, building on synergies between the goals and leveraging the nexus approach has opened up a plethora of opportunities. Adoption of 'Climate Smart Agriculture' in several states has demonstrated the ability to save water and energy while raising yields in a cost-effective manner. For example, System of Rice Intensification (SRI), a technique of rice cultivation without flooding fields, has benefitted farmers in Andhra Pradesh, Tripura, West Bengal, among several others, delivering a higher yield of rice per unit of land, while reducing the use of water by 30 per cent to 50 per cent (Figure 2).[15]

Similarly, other solutions such as the use of solar cold storage chains to improve agri-infrastructure could have multidimensional benefits, such as helping achieve food security, positively contributing to climate action, and optimizing the use of land resources.

Figure 2: Positive impact of SRI on multiple goals

Mobilizing finances for nexus-based solutions like climate smart agriculture, can directly feed into several interconnected SDGs—providing a compelling case for it, while also driving overall efficiencies.

Internalize the Externalities

The economics of product pricing has evolved over the past few years with a significant focus on 'internalizing the externalities', or taking into account the impacts of all key ingredients, their collateral benefits or damages, that go into producing a good or service. This approach of accounting for costs that were omitted or unacknowledged earlier ensures that externalities form a key part of all financial valuations and decision-making. Specific to sustainability, this includes monetization of natural resources that are freely available (or are sourced at a nominal cost), and costs associated with the future impacts of producing a good or service.

So far, one of the prime deterrents to sustainable finance in India is the perceived unattractiveness of sustainable investments when compared to contemporary investment opportunities. This can be addressed by adopting some key aspects of 'internalizing the externalities':

Natural capital accounting

Natural capital constitutes a significant share (36 per cent) of total wealth in developing countries.[16] Considering natural capital as a critical asset and placing a value on it is a critical first step in internalizing externalities. Natural capital accounts can provide crucial information for the better management of the economy such as providing statistics on the country's natural resources like water, assessing the value of competing land uses, modelling sustainable growth scenarios, and balancing economic growth while protecting natural ecosystems and assets.

Carbon pricing

Internalizing the costs of future environmental damage by putting a price on carbon emissions is another important step in accounting for externalities. While India has a carbon cess associated with coal, and an equivalent of cap-and-trade mechanisms through the Perform, Achieve and Trade (PAT) scheme, the price of carbon has virtually remained unchanged due to the challenges in effective implementation. A focus on cultivating a conducive market ecosystem would ensure a carbon price more reflective of its future impacts on the growth potential of India.

Instituting reliable models for internalizing externalities, including natural capital valuation, carbon pricing and climate forecasting, would prove transformational in defining the resource, carbon and social costs that are appended to existing financial costs. Financial institutions would be able to better streamline their investments, subjecting them through stress tests on climate and social parameters to de-risk their portfolios and recalibrate financial exposures.

This becomes all the more evident in the case of private investments. While sectors such as green energy stood as an exception attracting private investments (mostly owing to the favourable policy interventions by the government), many other sustainable investment opportunities stand unrealized.

Re-engineer the Financial Architecture

Globally, the financial system has evolved continuously to emerge as a highly resilient system, with each financial crisis it has faced. The regulatory system has been serving as the stronghold for centuries, and has a key role to play in re-engineering yet another transformation of the current financial architecture.

A robust regulatory system supported with timely evidence-based reforms and implementation mechanisms can drastically propel India as a leader in sustainable finance. This would require concerted effort from all stakeholders.

Promote sustainable practices in the financial sector

The mobilization of funds from the private sector is heavily incumbent on changing investor mindset from viewing climate change and sustainability as a cost factor to considering it an investment imperative.

Climate change, for instance, has had a very real impact on financial assets the world over. According to some estimates, inflation-adjusted losses from weather-related loss events, globally, has seen a threefold rise from an annual average of around $10 billion in the 1980s to around $50 billion over the past decade.[17] It is also estimated that in 2012, global investors were exposed to $4 trillion worth of stranded fossil-fuel based assets which were rendered 'unburnable', thanks to the Paris Climate Agreement[18] of not exceeding global warming of 2 °C.

Accounting for climate and socio-environmental risks, recalibrating the cost of capital and de-risking the economy from the Carbon Bubble is the need of the hour.

This can be done by developing a comprehensive 360-degree risk mitigation framework aimed at creating a level playing field for investors and institutions in India. Such a framework will not only help de-risk the economy, but will help attract much needed finance into capital intensive, sustainability-linked sectors.

Mainstreaming sustainable finance also requires the implementation of tools and mechanisms such as guidelines for financial and non-financial disclosures, standards for sustainability reporting, and sustainability indices as recognition for green investors.

Develop innovative financial products and tools, and leverage capital markets for sustainable development

The growing emphasis on sustainable finance over the past decade has seen an increase in the financial flows which can be attributed to the development of innovative financial products and innovative application of existing products.

Specific to green debt, three innovative mechanisms are of importance that have played a significant role and have vast untapped potential—Green Bonds, Credit Enhancement and Blended Finance. With the renewable sector taking the centre stage in these products, there is a need to increase focus on other emerging sectors like water, energy efficiency, smart cities, sustainable MSMEs, e-mobility, affordable housing, sustainable infrastructure for agriculture, and so on.

For SDG financing, however, there is a significant void that needs to be filled in employing innovative financial tools for sustainable development. For example, similar to the green bond mechanism, a sustainable bond mechanism to finance SDGs alone still remains unexplored in India. SDG financing received an encouraging boost recently, when the International Finance Corporation (IFC) issued an SDG-linked bond.[19]

Sovereign bonds could augment the much-needed public finances at the central government level. The recent successful issuances by Poland (€750 million green sovereign bonds[20]) and France (€7.5 billion green sovereign bonds[21]) provide evidence of the feasibility of such mechanisms. For urban local bodies, green and sustainable municipal bonds provide significant untapped opportunities to raise the much-needed finances required for sustainable infrastructure development from capital markets. In developed nations such as the

US and other European nations, the Municipal Bond has established itself as a significant source of raising finances for local bodies. Though it remains under-developed in India, the instrument has seen some application recently, with the Pune Municipal Corporation (PMC) raising ₹200 crore for the smart city project through municipal bonds in June 2017[22]—the first local body in India to issue such bonds in nearly one and a half decades. Support from policymakers and regulators, formation of a national body that can act as a financial intermediary and issue municipal bonds on behalf of members, and removal of the fixed cap on coupon rates—allowing bonds to be issued at market rates—would be some critical steps towards mainstreaming this instrument.

Aggregation and securitization are other underutilized mechanisms that can prove crucial in channelizing mainstream finance at cheaper costs to small-scale projects. One of the main barriers to sustainable finance, in India in particular, has been the lack of appropriate channels that could ascertain flow of finances to projects that lack scale and are geographically scattered. Such projects need to be aggregated in order to attract institutional investors.

It is evident that the strengthening and effective leveraging of capital markets is crucial to channelize private finances for sustainable development. However, compared to other developed and developing nations, the Indian bond market is still underdeveloped and largely remains a market for highly rated, plain vanilla instruments. In addition to strengthening markets through policy reforms, the need of the hour is to promote the development of innovative instruments by financial institutions, corporates, public sector enterprises and municipal bodies. The growth of the Indian green bond market from its inception in February 2015 to $3 billion by the end of 2016, provides[23] evidence that by demonstrating the success and effectiveness of innovative tools, they could give rise to a niche market of their own.

Blended finance is fast emerging as another effective mechanism for leveraging public finance to crowd in private investment, and represents an enormous opportunity across the spectrum of sustainable development, with applicability ranging from promoting climate smart agriculture and renewable energy adoption to poverty alleviation.

Incentivize Disruptions

There is a need to leverage technology and the digital revolution to create disruptive financial innovations to tackle India's challenging climate and development goals. The government has demonstrated the transformative power of technology in impacting the bottom-of-the-pyramid, through programmes such as the PMJDY which leveraged the Aadhaar (biometric identity system) and mobile telephony to disburse ₹1.6 trillion ($ 25 billion) to 329 million beneficiaries through Direct Benefit Transfers (DBT).[24]

Innovation is key to create new and tailor-made financial products and services to cater to bottom-of-the-pyramid and low-carbon businesses. Financial institutions need to be incentivized to utilize technology and develop innovative financial mechanisms targeting climate adaptation, financial inclusion, and other sustainability driven sectors in need of customized solutions.

Impact Assessment

Measuring the impact of policy interventions requires robust mechanisms to track the flow of finances towards SDG and climate related initiatives. There is a need to develop climate and SDG markers that feed into a consolidated, national scorecard which tracks the interlinked expenditure and impact of all government initiatives.

Internalizing the externalities will form another important prerequisite for measuring holistic performance. Natural capital assessment and valuation, climate modelling and similar activities will help provide critical indicators to measure social and environmental return on investment of actions and usher in a truly sustainable future for India.

These approaches, together, are critical in assessing the effectiveness of current policies, and for undertaking course corrections that may be required to achieve short and long-term socio-economic and environmental goals undertaken by the nation.

Transforming India into the primary investment destination for SDGs and climate action calls for a unified vision, cohesive approach and coordinated execution strategy between all levels of the country's governance system and stakeholders.

The development of robust financial models and mechanisms that ensure effective translation and implementation of federally envisioned national policies, at the state and local levels, are essential to summon the monumental flows of sustainable finance needed to achieve India's unique climate and developmental goals. Driving sustainable finance in India would also require the active participation and partnership of the private sector and the international community. Identifying synergistic approaches that incentivize private players to invest in sustainability oriented sectors, and designing effective frameworks for accessing and utilizing international climate and development funds are critical aspects in reorienting the financial system towards sustainability. Powered by incisive policy interventions, sustainable finance will help power and propel the next phase of India's new, future-ready economy.

◆

Rana Kapoor is the managing director and CEO of YES BANK, India's fourth largest private sector bank, and the chairman of the YES Global Institute.

Resources

1. https://www.livemint.com/Politics/o4YMXVfJKtcCfgEasBUvjO/World-Bank-projects-Indias-FY19-GDP-growth-at-73.html
2. https://www.oecd.org/eco/surveys/INDIA-2017-OECD-economic-survey-overview.pdf
3. Ibid.
4. http://economictimes.indiatimes.com/news/economy/indicators/

indias-per-capita-income-rises-9-7-per-cent-to-rs-1-03-lakh-in-fy17/
articleshow/58930178.cms

5 http://niti.gov.in/writereaddata/files/Final_VNR_report.pdf

6 http://www.firstpost.com/india/life-expectancy-in-india-on-the-rise-
but-quality-health-care-services-inadequate-2790442.html

7 http://www.livemint.com/Politics/Tpqlr4H1ILsusuBRJlizHI/India-to-
see-severe-shortage-of-jobs-in-the-next-35-years.html

8. http://pib.nic.in/newsite/PrintRelease.aspx?relid=128403

9. Ibid.

10. http://www.devalt.org/images/L3_ProjectPdfs/AchievingSDGsinIndia_
DA_21Sept.pdf?mid=6&sid=28

11. http://www.moneycontrol.com/news/business/economy/union-budget-
2017-18-allocation-to-different-sectors-950000.html

12. Compiled from Climate Bond Initiative database.

13. Ibid.

14. https://www.businessgreen.com/bg/news/3025538/global-green-bonds-
market-expected-to-surge-to-usd200bn-in-2018

15. http://www.thehindu.com/opinion/op-ed/more-rice-from-less-water/
article6183223.ece

16. http://www.worldbank.org/en/topic/environment/brief/environmental-
economics-natural-capital-accounting

17. http://www.bankofengland.co.uk/publications/Documents/speeches/
2015/speech844.pdf

18. http://www.carbontracker.org/report/unburnable-carbon-wasted-
capital-and-stranded-assets/

19. http://treasury.worldbank.org/cmd/pdf/IBRDInvestorPresentation.pdf

20. https://www.bloomberg.com/news/articles/2016-12-12/europe-s-coal-
champion-offers-world-s-first-sovereign-green-bond

21. http://timesofindia.indiatimes.com/home/environment/the-good-
earth/france-issues-first-green-bonds-with-record-7-billion-euro-sale/
articleshow/56776221.cms

22. http://timesofindia.indiatimes.com/business/india-business/
pune-raises-rs-200-cr-in-first-municipal-bond-issue-in-14-yrs/
articleshow/59221950.cms

23. https://www.climatebonds.net/bonds-and-climate-change-2016-india-
edition

24. http://niti.gov.in/writereaddata/files/Final_VNR_report.pdf

SECTION 4
Building Brand India

Creating Indian Multinationals: Good for Business, Great for India

Gautam Kumra and Anu Madgavkar

Bound together by trade and information, the world is more connected than ever before. Multinational companies (MNCs) play a major, even outsized role in forging these connections—and India can punch above its economic weight globally by facilitating the growth of Indian MNCs.

We believe that our government and business leaders can take purposeful steps to encourage the creation of global champions. By doing so, India can improve growth and productivity—and therefore the prosperity of its people.

The Case for More Indian MNCs

In 2014, the value of goods, services and financial flows, exceeded 80 per cent of GDP for 121 countries, up from 72 countries in 1990.[1]

There is evidence that globalization and prosperity are linked. The McKinsey Global Institute (MGI) has compiled a 'Connectedness Index' of 118 countries, which considers the flow of goods, services, capital, people and data (in absolute terms and as a share of the domestic economy). The index shows an increase in all types of flows, and that countries that ranked high on connectedness also tend to have high incomes. The MGI concluded that global flows increase GDP over the long term by raising productivity, and eventually increase employment.[2]

The index rated Singapore as the most connected economy in the world, with a 'flow intensity'—the goods, services and financial flows as a share of GDP—of 452 per cent. The Netherlands, the US, Germany and Ireland round out the top five; all are also high-income. The next five are the UK, China, France, Belgium and Saudi Arabia.[3]

India, by contrast, ranks only 30th on connectedness, well behind several of its peers, including China (7th) and Malaysia (20th). MGI estimates suggest that India's GDP would have been $1.2 trillion (58 per cent) higher by 2014, if it had accelerated its participation in global flows to match the top-quartile countries over the past 10 years.[4]

To improve its connectedness—and therefore its global competitive position—India needs to build successful, homegrown MNCs. Large multinationals have been leaders of globalization, benefiting both themselves and their home markets. From 1970 to 2007, MGI found that the 2,000-plus multinationals in the US accounted for less than 1 per cent of all companies, but more than 40 per cent of national labour productivity growth, 30 per cent of real private-sector GDP growth, and 25 per cent of private-sector employment.[5] Further, export-savvy MNCs and SMEs contribute to better balance of payments. For India, with a current account deficit of 2.4 per cent,[6] and a high dependence on imports for crucial inputs such as energy, strengthening exports is important to maintain economic stability. Further, our research shows that as global connectedness increases for Indian companies, so do profitability and scale (Figure 1). Thus, it is important for Indian companies to look for opportunities overseas, even as they continue to serve the large, fast-growing domestic market.

There are several instances of Indian firms globalizing and transforming themselves into world-class companies, particularly in information technology (IT) and pharmaceuticals. After the economic liberalization of the 1990s, IT companies expanded overseas, creating new jobs in India, opening the Indian market

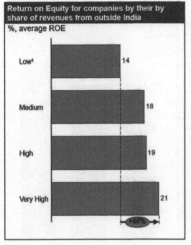
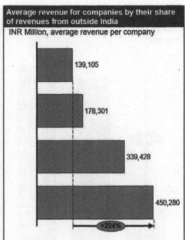

Figure 1. Profitability and size of companies in India rises as global orientation increases

Source: Capital IQ database; data on Indian and international (exports and overseas subsidiary) revenues of a sample of 209 companies with market capitalization of more than ₹5,000 crore in 2017, across nine sectors.

to global technology, and enabling India to move up the ranks on services flows (rank 10 of 118).[7] The IT sector continues to get over 90 per cent of its revenue from outside India and accounts for nearly 8 per cent of the GDP.[8] In pharma, in large part due to their lower production costs, Indian companies manufacture 20 per cent of the world's generic drugs.[9] This success also helped bring low-cost drugs to millions of Indians. Indian companies are also taking steps to go global in other sectors, such as automotive, mining, steel and telecom.[10]

Clearly, MNCs can and do thrive globally. The problem is that there are not enough of them and many of those that do exist have not attained true global scale. Of the 100 largest MNCs from emerging markets, only eight are Indian, while 41 are Chinese.[11] There is clearly significant potential for Indian multinationals to grow in number and significance (Figure 2).

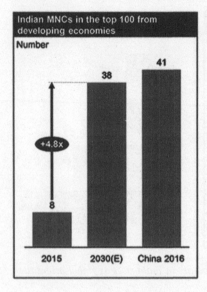
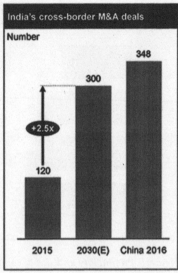

Figure 2. In the next fifteen years, we expect the scale of Indian MNCs to grow ~5X

Source: McKinsey Global Institute analysis

Towards a Global Future

MGI's research has shown that emerging markets like India are in a good position to grow world-class MNCs.[12] Companies in emerging markets often face price-sensitive and demanding domestic customers, and have to cope with difficult distribution networks. Therefore, they develop unique capabilities that can help them succeed away from home. Indeed, developing a dominant position in the home market has proved to be one of the four factors that characterize successful emerging-market MNCs. The other three are creating a unique value proposition; capturing value from joint ventures (JVs) and mergers and acquisitions (M&A); and developing a global organization.

Build a dominant position in the home market: A vast majority of global champions, studied by MGI, built a dominant position in their home markets, with strong profitability and cash flows, before they decided to globalize. These include giants like China's Huawei and South Korea's Hyundai and Samsung. Alibaba, the Chinese online retailer, has become one of the top six retailer companies globally in terms of market value,[13] on the back of its domestic success in China, the world's largest Internet market.[14] Cracking the large and complex home market ($5.6 billion in profit in 2016[15]) gave Alibaba the financial muscle necessary to invest outside China. It now sells to people in more than 200 countries,[16] and is more profitable than Amazon—in terms of both net income and margins, in spite of lower revenues.[17]

Create a unique value proposition: Successful companies typically create distinctive capabilities and make these the basis of business models to be used worldwide. Samsung, driven by very demanding high-tech consumers and intense domestic competition, developed superb product design skills. It also became adept at turning those designs into manufactured products. The company used this skill to build its brand in global markets and adapt its products quickly to local tastes.[18] Indian IT companies took advantage of the country's low-cost, high-quality labour to win a large share of the global market for outsourced IT services, through a unique yet scalable global delivery model.

Capture value from JVs and M&A: Multinational companies typically choose this direction to build scale, gain access to customers, and create superior operational systems as quickly as possible. Our research also indicates that firms that are serial 'programmatic' acquirers—that is, those that make many strategic medium-sized acquisitions—tend to have higher revenue than those that chose to expand organically or relied on one big acquisition. Successful acquirers anchor M&A in themes that support corporate strategy, place equal emphasis on financial and strategic due diligence and focus relentlessly on value creation and speed to value. They have well-established M&A operating models, with strong governance and clear role assignment.

For example, Chinese e-commerce giant Tencent has spent over $60 billion across 75 acquisitions since 2012,[19] making strategic investments across 'ecosystems'—payments, cloud, AI & retail— that strengthen the company's core online presence.[20] Partnerships are executed with leading businesses and content providers across categories within each ecosystem,[21] thereby expanding Tencent's 'pan-entertainment' empire.

Develop a global organization: It is critical to have a core team that understands the company and also has diverse experiences, which help them customize offerings and operations for local markets. Companies that are keen on globalization must also rethink their organization structure. ABB, a Fortune 500 engineering conglomerate from Zurich, has over 100,000 employees across 100 countries,[22] and has acquired or has a minority stake in over 60 companies.[23] In order to manage an increasingly complex organization, ABB restructured itself in January 2017 and created four simplified customer-facing divisions. Each division functions across geographies and companies as entrepreneurial departments with a view to drive greater profitability and accountability. These divisions are assisted by crosscutting supply chain management, research centres and digital capability, in order to leverage economies of scale and global capabilities.[24]

Role of the Government

The government, with its actions and policies, could consider ways to create an environment where all of India's businesses can compete with the rest of the world on a level playing field.

The most important priority is to foster a domestic market that nurtures efficiency, so that Indian companies are ready to succeed when they venture outside. The government has recognized this as a strategic priority, and has been working to improve the country's business environment. In the World Bank's 2017 'Ease of Doing Business' index, India ranked 100th out of 190 economies, up from 130th last year. The value of a supportive business environment is clear: New Zealand, Singapore, Denmark, South Korea, Hong Kong, the US and the UK top the rankings.[25] To improve, India needs to identify strategic areas and then target policies to address them. These include four priorities:

Reduce the cost of doing business: While the government is trying to improve the ease of doing business, it is equally important to focus on the cost of doing business. Power and logistics are two areas of concern. For several industries, such as cement and basic materials, these two sectors account for more than a third of their costs.[26] Making them less expensive is critical to enhancing their global competitiveness. In both areas, evolving technologies can help capture efficiencies: For example, optimizing the grid to reduce outage, or using e-tolling to reduce time and money spent at toll booths. Beyond technology, continued reforms in infrastructure provision would be necessary as the current cost disadvantages to Indian businesses are considerable. On a purchasing-power parity (PPP) basis, the industrial power tariffs of developed economies are 10 per cent of India's and in China, a third of India's.[27] The reliability of power is another problem. The average utility customer in India suffers 175 hours of power outages a year, significantly higher than in Malaysia where the average is 0.8 hours.[28] To lower the cost of power and enhance its reliability, India could improve the financial health of distribution companies; lower the economic and non-economic barriers on open-access; and focus on cheaper sources of energy through harvesting alternate sources of energy. The Ujwal DISCOM Assurance Yojana plan, which addresses operations and bill collection; the Integrated Power Distribution Scheme (IPDS) for urban power distribution; and the initiatives on rural power distribution are steps in the right direction, but need to be accelerated. In India, logistics comprises 14 per cent of GDP, much higher than in the US or Europe where it is 8–9 per cent.[29] McKinsey's research suggests four levers to help bring this cost down.[30] Indirect costs, like inventory carrying cost, damages & losses in transit, account for around 40 per cent of logistics cost in

India (vs less than 10 per cent in developed countries). These costs are driven by high lead time variability in our supply chains. Decreasing this variability can cut inventory costs significantly. Even as we focus on reducing cost of movement in major commodities, improving the agricultural supply chain—especially across warehousing and transportation—could be a key factor. There is a need to understand the extent to which we can shift the modal mix. Railways carry one-third of the country's cargo (33 per cent). However, most of the cargo routes are less than 800 km, affecting the efficiency of railway transport on these routes. On that basis, it is estimated that the share of railways in the modal mix can go up only by about 5 per cent. Any further shifts in mix away from roads will have to be driven by investment in ports and coastal areas to increase the share of waterways. There is high focus on improving the quality of roads and trucks since roads will continue to carry the maximum share of cargo. To maximize the return on the investments here, it is important to invest in increasing the number and quality of Indian drivers by opening training schools, boosting wages and benefits, and investing in monitoring technologies for real-time feedback. Revisiting the logistics system from beginning to end, just as companies experience it, and then strengthening each link, will help improve the competitiveness of Indian enterprises.

Create a single domestic market: In the US and Germany, which are both federal systems like India, goods and services move seamlessly across states. The EU, which has had an almost entirely free internal market for twenty years, has also illustrated the benefits of such integration. These include lower costs (through the elimination of tariffs and regulatory barriers) and higher productivity (through greater competition and economies of scale). In India, however, many important areas like construction permits, access to utilities, labour laws, and land use and acquisition are governed by the different states with widely varying effects. For example, it can take eight times as long in one state compared to another to get access to land.[31] Such variations are common and force firms to spend a great deal of time getting multiple clearances. Moreover, the different strengths (and weaknesses) of different states make it difficult for companies to scale up or to operate nationally. GST is an example of a unified regulation that is expected to benefit Indian businesses in the long run by making them more cost-efficient. Similar steps can be taken in other areas, such as the creation of model rules and regulations, unified compliance requirements, and digital platforms that create consistent norms and communications between business and government. These could help create a larger, more unified national market, and help businesses achieve the expertise and economies of scale that are so important to succeed globally.

Concentrate on multiplier sectors: Industries such as construction are important by themselves but since they also contribute to other sectors like manufacturing and transport, they have a disproportionate effect on growth, output, income and employment. Therefore, the government can boost growth and competitiveness by prioritizing the development of these sectors. The enhanced growth opportunities that ensue will benefit not just India's current and potential MNCs, but all businesses that are competitive enough to tap into the expanding market. India's construction industry absorbs a majority of the output in sectors such as steel, paint and glass.[32] In residential construction, a one-unit increase in final demand results in a fivefold increase in cumulative revenue for the economy.[33] From the continued budget allocations, the government could improve access to land for the housing sector by making land titles clearer and making it easier to register property rights. In addition, the government could put greater focus on infrastructure development in industrial clusters, so that construction also leads to a multiplier effect on investment and job creation, which in turn sustains demand for housing.

Improve the overseas environment for Indian businesses: The government can help Indian companies as they seek to expand overseas in small but useful ways. It has already repositioned India's foreign offices to become economic as well as geopolitical ambassadors. India could do more along these lines; consider that the British Foreign Service has about 4,000 officers,[34] compared with 600 for India.[35] It could also emulate groups such as Austrade and Great, created by Australia and the UK respectively. These groups will help homegrown firms to globalize through market research, advisory services, country visits, and trade missions.

The World Bank has predicted that by 2030, India's share in global investments will double, making it the second-largest investor in the developing world (after China).[36] But these are simply projections; to make them a reality, India needs to take purposeful action to improve its connectedness. Building a cohort of successful domestic businesses that can compete globally is a vital part of this strategy. China, Japan and South Korea have all shown the value of this approach. Their MNCs have been at the forefront of their efforts to connect with the world, and have helped these countries—and their people—prosper. Why not India?

◆

Gautam Kumra is the managing partner of McKinsey India, based in Delhi. Anu Madgavkar is a partner at McKinsey & Company, India and the McKinsey Global Institute, based in Mumbai.

Endnotes

1   Manyika, James; Lund, Susan; Bughin, Jacques; Woetzel, Jonathan; Stamenov, Kalin; and Dhruv Dhingra, 'Digital globalization: The new era of global flows,' McKinsey Global Institute, February 2016.

2   Ibid.

3   Ibid.

4   Ibid.

5   Cummings, Jonathan; Manyika, James; Mendonca, Lenny; Greenberg, Ezra; Aronowitz, Steven; Chopra, Rohit; Elkin, Katy; Ramaswamy, Sreenivas; Soni, Jimmy; and Allison Watson, 'Growth and Competitiveness in the United States: The Role of its Multinational Companies,' McKinsey Global Institute, June 2010.

6   Reserve Bank of India, https://www.rbi.org.in/Scripts/BS_PressRelease

Display.aspx?prid=41684

7   Manyika, James; Lund, Susan; Bughin, Jacques; Woetzel, Jonathan; Stamenov, Kalin; and Dhruv Dhingra, 'Digital globalization: The new era of global flows,' McKinsey Global Institute, March 2016.

8   National Association of Software and Services Companies (NASSCOM), 2016.

9   Indian Brand Equity Foundation, https://www.ibef.org/industry/pharmaceutical-india.aspx

10 UNCTAD's Top 100 non-financial MNC's from developing countries include Indian MNC's such as Reliance Industries Ltd, Tata Motors Ltd, Tata Motors Ltd, and Bharti Airtel Ltd.

11 UNCTAD.

12 Kaka, Noshir and Madgavkar, Anu, 'India's ascent: Five opportunities for growth and transformation', McKinsey Global Institute, August 2012.

13 Forbes Global 2000 list.

14 UNESCO, http://www.unesco.org/new/en/media-services/single view/news/china_india_now_worlds_largest_internet_markets/

15 Statista.com, https://www.statista.com/statistics/298844/net-income-alibaba/

16 Lashinsky, Adam, 'How Alibaba's Jack Ma Is Building a Truly Global Retail Empire,' *Fortune*, 24 March 2017.

17 Statista.com, https://www.statista.com/statistics/266288/annual-et-income-of-amazoncom/

18 Sinha, Jayant, 'Global champions from emerging markets', 2005.

19 http://www.scmp.com/business/companies/article/2098548/tencent-leads-baidu-alibaba-when-it-comes-ma-deals

20 2017 Fourth Quarter and Annual Results Presentation, Tencent, 21 March 2018.

21 2017 Fourth Quarter Corporate Overview, Tencent, 21 March 2018.

22 http://new.abb.com/about

23 http://new.abb.com/investorrelations/strategy/acquisitions-and-disposals

24 ABB: Next stage of unlocking value, ABB Group Press Release, 4 October 2016

25 'Doing Business: Measuring Business Regulations,' World Bank, 2017

26 Conversations with experts across industries.

27 Enerdata.

28 Power Reliability Data, Enerdata, 2015.

29 Netzer, Thomas; Gupta, Rajat; Jambunathan, Sriram, 'Building India-Transforming the nation's logistics infrastructure,' September 2010.

30 Mundra, Neelesh; Singh, Abhinav; Uthpala, Raghavendra, 'Debunking India's Logistics Myths', *Mint*, 23 March 2018.

31 Business Reforms Action Plan 2017 indices, http://eodb.dipp.gov.in/

32 'Construction industry: Contributing to Make in India,' The Associated Chambers of Commerce (ASSOCHAM) and Industry Thought Arbitrage Research Institute (TARI), 2015.

33 'Impact of Investments in the Housing Sector on GDP and Employment in the Indian Economy', National Council of Applied Economic Research, April 2014.

34 https://www.gov.uk/government/organisations/foreign-commonwealth-office/about/recruitment

35 Ministry of External Affairs; http://www.mea.gov.in/indian-foreign-service.htm

36 'Capital for the Future: Saving and Investment in an Interdependent World,' Global Development Horizons, World Bank, 2013.

Atal Innovation Mission: Building Blocks for an Innovative India

Tarun Khanna

I want to manage heavy traffic in New Delhi, India. Thousands of people die in India amidst heavy traffic while on their way to hospital. I want to change this!

How will I do it?

Maybe by connecting ambulances with our traffic lights through IoT, or by creating special elevated roads for ambulances, or by developing smart ambulances that could rise up on a road full of traffic, or something else!

I will build a solution and test it. I want to do this, I want to change India and I want to develop a new India, an Innovative India.

—Class VII student from a public school
New Delhi, India

I was amazed to hear the audacious and endearing goal of this young school student during a visit earlier in 2017 to one of the early Atal Tinkering Lab (ATL) in a public school in south Delhi. The boldness and exuberance is mesmerizing, the can-do attitude, refreshing. To me, it was the best telltale sign yet of a grass-roots movement that the Atal Innovation Mission (AIM), under the auspices of NITI

Aayog, is trying to catalyze and nurture.

'Catch them young' is a phrase often used by sports scouts responsible for identifying the next generation of world-beaters. Sports superstar Lionel Messi was signed by FC Barcelona's Youth Academy when he was barely thirteen years old. But can this analogy be brought to the field of innovation? How do you train the youth of the nation to be innovative from an early age, especially in the context of an education system that has traditionally prioritized rote learning over creativity? In July 2017, 600 students from more than 50 schools across the Delhi National Capital Region partook in a two-day Tinker festival, under the ATL initiative of AIM. This one-of-its-kind initiative, targeted at students from classes VI through XII was focused on channelling their innovative spirit. India is no stranger to student-led innovations, but has to step up its game.

Numerous students represent India every year at International Innovation competitions like the Intel Science and Engineering Fair that aim to identify student innovators across the globe. There are encouraging signs, like the example of Shreyas Kapur, a student of Modern School, Delhi, who won the 'Google Thinking Big Award' at the Fair in 2016 for his project 'Cellphone-based Optometry using Hybrid Images'—cost-effectively diagnosing eye ailments using a smartphone application.

The students participating in the tinkering festival started with a blank slate. Over two days, they were trained in the concepts of ideation, design thinking, defining problem statements, using CAD tools, prototyping and in the basic workings of robotics and electronics. The results: A vehicle that can sense an obstacle twenty feet ahead, home anti-theft systems, efficient drip irrigation machines that sense the moisture level in soil, and automatically release desired quantity of water, thereby preventing wastage of water, and so on.

The best examples turn kids' fun and excitement into creative adventures. Recently, a ten-year-old girl was inspired by the Indian blockbuster movie, *Baahubali,* in which the hero had a chariot that helped him defeat his enemies. Her workshop mentor helped her print a chariot using a 3D printer. The point here isn't that there is a big problem being solved, but the young girl now is engaged with the act of turning imagination into a prototype that is meaningful to her.

Promoting Innovation and Skill Development

Giving a call from the ramparts of the Red Fort to the nation to 'Come, Make in India' on Independence Day in 2015, Prime Minister Modi emphasized the need for providing employment and transforming India from a country of jobseekers to job creators. This vision exhorted the nation to foster innovation and enhance skill development. It was given concrete shape during the budget speech of 2015–16, when Finance Minister Arun Jaitley announced the intention to establish AIM at NITI Aayog. It was conceived as an innovation promotion platform that sought to promote entrepreneurship, and an initial sum of ₹150 crores was earmarked for this purpose.[1]

Late in the spring of 2015, I had the honour and privilege of leading an Expert Committee on Innovation and Entrepreneurship. Our mandate was to work out the detailed contours of AIM. The committee was pulled together in rather short order, with representation from an intentionally diverse set of individuals, including entrepreneurs, financiers, scientists, academics and people with experience liaising with the government. Over four months, the Expert Committee worked almost continuously meeting physically in New Delhi, Bangalore and Boston, punctuated by several virtual interactions. It undertook a comprehensive review of the existing ecosystem and infrastructure in the country to be included along with the recommendations of the report. It also took a big-tent view of entrepreneurship, to think of the innovation and creativity that underlie successful entrepreneurship in a variety of walks of life, far-transcending the exciting but ultimately rather limited remit of India's current entrepreneurial hotspots in information technology and e-commerce. We also sought to learn from successful similar endeavours globally, including Chile, China, Israel and the US.

These deliberations led to a conceptual model of the 'AIM

Pyramid' whose three layers (immediate peak layer, interim layer, and long-term foundational layer) identified actions with payoffs becoming apparent over varying time horizons. The immediate peak layer seeks to highlight measures with quick payoffs that can expedite the development of an entrepreneurial and innovative culture in India. The suggested recommendations include innovation mechanisms on the lines of X-Prize and SBIR,[2] support to early-stage ventures through business incubators, and access to capital at the seed funding and angel stage. The interim layer suggests recommendations like embracing digital platforms to encourage the public and private sectors, reforming the archaic education system and putting emphasis on work-related skills, improving the ease of doing business by simplifying regulations, and emphasizing a more stringent intellectual property rights regime. The long-term foundational layer seeks to remove the deep-rooted cultural impediments to entrepreneurship. This requires a long-run, attitudinal shift which will come over time, with progress on the interim and immediate peak layers. For example, India needs to become more receptive to risk-taking, not stigmatize failure and

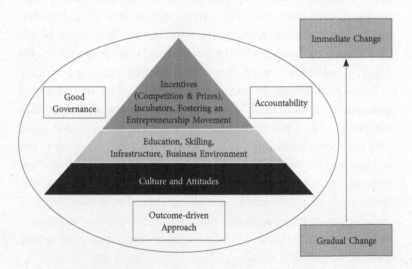

Figure 1. The AIM Pyramid Framework to Examine Entrepreneurship

recognize the skill sets of talent without engineering backgrounds or without degrees from elite institutions. In this foundational layer is also the issue of finding ways to reduce the mutual mistrust between the government and the private sector.

With the basic foundation and core mantra of the mission in place, the next step was to gather a team trusted to take forward and execute the recommendations of the Committee. The mission High Level Committee, AIM's governing body, unanimously decided to draw from a pool of willing private sector professionals to run the mission. An eclectic team of driven individuals thus assembled, leaving their higher-paying jobs, with the common goal of building the entrepreneurial ecosystem in the country. The team comprised a former Wall Street investment banker, a Medtech innovator-entrepreneur, a venture capitalist, a specialist who had worked at incubators, and an expert on intellectual property, all marshalled by a seasoned executive with an illustrious career spanning three decades leading an IT behemoth. The team, eventually expected to grow, likes to think of itself as a small, scrappy start-up within the NITI Aayog, albeit a well-funded one. While the jury is still out, success of this team could contribute to refining the template (first created by India's Unique ID Authority, Aadhaar, initially under Nandan Nilekani) of integrating private sector expertise into government initiatives.

A Silent Revolution in Skilling India

AIM's proposed initiatives are targeted at these different stages of innovations: Applied research, technological progress, prototyping, piloting, and production and marketing. The encompassing theme here has to do with contributing to a grass-roots innovation mindset. With this goal in mind, AIM is setting up ATLs across India. The labs, which are meant to be dedicated workspaces where students learn innovation skills and develop ideas, are audacious in their scale and ambition. These labs acquaint students with state-of-the-art equipment such as 3D printers, robotics & electronics development tools, internet-of-things (IoT) toolkits, emerging sensor technologies, and so on. The lab activities are designed to spur creativity, and to go beyond regular curricular textbook learning. The labs will let students explore skills of the future such as design and computational thinking, adaptive learning and artificial intelligence.

AIM has already set up more than 900 such labs across India, and plans to establish 2,000 by 2018. These labs are spread across the length and breadth of India and include two in Jammu & Kashmir, two in Port Blair in the Andaman Islands, several in the Northeast states, and already cover 388 (of India's 705) districts, across 79 of the designated Smart Cities.

ATLs are being established in schools which are passionate about science and innovation—government as well as private. More than 40 per cent of these labs are in government-funded public schools.

Each selected school is provided grant-in-aid that includes a one-time establishment cost of ₹10 lakh and annual operational expenses of ₹10 lakh for a maximum period of 5 years. Specialized support is also made available to the labs. Each is managed by an ATL in-charge who is being trained to operate the equipment. Furthermore, the progress of each lab is to be monitored by an advisory committee comprised of the principal of the school as chairman, an ATL in-charge (typically one of the school teachers), two representatives from the local community and two parents.

The initial results from these innovation labs have been very encouraging, so much so that the prime minister referred to the ATLs as a silent revolution in skilling India.

While the physical infrastructure for these labs has been identified and put in place, their success will hinge to a large extent on building an ecosystem for student innovators to thrive. To achieve this, AIM has adopted a two pronged approach: a) Interventions through partnership with corporations and institutions and b) Building a network of dedicated mentors.

To ensure that the ATL in-charge understands the philosophy of these labs, and is suitably technically and cognitively equipped to guide students, AIM has been organizing training workshops across India.

Called 'Unbox Tinkering', supported by two large technology firms, these workshops will last over 100 days and are being conducted at 10 hubs. Several other initiatives, including tinkering festivals, tinkering marathons etc. are being put together through corporate partners to provide a platform to showcase and recognize student innovations.

To maximize the impact of these innovation labs, AIM has recently launched Mentor India.[3] Envisaged to be the largest formal volunteer mentor network in India, Mentor India is aimed at engaging leaders who can guide and mentor students in these labs. The concept takes inspiration from India's proven track record of being a volunteering nation where national level volunteering programs like Teach for India have become a huge success. Since its inception, this strategic nation building initiative has garnered strong support, with more than 90 schools already adopted across India by corporates and institutions for end-to-end mentoring and other support. Reassuringly, companies are supporting tinkering efforts in smaller cities and town. For example, one tech giant has agreed to support all labs in Bhubhaneswar and Nagpur, as well as in several smaller tier 3 and tier 4 towns like Bhagalpur, Gaya, Golaghat and Jogindernagar. Furthermore, the All India Council for Technical Education (AICTE[4]) will facilitate ATLs access to mentors through its own network.

In addition to corporates, Mentor India is also a call to professionals, academics and students in their individual capacity to join AIM in preparing our next generation for a world of continuous innovation. Given that these labs are intended as places of exploration, mentors are expected to be enablers rather than instructors. Mentors contribute technical know-how, design thinking and experiential knowledge of business. A modest but important ongoing commitment of 1–2 hours per week is expected from the mentors. More than 40 of India's top thought leaders have signed up as Super Mentors for this initiative, and the list is growing every day.

India has more than 140 incubators and accelerators, according to a recent NASSCOM report,[5] and has seen a 40 per cent YoY growth (in number) in 2016. One may not be faulted in wondering, why then is AIM seeding more incubators? It turns out that more than 40 per cent of existing incubators are concentrated in Bengaluru, NCR and Mumbai; further, most of them have a technology focus (Big Data/Analytics and Cloud, followed by core technology such as IoT, 3D manufacturing, machine learning and artificial intelligence). New incubators and accelerators are shunning the 'me too' approach and focusing on niche areas e.g. fin-tech, healthcare, retail etc. Yet, India needs its incubators to support activity that is much more diverse. Thus, AIM will catalyze incubation capacity in specific sectors such as manufacturing, transport, energy, health, education, agriculture, water and sanitation, etc.

Take the example of Tirupur, about 50 km east of Coimbatore in Tamil Nadu. This historic town, dating back to the Chera and Chola dynasties, is today the knitwear capital of India, accounting for more than 90 per cent of India's $3 billion of cotton knitwear exports. The 400,000 individuals employed in this cluster, many part owners of small businesses, provide a wonderful foundation atop which to layer even more innovation.

Here, AIM is establishing an incubation sector focused on textile manufacturing in partnership with a pre-existing Atal Incubation Center. In collaboration with higher educational institutions, R&D institutes, corporate sector, alternative investment funds registered with SEBI, business accelerators, and interested groups of individuals, AIM targets establishing incubators and providing them cumulative grant-in-aid of up to ₹10 crore for a maximum period of five years to cover capital and operational expenditures. Further, AIM also envisages supporting Established Incubator Centers (EICs), and helping them scale up, by providing cumulative grant-in-aid of up to ₹10 crore in annual instalments for a maximum period of five years. So far, the AIM team has scaled up six established incubators, and is in the process of setting up thirteen greenfield incubators.

A crucial work-in-progress aspect of the ATLs and various incubators concerns their governance. It is vital that we have well-articulated success metrics and that we evolve the discipline to hold recipients of public money accountable for its efficacious use. Labs and incubators that do not show evidence of learning and progress should be retired, and new ones brought online.

Another aspect of AIM is the challenge of inducements, financial and otherwise, to innovate. In 1920, Mahatma Gandhi announced an open challenge to manufacture a machine doing ten times (later revised to five times) the work of the common charkha. While none of the six submitted ideas met the condition and hence failed to win the prize money of ₹5,000, what was fascinating was that the submissions came from even as far as Sialkot. Incentives have long been used as a tool to encourage innovation in the developed world. The Orteig Prize was a reward offered to the first Allied aviator(s) to fly non-stop from New York City to Paris or vice versa. Most recent such grand challenges have been an offshoot of the Ansari Prize—which incidentally was inspired by the Orteig Prize. The hallmark of most of these challenges has been the emergence of relatively unknown innovators, like Charles Lindbergh (winner of Orteig Prize) or Team Indus (contender for the Google Lunar XPrize). Furthermore, these challenges have led to considerable investments in the associated sectors, far exceeding the value of the prize. In India's context, incentivized innovation could be used in particular to expedite rural development and social inclusion. Towards this end, AIM has been working on two programmes, expected to be launched in coming months, namely Atal Grand Challenges and Atal Vikas Challenges.

Atal Grand Challenges are aimed at finding ultra-low-cost solutions to India's most intractable problems. Six challenges, in the areas of universal drinking water, better batteries that can work with other forms of renewable energy, affordable housing, medical diagnostics, infrastructure and waste management, each with prize money ranging between ₹10 crore and ₹30 crore, will encourage the use of technology to empower the disenfranchized. These challenges, with precisely defined technical specifications to be solved over a precisely defined time horizon, could also have a ripple effect on innovation and problem-solving in the country. The substantial cash prize will motivate researchers, students, and even amateur innovators in the country to find solutions for the nation's most pressing challenges.

Atal Vikas Challenges are aimed at catalyzing an innovation ecosystem led by high-technology focused start-ups and micro, small and medium enterprises. Modelled on the hugely successful SBIR scheme in the US, the scope of this programme extends to developing an institutional mechanism and structure to channel potential innovative ideas for products and technologies from start-ups and MSMEs on their own or along with R&D organizations, academic institutions and even individual innovators. While India's science and technology institutions do vibrant work—witness for example Indian Space Research Organisation (ISRO) in space, All India Institute of Medical Sciences (AIIMS) in medicine, National Centre for Biological Sciences (NCBS) in computational biology among others—they lack the capability to connect their insights to the world of practice. This is a capability that society needs to cultivate, as it is the ballast for the long-run evolution of the entrepreneurial ecosystem. Atal Vikas Challenges are a small step in the direction of encouraging this connection between science and practice. Applicants showing capability, intent, and promise to be able to translate technologies into products will be awarded grants of up to ₹1 crore as they meet various milestones.

Enthused by early successes, the AIM team is powering forward on many fronts including mobile tinkering labs, inspired by the concept of 'Science on Wheels', and Community Innovation Labs to bring innovation to remote and infrastructure compromised areas, and further support ATLs there. AIM is also conceiving of so-called Innovation Freeways, i.e. specialized innovation hubs in emerging technology areas such as FinTech, AI & Automation, AgriTech, BlockChain etc. that can provide a critical corpus of know-how atop which others can build.

AIM should aspire to be the enabling platform for all things related to innovation and entrepreneurship in India, fostering connections both to the science establishment and the corporate environment. This will nurture the can-do attitude among India's youth towards which our attention is directed by the quote from the seventh grade student at the beginning of this essay.

◆

Tarun Khanna is Jorge Paulo Lemann Professor at Harvard Business School and Director, Lakshmi Mittal South Asia Institute at Harvard University.

Endnotes

1 The budget announcement also included establishing Self-Employment and Talent Utilisation ('SETU')—a techno-financial, incubation and facilitation programme to support all aspect of start-up businesses, and other self-employment activities, particularly in technology-driven areas. SETU had an initial budget of ₹1,000 crores. Subsequently on the recommendation of Expenditure Finance Committee, AIM and SETU were merged as one program under Atal Innovation Mission.

2 The Small Business Innovation Research (SBIR) program is a US based program that encourages domestic small businesses to engage in R&D that has the potential for commercialization, thereby stimulating high-tech innovation in US.

3 Khanna, Tarun, 'Mentoring young India: Tinkering Laboratories—NITI Aayog-promoted open-innovation workspaces in high schools—has the potential to ignite entrepreneurship from below', *The Indian Express*, June 2017.

4 All India Council for Technical Education (AICTE) is the statutory body and a national-level council for technical education, under Department of Higher Education, Ministry of Human Resource Development. AICTE encompasses over 10,000 technical institutes across India, spread across fields of engineering, management, architecture and pharmacy.

5 'Indian Start-up Ecosystem Maturing', Edition 2016, NASSCOM-ZINNOV Report

Boosting R&D and Innovation to Catalyze India's Growth and Competitiveness

Nivruti Rai

India is on the move and it is tremendously encouraging to see a deep commitment and resolve from all stakeholders (businesses, academia, government and policymakers) to drive progress. Especially encouraging is the collective focus to enable the country's rapid growth through relevant, strategic and innovative policy interventions.

For India to fulfil its high-growth aspiration, it will need to move up the value chain and improve productivity in an inclusive manner across the population. This entails a transformational shift to delivering higher-value goods and services in a globally competitive manner. It also involves a multipronged approach by making innovation the fundamental driver of growth, supported by increased investments in human and physical capital.

Against this backdrop, focus on accelerating Research and Development (R&D) and innovation is a critical imperative. Innovation, driven by R&D, forms the backbone of a globally competitive and knowledge-driven economy. The constant flow of R&D investments boosts innovation and breakthroughs in the form of products, services and business models that drive growth, create high-end jobs, and enhance the country's progress.

The traction towards this has been stimulating for the Indian ecosystem. According to a report,[1] India has moved up six places to 60th among 130 nations on the Global Innovation Index (GII) in 2017.

A Conducive Environment

Growing R&D centres: India has one of the largest numbers of Global In-house Centres (GIC) for R&D. As per a study by Zinnov[2] titled 'India GIC Landscape Study 2016', the GICs in India today represents a $23.1 billion industry with over 1150 MNCs across the country. The number rose from 928 MNCs with 1,165 R&D centres in 2015 to 943 MNCs with 1,208 R&D centres in 2016. These centres are now becoming value providers and innovation hubs, enabling digital transformation and converging into centres of excellence.

According to another Zinnov study,[3] engineering R&D market in India is estimated to grow at a CAGR of 14 per cent to reach $42 billion by 2020. India accounted for 40 per cent ($13.4 billion) of the total $34 billion of globalized engineering and R&D in 2016.

A powerhouse of IT services: India continues to be a destination for global companies for IT outsourcing services. Over the last 25 years, the Indian outsourced IT services space has evolved rapidly to become a robust industry with maturity and ability to scale. Some of the key advantages offered by this industry include breadth and depth of competencies, ability to scale, diverse talent pool and the sustained cost advantage.

The fastest growing and world's third largest start-up ecosystem: India[4] is today the fastest growing and third largest start-up ecosystem in the world, after the US and the UK. These start-ups are mostly in the areas of app development, software and e-commerce. We are beginning to see the emergence of hardware and systems start-ups in the areas of Artificial Intelligence (AI), Internet of Things (IoT), augmented reality (AR), virtual reality (VR) and connectivity catering to industry verticals like industrial automation, healthcare, education and entertainment.

Strengthening industry-academia connect and breakthrough research: The academia has been working very closely with the industry to bridge the skills gap by developing relevant curriculum including setting up labs in growing areas like AI, IoT and communication. In addition, there are collaborative efforts to work on mutually important research areas with a focus on their relevance and application to India. According to a survey by Springer Nature,[5] India ranked second amongst the countries with the highest increase in contribution to high-quality scientific research just next to China. Some of the Indian academic institutions have gained a position among the top 100 highest performers across the globe. They include the Council for Scientific and Industrial Research (CSIR), Indian Institute of Science Education and Research (IISER), Tata Institute of Fundamental Research (TIFR), Indian Institute of Science (IISc) and Indian Institutes of Technology (IITs).

Increased focus on innovation: Innovation has been the cornerstone for India's path to digital transformation. There have been key initiatives to foster innovation, design capability and technology creation and adoption. Programmes like 'Digital India', 'Startup India', 'Design in India' and 'Skilling India' are primarily helping build a digitally empowered society and knowledge economy. With increased focus on innovation and R&D, India is aiming at achieving higher GDP growth.

Demographic dividend: India is fortunate to have demographic dividend with a large number of youth entering the job market every year. A World Economic Forum report[6] says India had 2.6 million Science Technology Engineering Math (STEM) graduates in 2016, while China had 4.7 million. By 2020, the average age[7] in India will be 29 and India is set to become the world's youngest country with 64 per cent of its population in the working age group. This demographic potential offers India and its growing economy an unprecedented advantage that economists believe could add a significant 2 per cent to the GDP growth. While this is a positive trend, it also requires focus from the government and industry to generate large-scale and high-end employment for all.

Advanced Technologies to Accelerate Transformation Across Key Sectors

Rising pace of technology-based disruptions: Technologies like AI, IoT, Autonomous Systems, Cloud, and next-generation communication technologies like 5G are poised to unleash the next wave of disruption that would impact people, businesses, as well as the economy. 5G will dramatically improve network capability, and help take advantage of the Digital India opportunity. Today, these technologies are real and are powering newer developments in various fields like robotics, AV, computer vision, language processing, virtual agents and machine learning. As new digital economies continue to rise across industries from biomedicine research to autonomous driving, generating a plethora of data, there is a great demand for high-performance computing (HPC) to advance systems for scalability and agility to support optimal data use in compute, storage, memory, network and security. According to a Gartner report,[8] smart machines, cognitive computing, AI, intelligent automation, machine learning and deep learning will enter mainstream adoption by 2021.

Enabling Key Transformations: Industry 4.0, Education, Agriculture and Healthcare

- **Industrial automation:** Also known as Industry 4.0, it blends computing with automation in a new and exciting way. It involves robotics connected remotely to computer systems that are run on machine learning algorithms with minimum human interference. It relates to a set-up called smart and connected factory where computing is used to monitor the physical processes of the factory and enable decentralized decisions. This entails machines communicating with each other and with humans in real time wirelessly.

- **Education**: The backbone of digital transformation needs fresh impetus. This includes teacher training programmes, citizen skilling programs, and building smart schools using digital technologies, connectivity, AI and machine learning systems. For instance, digital technology can increase the reach at a fraction of the cost as compared to conventional teaching methods. AI can deliver personalized education by offering customized learning modules that cater to specific goals across different grades, identifying performance and improvement areas for each student.

- **Agriculture**: In India's rapidly developing economy, agriculture is expediting food production and catering to the ever-growing population. It is poised to benefit the most from these technologies. To help proliferate smart farming in India, it is critical to establish a comprehensive rural broadband network that provides real-time information to farmers and rural institutions. Farmers may increase crop yield based on real-time insights from weather and soil data, producing more food, even in unpredictable climatic conditions.

- **Healthcare**: This critical sector can be optimized from curative to preventive care, with patient centricity via data-driven, efficient technologies. Real-time sensing and advanced analytics will enable doctors to diagnose conditions early and more accurately. It helps prescribe personalized precision medicine, leading to faster treatment, saving more lives. Improved connectivity has provided the masses with accessibility that enables them to manage their own health through apps, basic remote healthcare and more. One way to increase data collection and citizen participation at the grassroot level is to have an AI system that is flexible and adaptive.

Pertinently, these exciting technologies, applications and usages hold tremendous promise for a country like India. The democratization of technology paves the way for a better and enriched society, fosters inclusive growth and spurs economic growth. Its success hinges on the very powerful and effective collaboration between the government, academia and the industry. It is important to harness available tech prowess and skills, and make the quest for innovation and disruptive technology-based business models proliferate across the country.

Success Recipe: Enabling R&D/Innovation to Deliver Higher Value
Ecosystem collaboration forms the bedrock to enable cutting-edge research and innovation towards propelling India's growth and competitiveness. It is essential that PPP strategize and create an ecosystem where next-gen technologies become mainstream.

Support to enable proliferation of robust digital infrastructure and 5G: The massive data and data-driven devices would require robust, secured and scalable digital infrastructure like connectivity, networking, compute capability and smart cities with optimal data protection and security. Availability of 5G infrastructure will be key to drive adoption of smart and connected devices. Ecosystem partnerships, end-to-end 5G-related hardware/software, products, and platform, supporting 5G standards and setting up of test beds will boost 5G rollout. The time is ripe for the government to focus on spectrum policies and regulations for its deployment. An early policy will help operators and the ecosystem prepare their products and services for 5G roll-out, and enable backhaul and network solutions to reach rural India on time. The industry and government must partner to accelerate technology, standards and spectrum. No one entity can move this technology forward alone. The industry must define, prototype and deliver early 5G products, solutions and use cases that will shape the market. For example, it is important for the industry to get the right regulatory support to be able to undertake trials of this technology, which will augment R&D and innovation capabilities of industry and start-ups. Moreover, similar support is required to enable development and deployment of technologies like drones, UAV (unmanned aerial vehicle) and automotive safety technologies.

Focused Initiatives: There is a need to identify clear national priorities on key technologies like electronic manufacturing, AI, Advanced

Driver Assistance System (ADAS) and next-generation communication and channelize these initiatives through an appropriate structure. That would help bring the government, academia and industry players together on a common platform to achieve these priorities. Moreover, India is a large market and once we strive to be a leader and early adopter of the technology, the definition will take into account local requirements delivering more value from these innovations for India.

Accelerating Skilling and Reskilling Opportunities

The rapid pace of technology advancement is fundamentally changing the skills needed for R&D and innovation. A stronger partnership between the government, industry and academia holds the key to developing a talent pool from India that is relevant for future technologies. It reinforces the need for policy interventions to provide impetus on skilling in the areas of AI, networking and manufacturing 4.0. It would significantly augment employment generation for high-end jobs, increase domestic economy and improve efficient delivery of services.

With 1.5 million engineers graduating ever year, the government in consultation with industry can create opportunities for them to pursue high-end jobs in the areas of hardware and systems engineering. The skills and competencies that are required to advance R&D innovation in India are System on Chip (SoC) design and integration, platform and software, graphics, AI, data analytics, computer vision and power/performance management.

Need for Structural and Regulatory Support

Government intervention is critical to solving structural and regulatory impediments that will help unleash the true potential of innovation. A few things that are important include:

Imports: Simplified process to import parts to augment test and validation of key technologies. This will be a key step towards boosting innovation and expediting technology development in the country.

IP protection: Protecting IPs and trade secrets is of paramount importance to the R&D ecosystem. The industry would need policy interventions to strengthen IP protection framework in the country. Other areas of focus can be enhancing provisions for progressive Intellectual Property Rights (IPR) regime, simplifying procedures related to new technology development like experimental licences, and streamlining processes for regulatory filings, tax laws and customs rules enabling easy movement of goods. These measures would not only resolve lingering problem areas in Indian IP law, but would also encourage local innovation and greatly enhance India's 'brand' as a destination for high-tech investment.

Single window agency for the issue of product regulatory licences: The appointment of a single window agency to issue various licences and approvals and also initiating a policy framework for certain new technologies will help in reducing the lead time and enabling rapid growth of R&D in India.

Continued traction for ease of doing business: It is exciting to see India remarkably moving up the World Bank's ease of doing business ranking by thirty spots.[9] This comes as a big stimulus for the industry, and the government's continued commitment to improving this further is essential.

There is a need to understand unique challenges faced by R&D innovation centres with regard to infrastructure, skills, governance, incentives and IP protection. Developing a framework that supports R&D centres will help unleash the technical and economic potential of the country. By taking the right measures, we can drive a quantum increase in capability and complexity of the R&D work in India that can be an enabler for 'Design in India' and 'Make in India'.

High-value engineering work that addresses product design and IP creation must be our next frontier. Technology has the potential to propel the country to the next level. It will enable us to become self-reliant in addressing our needs and will drive us into global leadership.

With a growth-focused government, vibrant technology ecosystem and availability of talented workforce, India has all the key ingredients to move up the value chain by creating a world-class design and R&D hub in the country. This would help catalyze India's rapid and inclusive growth to become an economic powerhouse.

◆

Nivruti Rai is country head of Intel India and vice president in the Data Center Group (DCG) at Intel Corporation.

References

1. http://www.cii.in/PressreleasesDetail.aspx?enc=ohAT5AOwK1ghBZzbkjJ3vgBg0N4BjAHYD0wDwzZc4Is=

2. http://www.prnewswire.co.in/news-releases/gics-in-india-represent-a-usd-231-billion-industry-india-is-emerging-as-a-top-destination-for-digital-gics-says-zinnov-616683484.html

3. https://www.ibef.org/archives/detail/b3ZlcnZpZXcmMzc2NTEmNDc2

4. http://indiatoday.intoday.in/story/india-ranks-3rd-in-global-startup-ecosystems-nasscom/1/497896.html

5. http://indiatoday.intoday.in/education/story/india-second-highest-growth-in-scientific-research/1/785117.html

6. https://www.forbes.com/sites/niallmccarthy/2017/02/02/the-countries-with-the-most-stem-graduates-infographic/

7. http://www.thehindu.com/news/national/india-is-set-to-become-the-youngest-country-by-2020/article4624347.ece

8. https://www.gartner.com/newsroom/id/3545017

9. http://www.business-standard.com/article/economy-policy/india-breaks-into-top-100-club-in-ease-of-doing-business-117103101285_1.html

Coastal Employment Zones: A Catalyst for Transforming Indian Manufacturing

Rana Hasan and Sabyasachi Mitra

It is widely acknowledged that for India to achieve inclusive growth, a vibrant manufacturing sector that generates large numbers of jobs—not only directly but also indirectly through upstream and downstream linkages with agriculture and services—is essential. Moreover, India's manufacturing sector needs to be better integrated with production networks globally.

This is for two reasons. First, notwithstanding India's large size, domestic demand is not sufficient to exploit the economies of scale that characterize the manufacturing sector. Consider, for example, the market for electronic goods. India's domestic market is estimated at around $65 billion while the global market is estimated to be around $2 trillion. The domestic market is simply not large enough to allow an expansion to the scale required for Indian electronics manufacturing to be globally competitive. More generally, with a share of only 1.7 per cent in world merchandise exports—much lower than China's (PRC) 13 per cent—Indian manufacturing needs to be much better embedded within the structure of global production networks. Indeed, even if world exports were to remain stagnant over the next decade, a share in world merchandise exports of, say 6 per cent would allow Indian exports to rise from $300 billion in recent years to more than $1 trillion.

Second, prosperity cannot be achieved without improvements in productivity and the production of better quality goods and services. There is no better impulse for driving firms to adopt better technologies and management practices than that provided through integration with global markets. Global markets not only provide a conduit for the flow of new ideas and techniques, the intense competition in which they operate also provides a 'disciplining effect' through both import and export competition.

Legacies of the Past

Indian manufacturing continues to operate under difficult circumstances notwithstanding the delicencing and trade reforms of the 1980s and 1990s. First, relative to high-performing East Asian comparators, India's infrastructure deficits, especially in the power and transport sectors, have constrained Indian manufacturing in terms of its competitiveness. Second, on the regulatory front, firms in Indian manufacturing have operated under some fairly onerous regulations. One area concerns labour regulations. Considering the restrictiveness that the country's numerous, overlapping regulations on labour place on the employment and adjustment of workers within and across firms, it should not be surprising that domestic and, especially, FDI has tended to bypass modern labour intensive manufacturing.

Finally, the Indian state seems to have had more limited success than the high-performing East Asian economies in grappling with market failures that arise from learning externalities—causing firms to underinvest in undertaking innovative activities—and the need to coordinate the investments of disparate private agents and the public sector. Such market failures can seriously constrain entrepreneurs from adopting new technologies, diversify production and seek new markets.

The combined effect of these factors has penalized operations in the formal sector and has incentivized entrepreneurs to operate at small scales and in the informal sector. The result is that India's manufacturing firms remain overwhelmingly small. The concentration of small firms is a problem because at small scales of operation, firms often get caught in a vicious circle of reliance on traditional, low-productivity technologies with limited earnings and low wages.

Therefore, it is not surprising that Indian manufacturing has long performed below its potential. The sector contributes only 16 per cent to India's GDP, vastly below the 40 per cent and 34 per cent that manufacturing in China and Thailand contribute. As for employment, in comparison to countries such as China and Malaysia where the manufacturing sector accounts for between 20 per cent and 35 per cent of total employment, the corresponding share in India has fluctuated between 10 per cent and 15 per cent. While India's employment share is not too different from a country such as Thailand, the quality of employment in Indian manufacturing is significantly lower, with the vast majority employed in low paying micro and small (and informal sector) firms.

Unlocking the Potential of Indian Manufacturing

A vibrant manufacturing sector needs much to support it including good infrastructure; access to appropriately located and serviced land; fast, predictable and coordinated decision-making by central, state and local government agencies; and streamlined regulations that are enforced predictably and swiftly. Moreover, in the case of more technologically sophisticated manufacturing subsectors, it requires an innovations ecosystem.

The government recognizes the importance of a dynamic Indian manufacturing sector and has launched the 'Make in India' programme in 2015. The programme encompasses a number of initiatives including efforts to improve the 'ease of doing business' through a simplification of administrative procedures at the central and state levels for both domestic and foreign direct investment. Recent efforts to streamline administrative procedures have enabled India to move up thirty places in the World Bank's recent Ease of Doing Business rankings, from 130th in 2016 to the 100th spot in

2017. This improvement has been driven by improvements in starting a business, dealing with construction permits, resolving insolvency, and getting electricity and getting credit, among other parameters considered by the rankings.

At the same time, the government's introduction of GST should do much to make India a unified market for domestic manufacturers; the new bankruptcy law should help bring faster resolution to insolvency issues; and the public contract dispute resolution bill should improve enforcement of contracts. An effort by the government at streamlining labour regulations is making progress; moreover, it has shown willingness to let states pass reform-oriented amendments to key pieces of legislation including the Industrial Disputes Act, Factories Act and the Contract Labour Act.

The 'Make in India' programme also dovetails with separate initiatives, such as increased public expenditures on infrastructure, the creation of industrial corridors anchored to major metropolitan cities and transport hubs, the Sagarmala initiative to spur port-led development, the 'Skill India' initiative to promote technical and vocational education, and the Smart Cities initiative.

By and large, the programme and the package of initiatives are sensible. However, for a sector as complex as manufacturing, a more geographically focused approach appears to be necessary given that the financial and political costs associated with providing better infrastructure and regulations (and better implementation of those regulations) are clearly large. As experience of the last several years has indicated, legislative reform on labour, land and tax related issues is quite difficult at the national level, and often even at the state level. A geographically focused effort centred on two-three large coastal employment zones (CEZs) represents a concrete way forward.

At the same time, there is an intimate link between industrial development and urbanization. Dynamic firms lie at the heart of economic development, and cities are almost always where they are to be found. Cities are the locations where the full range of players—encompassing entrepreneurs, workers, financiers, scientists and technologists, and technocrats and policymakers—live, work and come together. However, it is not just any agglomeration of people that will do. Well-planned cities are critical in enabling individual sparks to build on one another and ignite growth. Poorly managed urban areas, on the other hand, often short-circuit the economies of agglomeration that enable cities to play their functions as engines of growth.

In this context, CEZs also represent an opportunity to test ways to better synchronize urban and industrial planning and make the most of the opportunities that urbanization brings.

Coastal Employment Zones: A Devise for Catalyzing Reform

It is useful to summarize some key features of CEZs as noted in various publicly available reports. First, CEZs are to cover a fairly large sized geographic area, for example, around 400–500 sq kms of area. Within this area, there will be various industrial clusters, including those for the manufacture of labour-intensive products with potential to create employment for less skilled workers. Second, employment generation will be a key feature of CEZs. For the jobs generated to be productive and well-paying, they will need to emerge in the context of (a) modern, (b) internationally competitive, and (c) formal sector employment. Hence, large scale manufacturing in labour intensive industries will have to play a key role in the CEZs. Third, the initial number of CEZs would be limited to two or three in order to ensure that limited resources are not spread thinly over too many zones. (As of now, it is envisaged that one of the CEZs would come up in Gujarat on the west coast and the other in Andhra Pradesh in the east.). Finally, in addition to infrastructure, CEZs will have to be characterized by an ecosystem that incentivizes private investment in manufacturing. Given the key role of large-scale, labour intensive manufacturers in providing jobs to semi or low-skilled workers, a part of the attractive ecosystem will involve the appropriate regulation of labour issues and design of any subsidies that may be there for firms and workers.

Key Design Features of Chinese Coastal Special Economic Zones

Within these broad parameters, there are several details of the design and functioning of the CEZs that will need to be worked out. A good way to think about these is to first consider the design features of what are arguably the most successful coastal employment zones anywhere in the world—i.e., China's coastal special economic zones (SEZs).[1] One can then consider which of these features can be adopted given Indian circumstances.

Size Matters

SEZs in China are observed to be fewer in number and significantly larger in size than those in India. The smaller SEZs like Shantou and Xiamen are in the range of 150–250 sq km, while the larger ones like Shenzhen and Zhuhai are in the range of 1,500–2,000 sq km. By way of comparison, multi-product SEZs in India are typically in the range of 5–15 sq km, with sector-specific SEZs being even smaller.

Infrastructure Matters

A key characteristic of SEZs in PRC has been the high quality of infrastructure available to investors. The logistics infrastructure has been especially remarkable with connectivity established through high-capacity rail connections, four-six lane highways and expressways; and modern airports and ports. Similarly, urban infrastructure encompassing housing, universities, schools and hospitals has also been developed.

Decentralized Decision-making on Regulatory and Institutional Issues

A remarkable feature of the institutional arrangements for planning, development, and operation of China's SEZs is the high degree of decision-making that rests with local governments. In the initial stages, the local government takes the lead in construction, development and management of the zones. Once the zone is developed, the typical models included establishment of a dedicated development company responsible for infrastructure development and management either under the local government/SEZ Committee or as an independent legal entity.

Moreover, the central government delegates powers to local governments and the SEZ Committees to attract, approve and manage investments in the SEZs in their jurisdictional area without need for approvals from the former. Delegation extends to even legislative authority, whereby SEZ Committees are empowered to make rules and regulations related to a wide range of issues including municipal issues, planning, land management, labour laws, wages, fiscal and non-fiscal incentives, business management aspects like profit repatriation, reduced duties on imports, etc., for their respective zones.

Towards an Effective CEZ Design

The large scale of operations and associated high-quality logistics and power infrastructure of China's SEZs have not only resulted in economies of scale for both developers and investors, but also helped attract global developers and large global anchor investors to set up operations in the zones. It is critical that the Indian CEZs be sufficiently large so that economies of scale and agglomeration can be best exploited.

The location of the zones is also important. In general, international experience suggests that setting up zones in remote areas and/or backward regions does not work (ADB 2015). Modern production requires the availability of a range of inputs that are unlikely to be available in backward regions, almost by definition. These include good infrastructure and the availability of workers of all skills and stripes and capable entrepreneurs. Moreover, a high degree of mobility for inputs and outputs to move seamlessly across borders and regions is needed.

In this context, the public pronouncements of the large size of the planned CEZs, and their location in Gujarat and Andhra Pradesh, where among others, connectivity to deep draft container ports and their placement within the influence zones of the Delhi Mumbai Industrial Corridor and the East Coast Economic Corridor, respectively, portend well for the future.

Moving beyond this, the two central challenges that need to be overcome relate to issues of access to land and an institutional design that is able to mimic the role that appropriately incentivized and empowered local governments have been able to play in the CEZ.

The Challenge of Land

Unlike China, where ownership of land resides with local government agencies, access to land has been a much more complicated factor in India. Indeed, many observers of the experience with SEZs point to issues surrounding the acquisition of land from farmers for industrial purposes as one of the single most important factors explaining the relatively lacklustre performance in spurring economic dynamism in the regions where they have been located (Mukherjee et al 2016).

There are essentially two ways to tackle the issue of land. First, the exact location of CEZs should factor in the availability of large tracts of land already vested with the government. Second, the tool of 'land pooling', which has been used successfully in states such as Gujarat and Haryana needs to be pursued. Fortunately, a legal framework already exists for the use of land pooling in the case of Andhra Pradesh, where the Andhra Pradesh Town Planning Act of 1920 and the Andhra Pradesh Urban Areas Development Act 1975, plus the new Andhra Pradesh Capital Region Development Authority Act (APCRDA) 2014 all allow for land pooling models to be used in some form. Of these, the land pooling scheme of the APCRDA is of particular interest as it involves voluntary participation of land owners, who get residential and commercial plots as well as monetary compensation in return for the land they surrender. While the APCRDA applies only to the capital region, new legal provisions could be inserted in a state-wide legislation. What seems extremely important is to conduct extensive stakeholder discussions that involve the presentation of credible plans for transforming areas covered by the CEZ and ensuring that these are deemed fair. Such a process certainly takes time. However, the effort will be well worth it.

Institutional Design for Planning and Managing the CEZs: Synchronizing Urban and Industrial Development

Manufacturing ultimately takes place in a particular location. If officials in that location do not have the incentives to ensure that firms located there do not grow, or if they do not have decision-making authority over the various inputs that firms need (such as roads, power, skilled workers, and decent housing and educational facilities for workers and their families), the growth prospects of firms and the location in question are bound to be more limited.

Admittedly, India has a very different structure of governance for cities and townships than China. As noted above, local government agencies in China have played the leading role in development of CEZs, from planning to implementation and even regulatory design. The reason they have been able to do so comes from the Chinese governance framework, where the performance of senior local government officials is largely assessed based on the extent of economic development in their area and the high degree of autonomy and empowerment they enjoy. In contrast, local government in India is mostly focused on the provision of urban/municipal services like water and sanitation. Economic development is largely the mandate of the state and central government. In addition, capacities also tend to be relatively weak in India at the local government level. But the key takeaway is that mechanisms for aligning the incentives of local officials with local economic development need to be strengthened and a way found to bring all the key decision-makers together.

In keeping with Indian realities, a different set of solutions is needed on the institutional design for planning and managing the CEZs. In a nutshell, the key challenge lies in recognizing that industrial and urban development go together, and that some mechanism is needed for synchronizing industrial and urban development plans. Otherwise, new industrial sites can spawn urban agglomerations characterized by sprawl and congestion, and significant unevenness in land prices that leads to sub optimal use of scarce land, with the overall effect that 'demons of density' chase away 'economies of agglomeration'. Anecdotally, this has become quite a common situation in India where development efforts are almost exclusively undertaken under the direction of state industrial departments with urban development departments having little say in planning.

Fortunately, an integrated approach is possible. A case in point is in Gujarat where the Industries and Mines Department enacted its own legislation, the Special Investment Region Act, incorporating provisions of the Gujarat Town Planning and Urban Development Act. In effect, the Gujarat Industries and Mines Department has subsumed all urban development functions, at least in the context of new industrial development. In addition, there are also examples of integrated urban-industrial complexes in Andhra Pradesh, Sri City being an example (as is Mahendra World City in Chennai).

Regulatory Framework for Attracting Investment and Generating Employment

India's business environment is often described as cumbersome and riddled with regulatory uncertainties for investors. It is critically important that CEZs clearly signal themselves as economic zones where streamlined regulations and their implementation is the norm. This would require CEZs to be managed by an empowered group of officials from both state and central governments. This would seem to be necessary for having a credible 'single window' clearance mechanism, backed by information technology enabled monitoring and back-end coordination between all concerned agencies for quickly sorting through various business decisions that have to go through the regulatory apparatus.

In addition to coordinated executive action by state and central government officials, certain legislative actions will be required. Especially from the perspective of encouraging labour-intensive manufacturing in the zones, a more flexible regime governing labour regulations must be given very serious consideration in the area under the demarcation of CEZs. No doubt, this can be challenging. But, once again there is precedence, as in the case of SEZs in Gujarat, or even the state-level amendments to the Industrial Disputes Act, Factories Act, Contract Labour Act that have been enacted by state such as Madhya Pradesh and Rajasthan.

Tackling Market Failures

Considerations of equity as well as possible market failures have given rise to a lot of policy interventions all over the world, and in this regard India is no different. A recent study points to over 300 schemes to promote development among enterprises in India (Mukerjee et al 2016). The difficulty of many of the schemes is that evidence for their efficacy is extremely limited. A key issue that the government has to consider is the effectiveness of these programmes.

Policymakers must be guided by various principles in designing and implementing different elements of industrial policy (IADB 2014). Some specific questions to guide policy interventions include: Why is it that the market does not do by itself what appears desirable? Is the policy intervention a proper remedy for market failure? Are institutions sufficiently strong to adopt the policy effectively? In this context, IADB goes on to present a useful typology of interventions based on: (i) A distinction between horizontal, or broad-based interventions versus vertical, or sector specific interventions; and (ii) the provision of public inputs versus market interventions. The least controversial interventions are those involving the delivery of public inputs of a broad-based nature. A one-stop shop for business registration is an example. Diametrically opposite are market-based interventions that apply to a particular sector. A tax exemption for the tourism industry is an example. The nature of such interventions makes them most prone to abuse or waste. This is not to suggest that policymakers shy away from the more complicated interventions. It does however suggest caution and that a lot of attention be paid to ensuring good design and implementation capacities.

India's favourable demographics, the entrepreneurial dynamism of its private sector, and a small but not insignificant cadre of well-trained managers, administrators and science and technology personnel, have enabled India to make the most of the reforms of the 1990s and grow rapidly over the last two decades. However, this growth needs to be sustained, and made more inclusive by ensuring that employment intensive sectors experience some combination of increases in productivity and/or employment.

In this context, India has embarked on an ambitious 'Make in India' programme. It is critically important that this programme succeeds. The CEZs could well play a catalytic role in spurring Indian manufacturing and doing so in a framework that promotes a better planned and more dynamic urbanization.

◆

Rana Hasan is a director in the Economic Research and Regional Cooperation Department, Asian Development Bank (ADB).

Sabyasachi Mitra is Deputy Country Director at the India Resident Mission, South Asia Regional Department, ADB.

References

1   Asian Development Bank, 'Can Special Economic Zones Drive Development?', Asian Economic Integration Report, Manila, 2015.

2   Inter-American Development Bank, 'Rethinking Productive Development: Sound Policies and Institutions for Economic Transformation', 2014.

3   Mitra, S., Hasan, R.; Sharma, M.; Jeong, H.Y.; Sharma, M.; Guha, A., 'Scaling New Heights: Vizag-Chennai Industrial Corridor, India's First Coastal Corridor', ADB, 2014.

4   Mukherjee, A.; Pal, P.; Deb, S.; Ray, S.; Goyal, T.M.; 'Special Economic Zones in India: Status, Issues and Potential', Springer Nature, 2014.

Endnotes

1   Indeed, China's special economic zones represent one of the most prominent tools used by its policymakers to jumpstart the industrialization process from a relatively weak economic base, open the economy to the world, introduce market oriented reforms, and even foster modern city and regional planning. They represent a tool for introducing institutional reforms in a geographically focused manner, largely insulated from prevailing domestic institutions. The success of this tool may be seen from the fact that by 2007, SEZs (including all types of industrial parks and zones) in China accounted for about 22 per cent of national GDP, about 46 per cent of FDI, about 60 per cent of exports, and generated more than 30 million jobs (Zhang 2012 as cited in ADB 2015).

The Big Urban Mobility Opportunity

G.V. Sanjay Reddy

British science-fiction writer Arthur C. Clarke stated, 'Any sufficiently advanced technology is indistinguishable from magic.' Scientists today are working on a number of technologies which feel like magic. The challenge for us as a society is to convert the power of this magic to real-life solutions, such that the benefits can be realized by the common man. To do this, we have to start by clearly identifying our current problem, be aware of the scientific magic under development, understand the application of this magic to solving our problem and then develop an implementation path which will provide real benefits to society. This is especially important for a developing country like India, where the latest technologies can be utilized to leapfrog beyond traditional constraints and deliver value to its citizens. One such problem we face today is urban mobility or the lack of it.

Cities today are the epicentre of all economic activity. In developed countries, as much as 80 per cent of the population lives in urban areas. Denser cities can potentially drive greater economic value. But they also need a well-oiled urban transportation system, not just to move people around, but also to keep them connected.

Urban mobility should be measured on a metric combining efficiency, affordability, health, safety and convenience. Increasing urbanization and rising incomes, combined with poor public transportation, has incentivized vehicle ownership. Personal vehicles are the most inefficient mode of urban mobility, as their actual usage is very low (4–5 per cent per year in USA,[1] UK[2] as well as India[3]). They are quite expensive, require significant parking space, and lead to increased infrastructure costs and travel times and worsening pollution in cities.

India faces a similar challenge, where lack of sufficient infrastructure has led to congestion and has reduced the average speed in most metro cities to around 20–30 kmph.[4] The study[5] conducted by ride sharing company Ola, highlights this challenging situation.

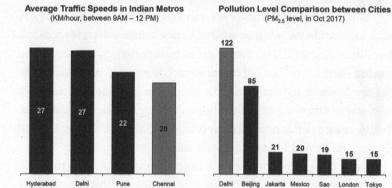

Average Traffic Speeds in Indian Metros
(KM/hour, between 9AM – 12 PM)

Pollution Level Comparison between Cities
($PM_{2.5}$ level, in Oct 2017)

Growing vehicular traffic also impacts the environment. As it can be seen from the chart, Delhi has worse air quality level than even Beijing, as per Numbeo[6] (a data aggregator). Research study[7] highlights that change of just 10 units of $PM_{2.5}$ decreases worker productivity by roughly 6 per cent.[8]

Indian roads lack safety as well. According to Geneva-based International Road Federation (IRF), India accounts for 10 per cent of global road accidents with more than 1.46 lakh fatalities annually—highest in the world.[9]

An aspirational 8+ per cent GDP growth and current urbanization level[10] of 33 per cent will eventually lead to developed country levels[11] of more than 75 per cent. The magnitude of the twin challenges of pollution and congestion will only get worse. We will not be able to solve these challenges just by building more roads and metro lines. Given the limited space in our cities, we have to improve the space efficiency of our urban transportation systems.

We need to think beyond the obvious to transport large numbers of people across large distances—it should be faster, cheaper, with better comfort and safety. Our ancient traditions suggest that the best way to find solutions to complex problems is by looking inwards. We don't need to look very far as our blood circulation system is appropriate to cull out learnings of a highly superior, smart and reliable transportation system—so simple yet so advanced.

Our vascular (or circulatory) system uses a three-dimensional (3D) structure inside the body, compared to our primary dependence on a two-dimensional (2D) system for urban transportation.[12] Analogous to the IoT there are millions of sensors which keep providing feedback to the brain, which in turn guides the heart to pump different quantities of blood to different parts of the body, carrying the relevant nutrients. It also manages the return transportation of the low nutrient blood through dedicated least resistance paths.

Even though incremental solutions will be insufficient to tackle our challenges, we have to continue to implement them to improve the current situation. But from the perspective of finding holistic and comprehensive long-term solutions, we should also put in place a framework to work on futuristic innovations to help us leapfrog at the right time.

Some of these potential future solutions include autonomous vehicles, drones (unmanned aerial vehicles), flying cars, magnetic pods, hyperloop, rocket travel, and many others.

Potential Solutions	Current Status
Autonomous Vehicle (AV)	First driverless car was introduced by Google in 2009 and has covered 1.3 million miles on normal streets by 2016, compiling a vast array of automated driving knowledge.

Drones/Unmanned Aerial Vehicles	US and European countries are framing guidelines for usage of drones across agriculture, telecom, infrastructure and e-commerce sectors.
Flying Cars	Airbus' self-piloting flying car concept 'Vahana' plans to offer modular functionality, which means it can operate both on ground and in the air.
Magnetic Pods	Israel Aerospace Industries[13] is testing suspended magnetic pods (called SkyTran),[14] a self-driving monorail designed to hover 20 feet above roads and travel up to 155 mph.
Hyperloop	Hyperloop will have[15] floating train pods using magnetic levitation technology in a tube operating at near-vacuum and gliding at an airline speed of 670 mph over long distances.
Rocket Travel	Elon Musk envisions long-distance travelling (between cities) on Earth by using the same rocket system which is being developed for the moon and Mars trips.

At the current juncture, some of the above forms of transportation may appear like 'magic'. But history suggests that the transformation driven by technology disruptions can be very rapid, once the inflection point is crossed. An example of this is the transition from horse carriages

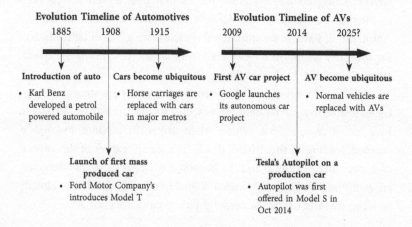

Evolution Timeline of Automotives			Evolution Timeline of AVs		
1885	1908	1915	2009	2014	2025?
Introduction of auto	**Cars become ubiquitous**		**First AV car project**		**AV become ubiquitous**
• Karl Benz developed a petrol powered automobile	• Horse carriages are replaced with cars in major metros		• Google launches its autonomous car project		• Normal vehicles are replaced with AVs

	Launch of first mass produced car			**Tesla's Autopilot on a production car**	
	• Ford Motor Company's introduces Model T			• Autopilot was first offered in Model S in Oct 2014	

to automobiles. Back in 1900, horse carriages were the[16] dominant means of transportation, even in New York, with almost no car in sight. But the initial seeds of a viable car had already been sown and the ecosystem started witnessing rapid competitive innovation. The first mass produced automobile, Model T Ford, was introduced in 1908. Within a short span of fifteen years (by 1915), the horses were retired and replaced completely by cars.

Similarly, the initial seeds for AVs and Drones (commercial) have already been sown and both are witnessing rapid innovation and implementation. Once the inflection point is crossed, it will cause significant positive disruption to urban mobility over the next 10–15 year period and therefore India needs to start preparing itself for this future.

Autonomous Vehicles

The benefits of AV adoption are enormous, and include cost effectiveness, greater safety, better vehicle utilization, less congestion and pollution, reduction of accidents,[17] easier access to differently enabled and old people and freeing up time of individuals for work or leisure.

In Feb 2016,[18] the US Department of Transportation (US DOT) officially accepted the AI powering Google's driverless cars as a 'driver'. Uber has already launched its first fleet of self-driven taxis in Pittsburgh. Germany has already designated a section of the A9 Autobahn in Bavaria for automated vehicle testing.[19] Similar initiatives for the early adoption of AVs are visible in the UK, France, Canada, Japan, Australia, UAE and Singapore.

At the same time, regulators around the world are struggling with issues related to system safety, privacy, data security, integrity and access. In a recent case, a Tesla vehicle when driven in 'autonomous mode' crashed, leading to the driver's death. The identification of the 'owner' and insurance of vehicle and the 'responsible driver' is also undergoing an evolution. Federal Automated Vehicle Policy in the US is already tackling these issues while creating policy guidelines for AVs.

Unfortunately, India's first response to this change has been more of fear than of exuberance. Given that 'driving of vehicles' is a significant employment contributor, our proclivity is to resist the change instead of embracing and leading it. We must realize that we cannot prevent the eventuality and it is better to lead the transformation, than to be a buyer of the technology and know-how from foreign players. We are already leading in the EV and renewable space and should do the same for AVs as well.

While the aim is to have an autonomous fleet, the process to reach that stage should be achieved in phases, as described in the chart below.

Design Stages to Achieve the Future of AVs

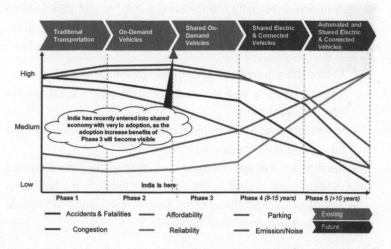

Out of the five outlined phases, India has already experienced the first two phases and recently entered the third phase where it has started using shared vehicles (through Ola and Uber). The transition to Phase 4 will happen in the next 8–15 years. In this phase, EVs will become omnipresent and will be connected and shared. The EV transformation is already underway, with governments around the world coming up with supportive policies to encourage investments across the whole spectrum of solutions from battery technology and EVs to charging infrastructure and renewable energy to feed electricity requirements.

In Phase 5, all vehicles would be autonomous, connected and shared. During each phase, cities will see congestion, emissions and traffic collisions going down over time, even as affordability and reliability will go up.

But to continue progressing on this path of evolution, we need to be proactive and provide the necessary policy support. To avoid iterations in policy and technical guidelines, government needs make the design and implementation process more collaborative. Inputs from private companies, technology start-ups, funding institutions, academic institutes should be invited and buy-in attained from the public, who will eventually use the services. AV would also need to be integrated with the smart city development mission. Key areas which need to be considered and refined at each phase would include:

- **Urban Transportation Elements:** Create automated gateway transits, roadway and in-vehicle sensors, connected highways and dedicated lanes.
- **Infrastructure:** EV charging stations, smarter street lights, and repair and maintenance booths.
- **Analytics:** Robust analytics platforms for performance measurement, real-time analytics and predictive management.
- **Architecture and Standards:** Automation standards, vehicle standards and open data standards.

Bringing in such a transformative change will also require an integrated effort across various ministries in the government. While transportation comes under the Ministry of Transport, true AV adoption will require policy evolution across transportation, power (for EVs and charging infrastructure), home (for security and privacy), telecommunications (for connected vehicles), science and technology (for R&D), HRD (loss of jobs), urban development and a few others. It also has to be a federal effort, involving the state governments as well as the municipal corporations in large cities.

Based on the discussed design framework and learnings from other countries, the implementation roadmap for India to achieve a leadership role in this revolution includes the following:

a. **Setup an institution to support AV adoption:** US DOT outlines best practices for the safe pre-deployment design, development and testing of AVs prior to commercial sale or operation on public roads. Similarly, Committee on Autonomous Road Transport for Singapore (CARTS) has set up the Singapore Autonomous Vehicle Initiative[20] (SAVI) to conduct R&D and testing of AV technology and applications.

Following such early movers, the government of India needs to setup institutions such as National Autonomous Vehicle Institute (NAVI) to coordinate and stimulate autonomous mobility technology supported by funding. NAVI's mandate would be to create an AV ecosystem, promote R&D and coordinate the deployment of AVs across the country. It will have to set the necessary standards and regulations for AV testing, manufacturing and deployment. It will also have to coordinate with multiple states, regional transit authorities and transportation companies, (auto manufacturers & logistics operators) and major stakeholders to consider the impact of AVs in their strategic plans. NAVI will have to engage in developing a national cyber-security strategy and standards as well.

b. **Guide AV adoption through various stage-gates:** Before putting the technology for public use, the effectiveness of autonomous technology needs to be tested and proven in smaller industrial setups of mining and agriculture. Thereafter, the government will have to make amendments in the Motor Vehicles Act to allow commercial trials on road. New smart cities and high-speed corridors could then become the starting point to test and commercialize this technology for public use.

Before opening it for wider use, roads will have to be equipped with road signs and marked lanes to help autonomous car's sign reading algorithm take the right decision.

c. **Assess AVs impact on employment:** A critical factor to be considered in all transformations is the impact on people involved and dependent on the existing system. While there will be substantial new jobs getting created over the long term, from a short-term perspective, the shift to AVs could lead to reduced job opportunities for drivers. Cab aggregators, radio taxis, car rental agencies, as well as private individuals and transportation services, are currently large employers of drivers in India. The apprehensions of these employees (many of them are self-employed entrepreneurs) need to be addressed. The government will need to build consensus around the benefits of this transformation and also invest in substantial reskilling and employment support for people losing jobs.[21]

d. **Include AVs in scope of future transportation projects:** India[22] will have to ensure that all new major transportation projects include a critical assessment of how they will support the deployment of AVs. Specific category of dedicated funding for projects should be provided to stimulate AV technology development, trials, testing and deployment.

e. **Promote private participation and industry development:** AVs are as much about technology as they are about automation. Our inroads into global technology networks, extensive talent pool and technology R&D set-ups, makes us well-placed to play an important role in this evolution. In addition to our engineering institutes, like the IITs, the government should encourage private companies (Indian as well as global automotive and technology players) and start-ups to develop and test solutions in India. Given the breadth of investments required across different innovative solutions and the need to eventually ramp-up to achieve countrywide transformation, private capital would be critical to drive this rapid change. Other than developed nations, in most parts of the world, the traffic conditions resemble the chaos prevailing on Indian roads. Hence, India could be a good testing ground for real-life conditions.

To start with, government-led institutions like IITs, IISc., etc. should come out with specific industry collaboration projects for key technologies involved in AV development. Such R&D could also be funded through a technology promotion fund.

f. **Support transition in related industries:** Currently, insurance companies provide cover to drivers. But for AVs, manufacturers and infrastructure providers will be the subject of liability. Personal car insurances will gradually come down and would migrate to product liability insurance.[23] There will be different risks that need insuring such as the risk of an algorithm failing or cyber-attacks relating to driverless cars.

g. **Frame national security and policing policies:** Similar to the Federal Automated Vehicle Policy in the US, NAVI will also have to focus on system safety, individual rights, privacy, data security, integrity and access related issues while creating policy guidelines for AVs. It will also have to frame rules to mitigate the potential misuse of AVs by criminals and terrorists.

Drones/Unmanned Aerial Vehicles (UAVs)

Drones[24] have a wide range of civilian applications across agriculture, remote sensing, law enforcement and many other sectors.[25] A spurt in automation technology, advanced design, mapping, visualization techniques, combined with advance robotics, digital cameras, GPS receiver chips, rechargeable batteries and machine learning, has opened up limitless applications of drones.

From the perspective of urban mobility, drones allow us to fully explore the third dimension (3D) of our environment. Drone taxi services as well as drone-based logistic delivery have the potential to completely disrupt the current transportation models, in terms of time, cost, convenience and fuel efficiency.

Despite several advantages, this technological revolution comes with a set of significant concerns, impinging as it does upon the proprietary, reputational, and security interests of individuals.[26]

Only a few countries like the US, UK, France and Germany have laid down comprehensive legislations to regulate the use of drones after thorough deliberation. For example, in the UK, recording of images obtained via drones could potentially breach the obligations contained in the Data Protection Act and the CCTV Code of Practice.

Given the benefits from deploying drones, India should be looking at proactively supporting drone usage to overcome many India-specific challenges, while ensuring appropriate regulations. While the eventual aim is to enable extensive use of drones for urban mobility and last mile logistics, the process to reach that stage should be achieved in phases, as described in the chart below.

Potential Design Stages to Utilize Advantages of Drones in Urban Mobility

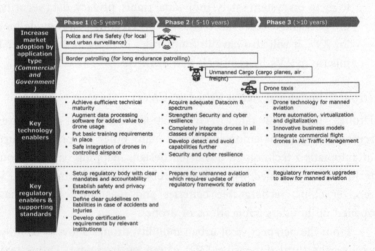

Source: SESAR—European Drones Outlook Study, 2016

In the first phase,[27] the focus must be on opening the aviation market to the civil use of remotely piloted aircraft systems in a safe and sustainable manner. This phase should identify and evaluate the most relevant applications for drones that could be done within Visual

Line of Sight (VLOS) and establish common training requirements. In addition, data processing capability required for drone operations will need to be strengthened along with the creation of technical regulations to support the development of drones.

In the second phase, we should acquire critical technical capabilities to focus on long endurance surveying beyond visual line of sight (BVLOS). This phase involves all type of operations at low altitudes in urban environment. Here, critical enhancement in 'detect and avoid' capabilities will be required as drones would execute operations in urban settings, including last mile delivery.

In the third phase, we should achieve acceptance of drone applications for carrying humans, with stronger automation and virtualization levels.

Despite the benefits, the Indian regulatory approach has been cautious towards drone applications. As per DGCA public notice of October 2014,[28] no non-government agency, organization, or individual would be permitted to launch an unmanned aircraft system for any purpose until the issue of binding regulations. The government has already issued a new set of draft guidelines in April 2016. It should proactively ease the relevant regulations, so as to allow for critical testing as per the design phases.

Based on the discussed design framework, the implementation roadmap includes the following:

a. **Make the Regulatory Process Collaborative:** The task to create a regulatory framework that supports the deployment of drone-enabled solutions should be participative and not be left solely with the DGCA. Tech innovation companies and start-ups should be involved to evaluate technological advancements and eventually lay the foundation of a legally coherent framework.

b. **Address Safety & Security Concerns:** Several technology solutions should be examined to detect airborne unmanned aerial systems (UAS) and pinpoint the location of the operator. Technologies to disable, jam, take control over, or potentially destroy a small

UAS also need to be available with the regulator.

This will need to include ongoing monitoring of all UAS and utilize high bandwidth telecommunication network to manage the big data support required.

c. **Address Privacy Issues:** Currently, Indian regulations lack clarity on this issue and the ambiguity in ownership of airspace above land continues. This needs to be addressed by future regulations.

d. **Incentivize Private Companies and Set Operating Standards:** Integration of commercial or civilian drones in national airspace will be difficult without developing right technical capabilities.[29] These include technologies to enable drones to sense and avoid other air traffic; manage low-altitude airspace and detect and prevent unauthorized use of airspace; mitigate risks to persons and property on the ground; provide secure command and control linkages between drone aircraft and their operators; and enable automated operations.

Private companies should be incentivized to develop solutions for the various technological challenges as well as developing solutions relevant to the Indian context.

Creating Magic Like Our Ancestors

Till now, India has been content with reverse engineering the various solutions which have been developed and implemented in Western countries. But a study of our great epics clearly highlights the visionary leadership of those times with regards to futuristic scientific inventions.[30] The Ramayana describes Pushpak Vimana as a double-deck, circular (cylindrical) aircraft with portholes and a dome.[31] Vaimanika Shastra, a fourth-century-BC text written by Maharshi Bhardwaj, detailed the operation of ancient 'vimanas' and included information on steering, precautions for long flights, protection of the airships from storms and lightning, and how to switch the drive to solar energy.

Clearly, India was at the forefront of advances in aviation technology using which we built all the futuristic vehicles back then. Unfortunately, somewhere along the way, we lost our scientific leadership. It is time for us to regain that leadership.

Today, our scientific talent and experience is at par with the world, our companies have expanded into global markets and the liberalized environment also allows for international collaboration and funding to spearhead new development. ISRO's Mass Orbiter Mission (MOM) is a good example of this.[32] MOM was lauded globally not only for achieving its mission, but for doing so at a fraction of the cost of similar space missions launched by NASA and the European Space Agency.

Instead of being content with 'reverse engineering' global solutions, India should foster a culture of 'Developed in India', which will encourage future champions to research and collaborate on solutions, not just for India, but for the world. In our epics, the rishis were well-known for achieving magical feats. It is now time that we unshackle our minds and give our scientists and entrepreneurs the freedom and encouragement required to create magic for people in India and across the globe.

◆

G.V. Sanjay Reddy is the vice-chairman of GVK Power and Infrastructure Limited.

Endnotes

1 http://newsroom.aaa.com/2016/09/americans-spend-average-17600-minutes-driving-year/
2 http://www.reinventingparking.org/2013/02/cars-are-parked-95-of-time-lets-check.html
3 Based on a study by Central Road Research Institute.
4 http://www.hindustantimes.com/opinion/how-smart-solutions-can-ease-traffic-jams-in-our-cities/story-1NM5NIpVJK6QxC4whkKuMP.html
5 http://www.huffingtonpost.in/2017/01/03/in-the-race-for-the-slowest-moving-traffic-among-indian-cities_a_21646157/
6 https://www.numbeo.com/pollution/compare_cities.jsp?country1=India&city1=Delhi&country2=China&city2=Beijing

7   http://www.nber.org/papers/w19944.pdf

8   http://www.businessinsider.in/The-pollution-outside-your-office-window-affects-your-work-in-a-big-way/articleshow/47749013.cms

9   http://auto.economictimes.indiatimes.com/news/industry/india-ranks-first-in-road-deaths-in-the-world/56221070

10 https://www.cia.gov/library/publications/the-world-factbook/fields/2212.html

11 http://www.un.org/ga/Istanbul+5/booklet4.pdf

12 TED Talk by Wanis_Kabbaj on "What_a_driverless_world_could_look_like"

13 https://www.wired.com/2014/06/israel-pod-transport/

14 http://www.businessinsider.in/A-new-self-driving-monorail-will-chop-2-hour-commutes-down-to-10-minutes/articleshow/52995360.cms

15 https://hyperloop-one.com/facts-frequently-asked-questions

16 https://www.mnn.com/green-tech/transportation/blogs/horses-horsepower-rocky-transition

17 US Department of Transportation – Federal Automated Vehicle Policy

18 http://www.techrepublic.com/article/our-autonomous-future-how-driverless-cars-will-be-the-first-robots-we-learn-to-trust/

19 http://www.telematics.com/germany-creates-its-driverless-car-legislation/

20 http://connectedautomateddriving.eu/wp-content/uploads/2017/02/3_Day2_PL10_WeeShann_CAD_final.pdf

21 Preparing for Autonomous Vehicles in Canada – by CAVCOE (Canadian Automated Vehicles Centre of Excellence)

22 Preparing for Autonomous Vehicles in Canada – by CAVCOE (Canadian Automated Vehicles Centre of Excellence)

23 Preparing for a Driverless Future – Nishith Desai Associates

24 http://www.firstpost.com/india/civilian-drones-despite-ban-flying-in-india-time-to-relook-blanket-prohibition-3782701.html

25 http://carnegieindia.org/2017/03/10/civilian-drones-and-india-s-regulatory-response-pub-68218

26 http://carnegieindia.org/2017/03/10/civilian-drones-and-india-s-regulatory-response-pub-68218

27 SESAR European drones Outlook Study, 2016

28 http://carnegieindia.org/2017/03/10/civilian-drones-and-india-s-regulatory-response-pub-68218

29 https://www.hsdl.org/?view&did=789767 (CRS Report, USA Policy Perspectives on UAVs)

30 https://www.bibliotecapleyades.net/vimanas/esp_vimanas_4.htm

31 http://www.hinduwisdom.info/Vimanas6.htm

32 http://www.hindustantimes.com/health/india-s-mars-orbiter-completes-1000-days-in-orbit-and-is-still-going-strong/story-fcswttvZZDtSq7BDzei3qI.html

Design Indian Cities for People, Not Buildings

Sanjeev Sanyal

The need to upgrade Indian cities is now finally receiving attention from researchers, policymakers and the media. With half the population likely to be living in urban landscapes within a generation, there is sense of genuine urgency. This is a big shift from fifteen years ago when urban issues were seen as peripheral in a largely rural country. Nonetheless, for someone who has spent many years working on urban issues abroad, the Indian approach appears peculiarly skewed to planning hardware—infrastructure, housing, industrial zones and so on. Urban software, when discussed at all, is limited to building codes and formal institutions.

The problem with this approach is that cities are not merely a collection of roads and buildings lorded over by municipal commissioners. Ultimately, cities are about people—their aspirations, jobs, quality of life and the agglomeration of human capital. This change in the frame of reference can profoundly impact the way we visualize our cities and manage them. The following are three illustrations of this people-centric approach to urban management.

Cities as Socio-economic Ladders

As our cities have expanded over the years, they have absorbed the surrounding agricultural lands. In some cases, old villages too have been swept away. However, in most cases, the old villages survive despite being engulfed by the expanding urban sprawl. Scattered across modern Indian cities, there remain enclaves where the contours of the old villages can be clearly discerned decades after the surrounding farmlands were converted into offices, roads, houses and shops. Yet, these urban villages have dramatically changed with the times. Despite being ignored by civic authorities, they play an important role in the evolving social and economic life of Indian cities.

Urban villages in most Indian cities are often tucked away behind a modern building complex. They make their presence felt in many different ways, however, as the source of vagrant cattle, as homes to armies of informal workers, as the place to visit if one wants to buy bathroom tiles or electricals. Many of these villages have been newly absorbed into the urban fabric but some are old and have been embedded in the city for generations. In Mumbai, the old villages of Bandra and Walkeshwar retain strong vestiges of their origins despite being located at the heart of a throbbing megalopolis.

For the purposes of this article, I will limit myself to Delhi's experience, although the story can be easily generalized. According to architect Ranjit Sabikhi, there are 106 villages within the city-state. They are many more in the wider metropolitan area if one includes Noida and Gurgaon. My studies suggest that, in general, these villages go through the following cycle:

- The farmers sell their land to the government or to a developer. Some of them fritter away their newly-acquired wealth, but most redeploy it in businesses that leverage the emerging urban landscape—transportation, labour contracting, supply of construction material and so on. Some of the more prosperous villagers buy themselves new homes and move out. However, they all usually retain their houses in the old village settlement. This settlement, dubbed as a 'lal dora' area, is exempt from usual municipal and building codes. The former farmers use the exemption to build a mishmash of buildings with little regard for safety or ventilation. These become home to construction workers and other service providers who move into the area. Thus, the village turns into a slum with the old villagers as slumlords.

- After about a decade, construction work in that particular area begins to wind down. The construction workers drift away to other sites. New migrants move in—security guards, maids, drivers and other people who work in the newly-built urban space. The commercial establishments too go through a parallel transformation. The shops selling construction material and hardware are steadily replaced by shops selling mobile phones, street food, car parts and so on. For the first time, we see private and, occasionally public, investment in amenities such as common toilets. As the migrants become more permanent, they bring in their families from their ancestral villages. This leads to an interesting supply-side response—the 'English Medium' school! In my experience, language is seen by the poor as the single most important tool for social climbing. Nathupur in Gurgaon is an example of a village that has moved recently from the first stage to the second stage. Next door, the village of Sikandarpur has shifted to the next stage by leveraging a nearly metro station.

- After another ten to fifteen years, the village goes through yet another transformation. By this time, the surrounding area is well-settled and open agricultural fields are a distant memory. We now see students, salesmen and small businessmen move into the village. Some of them may be the newly educated children of migrants, but they are now a higher social class. The old villagers still continue to be the dominant owners of the land but they now begin to invest in improving their individual properties in order to elicit higher rents (after all, they now have a location advantage in the middle of the growing city). In many instances, the owners have become politically important enough to lobby for public investment in basic drainage and sanitation. In my experience, public transport connections have a strong positive effect on the economic dynamism of the slum. The shops upgrade themselves and the old street-food sellers become cheap restaurants.

- The final stage in the process of transformation is that the old village gentrifies. This can happen in a number of ways. Since the early 1990s, Hauz Khas village has become a warren of boutique shops, art galleries and trendy restaurants. Mahipalpur, near the international airport, has seen an explosion of cheap hotels in the last decade. Similarly, Shahpur Jat has become home to numerous small offices and designer workshops. In many cases, the old villagers have encashed their real estate and the ownership pattern has become much more mixed. The areas now grapple with the problems of prosperity such as inadequate parking.

The evolution of urban villages reminds us that Indian cities, including slums, play an important role as socio-economic ladders. As illustrated above, the process of evolution has a big positive impact on the economic and social development of both the old villagers as well as new migrants. Yet, this process is rarely taken into account in the urban discourse (except perhaps as a problem). Moreover, there are two important lessons. First, the process of adaptation depends on decades of steady investment by the owners. This is only possible because private property rights are clear in the former villages. This is why the same process of evolution does not easily take root in squatter slums (like in Mumbai's Dharavi). Policymakers must take these into account as they plan interventions aimed at making India 'slum-free'. Second, public investment in the 'commons' speeds up the development process. Amenities such as common toilets, public transport and drainage can have an important impact on the quality of life of residents and speed up the pace at which they climb the socio-economic ladder.

Using Universities to Cluster Human Capital

Around the world, universities are the stuff that makes great cities. Imagine Boston without Harvard, MIT and the myriad other institutions that are clustered around the Boston-Cambridge area. In Britain, Oxford and Cambridge are vibrant urban centres that derive their vigour almost entirely from playing host to famous universities. In each case, the universities are an integral part of the urban landscape and are consciously leveraged by their host cities.

Yet, Indian cities do not think of their universities and research institutes as important drivers of urban growth. At most, they are seen as places for teaching students. Their importance for clustering human capital and driving innovation is simply not seen as part of the overall urban strategy. Indeed, universities built after Independence have been sealed off on campuses, often in distant locations, that deliberately discourage interaction with the wider city. Thus, Kanpur and Kharagpur benefit little from being hosts to a prestigious institution like the IIT. This is absurd.

As already pointed out, urban development is not just about the 'hardware'—buildings, roads, plumbing and so on. It is the people, their social/economic activity and their continuous interaction that bring cities alive. Successful cities are those that can cluster human capital and encourage innovation, creativity and exchange of ideas. This has always been true. Think of the great cities of the past: Athens, Rome, Constantinople, Alexandria, Ujjain and Varanasi. However, this factor has become even more important in the twenty-first century. Never before has the economic value of ideation and creativity been greater. In short, the 'software' is critical to the evolution of a city.

Universities are key to the software of a city. They attract young talent, encourage the churn of ideas and trigger innovation. The physical infrastructure of the university provides the venue for conferences, seminars and cultural/sporting events that allow for intense human interaction. Note how NYU played an important role in regenerating Lower Manhattan in the 90s.

Next-generation global cities recognize this dynamic and use it actively as part of urban/national economic strategy. For instance, Singapore has built out a number of new institutions like Singapore Management University over the last decade. In most cases, these have been clustered in the middle of the city rather than on remote campuses. The city benefits from having a throughput of young people in the city-centre. At the same time, the university benefits from easy access to industry, government and urban 'buzz'.

Prior to Independence, the urban role of universities was appreciated. The colleges of Bombay and Calcutta Universities were built into the city much like the colleges of London. Even Delhi University, although built as a separate campus, was still seen as a part of the overall urban fabric. There were even important towns like Allahabad and Aligarh that were driven largely by their vibrant universities, much like Oxford and Cambridge.

Contrast this to how tertiary education institutions were built after Independence. All the IITs and IIMs are large, sealed campuses, built originally outside the city. The model was the industrial-era factory township. The physical walls that surround them have continued to barricade them off socially and intellectually from their host cities even where urban growth has brought them inside the city. How different from the urban campuses of MIT and Harvard Business School. This is a loss to both sides.

This issue is currently not even considered worthy of attention and debate in India. Thus, the establishment of a new university or institute is still about acquiring large tracts of land, often hundreds of acres, and then building out stand-alone buildings. If anything, success is measured by how much land has been acquired rather than the quality of education/research.

This is a very wasteful process at many levels. First, it is unnecessarily converting productive farm and forest land. Why does IIT Jodhpur need 852 acres, 24 km away from the town, for teaching a few thousand students? Second, it requires the creation of expensive infrastructure in isolated locations, including staff housing, convocation halls and seminar rooms. How many times a year is the convocation hall used by the institution itself? In a city location, these facilities would have added to the overall urban infrastructure. Third, such remote campuses are inconsiderate of the social, educational and career needs of the families of the faculty and staff. This is a major constraint to finding good faculty. We cannot build universities as if they are industrial-era factory townships where the wives stay at home and the children study in the company school. Finally, and most damagingly, these campuses are unable to generate the externalities that one would associate with a good academic/research institute. Students come and leave. There is no clustering or interlinkage with the real world.

As we build new institutions, we urgently need to stop thinking of them as fenced-off factory townships. We do not need more Kanpurs and Kharagpurs. If India wants to play on the global stage, it needs to create its very own Bostons and Oxfords.

Urban Design Strongly Influences Women's Safety

Urban crimes, particularly those directed at women, have been a cause of growing outrage in India over the last couple of years. Given the frequency and nature of some of these crimes, the outrage is entirely justified. But why are we witnessing such a sharp increase in crimes against women? Conventional wisdom is that this is due to outdated sociocultural mores and traditional patriarchal attitudes. However, there is reason to believe that such factors play no more than a small role in feeding this problem compared to a major flaw in the way we design our cities today.

Take, for example, Kolkata, a city that was once famed for being safe for women but has steadily become less safe for women since the early 1980s. Is this because Bengalis have suddenly become more patriarchal? Indeed, there is no evidence that crimes against women are greater in the more traditional Indian cities like Madurai, Udaipur, Ahmedabad, Surat or Thiruvananthapuram.

Instead, the increase in crime is being reported from the more 'modern' cities like Delhi-National Capital Region (NCR) and Mumbai. Even within Delhi, it is remarkable that all the high-profile incidents occurred in the newer parts of the city and not in traditionalist Old Delhi. Clearly, 'traditional attitudes' is not the full story. Even Guwahati has seen a rise in crimes against women in recent years, including a televised mob lynching. This is clearly not due to traditional social mores as women have traditionally enjoyed high social status in Assam and other northeastern states. The recent trend, if anything, is a deviation from traditional values.

Violent urban crime, including those targeted at women, are not unique to India. Cities in the US witnessed a sharp deterioration between the 1960s and 1990s. Jane Jacobs, one of the greatest urban thinkers of the twentieth century, closely observed this period of urban collapse and concluded that the key factor that kept cities safe was 'eyes on the street'—the fact that people were watching.

Note that eyes on the street is not about having a crowd. A road with heavy traffic may have a lot of people, but they are merely passing through and not engaging with their surroundings. In contrast, a street vendor or an old retiree on a park bench is likely to be observing what is going on.

In the Indian context, the eyes on the street were traditionally provided by the ecosystem of the 'nukkad'—the local barber, the grocery shop, the paanwallah, the chai-wala, the nosy neighbour and so on. This general model has many variants ranging from the 'pol' in Ahmedabad to the 'para' in Kolkata.

The problem is that modern urban planning has completely disregarded this 'software' aspect of the city. In the pursuit of a modernist, aesthetic ideal, planners segregated the multiple activities that give life to urban ecosystems. Commerce and street life were deliberately zoned away from where people lived, thereby leaving few spaces for informal social interaction.

So, when Kolkata expanded into Salt Lake in the 80s and then more recently into Rajarhat, the 'para' did not follow since so-called planning made no provision for the locals to gather together for the evening adda at the 'rock'. Not surprisingly, the newer areas remain more crime-prone than the old city. We find the same phenomenon in other parts of the world. It is no coincidence that the hopelessly crime-ridden 'banlieues' of Paris were built using the ideas of the same Le Corbusier who continues to dominate Indian urban thinking.

It is important to take Indian urban thinking away from the hardware-centric view of cities to a more people-centric view. Three case studies were used above to illustrate how a people-centric approach is fundamentally different from the current approach; it takes a much more organic view of the city and the focus is on how people come together and interact. In this model, the job of urban design and management is to positively influence this human clustering and interaction as well as to allow dynamic evolution over time. There is more than adequate evidence from successful global cities and from premodern Indian cities to support this approach.

◆

Sanjeev Sanyal is currently Principal Economic Adviser to Government of India.

Building the Smart Grid of the Future

Sumant Sinha

Today, a consumer should be able to produce clean energy using solar panels on her rooftop, use it to power her home and electric vehicle, store the excess amounts in lithium ion batteries, and sell it to the grid as and when the system-wide demand for electricity goes up. In India though, we are still a few steps behind.

Our basic electricity services are lacking. The average electricity consumer has to deal with a host of issues despite numerous technological advances. Imprecise and improper electricity bills, meter issues, unreliable power, blackouts, long-duration power cuts and lack of digital interfaces are all commonplace and accepted by consumers as the normal way of life. Then, of course, there are the 300 million Indians who don't even have electricity connections to begin with.

The literal one-trillion rupee question, therefore, is how do we leapfrog from where we are to where we should be—where all of us not only have reliable electricity connections, but also advanced and dynamic digital capabilities that allow us to optimize our energy use.

State of the Indian Electricity Market

In a discussion about the future, it is always helpful to take a step back and get a view of the past. India has seen just about moderate growth in electricity generation capacity since 1950. From 1,300 megawatts

(MW) around the time of Independence to a healthy 330,000 MW in 2017, capacity has grown at a CAGR of 8 per cent in the years in between. On the transmission side, the country started with a base of 23,000 circuit kilometres of long-distance transmission lines in 1950, and moved up to 9.3 million circuit kilometres by 2014, at a CAGR of 9 per cent.[1]

Meanwhile, consumption numbers—a good proxy for the reach of distribution networks—have grown at a CAGR of 6 per cent in roughly the same time frame. Around the time of Independence, the average of some 300 million Indians consumed 15 units of electricity a year, which reached 1,000 units a year for the average of 1.3 billion Indians in 2014.[2] This was four times less than what the average Chinese consumed in 2014—and China started at the same base as us seven decades ago.[3]

Obviously, this average includes those who have been stonewalled from the electricity grid, and if it were to exclude them, it would go up. As it were, the typical upper-middle class Indian in the metropolitan diamond of Delhi, Mumbai, Bengaluru and Kolkata consumes nearly at par with, if not more than, her counterpart in the developed world. But this fraction of society is a tiny sliver, and, despite the overall steady growth in numbers, the majority of India's population suffers from electricity poverty.

Imagining Consumer Experience in the Grid of the Future

At the outset, all consumers should be connected to the grid of the future, have 24×7 access to it, and be able to consume as much power as they need (assuming that beyond a minimum threshold, they have the financial resources and willingness to pay for what they consume). No questions asked. From a specific consumer perspective, here is what a consumer should be able to do in the grid of the future:

First and foremost, have a digital repository of her consumption data. Today, if a consumer were to be overcharged on her electricity bill, she would have no choice but to rely on the handwritten record of meter readings that distribution company (DISCOM) officials note in their journals on their bimonthly meter inspection checks. This non-digitized practice is fraught with inefficiencies and errors. Consumers should have access to digitized, granular consumption data. This is in the best interest of DISCOMs to capture as well, as the large data sets that are generated can be mined later through big data techniques for valuable consumer insights.

Second, choose the source of her electricity. What this means is the differentiation of carriage and content–carriage is the set of wires that distribution companies own, and content is the electricity that flows through it. Today, both are monopolized by DISCOMs—they own the wires, and they decide who to buy electricity from. Consumers have no say in the process. Ideally, they should be able to choose who they want to buy electricity from and what the source of those electrons should be, whether renewable or not. This would have the added benefit of reduction in consumer prices as electricity generation companies would bid aggressively for business and begin to eat their margins to win customer contracts in competitive markets.

Third, have digital insights into her electricity use. Some utilities in the US, like PEPCO in Washington DC, or Oklahoma Gas & Electric in Oklahoma, for example, use software that parses already available meter data to make fairly accurate statistical predictions of electricity use patterns—of appliances like TVs, refrigerators, computers, lights, etc.—and recommend targeted and customized best practices and suggestions for energy savings. Here is a sample case of how this works. The software figures out what percentage of the overall electricity consumption is attributable to the use of a customer's refrigerator and whether or not that is in line with the load profile of other, similar customers in the region. If the percentage electricity use of the refrigerator is unusually high in comparison to that of the others (which would happen only if it is an old, inefficient model), then the utility sends an intelligent recommendation to the customer telling her that her refrigerator should be replaced, along with the economic benefits of doing so. In some cases, like in PEPCO's, the utility also offers targeted subsidy for the phaseout of inefficient equipment.[4]

Fourth, be able to ship the captive electricity she produces on her premises (in most cases through rooftop solar panels) back to the grid or to her neighbours. This kind of an arrangement is called net metering where consumers are adequately compensated for the electricity they send back to the grid. While regulations have been laid out to promote net metering in India, DISCOMs have been hesitant to implement the same on the ground. Today, if an industrial establishment produces excess electricity through rooftop solar, it will, in most regions, still not be able to send the electricity back to the grid, let alone receive credit for it. We therefore need to upgrade grid networks for the effective bidirectional flow of electricity.

Fifth, have the ability to control her electricity use remotely through her phone, tablet or computer. This would mean having a DISCOM-authorized smartphone application that would allow her to see her power consumption in real time, pay her bills online and also provide her with the functionality to make adjustments to electricity-heavy equipment like air conditioners and television sets (turn them on/off, set timers, and adjust temperatures remotely). This can potentially serve as the bedrock for future large-scale demand response programmes.

Finally, get her DISCOM to install a smart meter at her home. A good start has been certainly made through the current central government's initiative to increase the penetration of smart meters by 4 million units in Indian homes.[5] Smart meters will allow DISCOMs to capture real time, accurate data on electricity consumption, and charge the right price for it—thus bringing us one step closer to the grid of the future.

Role of Renewable Energy and Other Infrastructure Trends

In addition to the capabilities that should be built into this system for enhanced consumer interaction, there are other trends that are reshaping electricity markets, some of which should continue to be encouraged.

First is the onset of large-scale renewables in the grid. Renewable energy—large-scale solar, rooftop solar, and wind—accounts for 6–7 per cent of electricity generation in India today. Considering renewables are now cheaper than thermal power by almost 20 per cent, all new capacity addition ought to be renewables based.[13] It is no surprise therefore that the current central government has set out ambitious targets for clean energy to account for 15–20 per cent of all electricity generation in India by 2022. In addition to better economics, renewables will aid India's efforts to contain climate change. They will also ensure cleaner air at home (something we need), have shorter construction cycles (6–12 months for a large solar plant, while over 24–36 months for a coal power plant), have less moving parts (therefore more reliable operations and maintenance), and reduce India's reliance on fuel imports (therefore have strategic value from a national security point of view).

DISCOMs today, however, are not ready to adopt large quantities of renewable electricity (at the 15–20 per cent levels targeted for by 2022). One of the drawbacks of renewables is the naturally variant characteristic of sunshine and wind speed which makes generation of electricity from these sources variable as well. However, this is a relatively straightforward problem to solve. In Germany, where renewables now account for more than 30 per cent of electricity generation, a five-pronged strategy to ensure a stable grid has been adopted: Redispatching mechanisms, balancing markets, demand-side peak-shaving, frequency regulation and feed-in management. All of these tools ensure that grid lines do not get congested, renewables are better controlled (for example, through battery deployments), and the system does not fall out of balance in making quick adjustments between demand and supply.[6]

Second, are the rapidly declining cost curves of battery storage. Cheap battery storage will change the dynamics of the electricity system and usher in the smart energy era. Since renewables can be potentially stored in batteries, the variability challenge will be solved entirely as grid operators will be able to simply switch around between renewables (when the sun is shining and wind is blowing) and batteries (when the two are not).

Third, and as hinted above, is the advent of demand response programmes. When we think about electricity capacity, we think about setting up power plants. But there is plenty of room to optimize energy consumption. Consider the following scenario: If an industrial facility can smartly choose when to turn its machines on, say whether at peak demand time or during off-peak hours, grid operators can distribute energy supply more evenly across a system. This can potentially reduce the burden on DISCOMs to buy more electricity from power plants at higher marginal costs during peak demand hours. Five years ago, managing a demand response programme required a lot of manual effort and collaboration between a DISCOM official and an energy manager at an industry facility. But now with smart software beginning to make sense (with a combination of smart metres, sensors and actuators), demand response programmes are becoming increasingly automated. Consider one among many examples, where on the eastern coast of the US, the local system operator, PJM Interconnection, runs a demand response programme of 10 gigawatts—which basically offsets the need to build 10 gigawatts of additional capacity.[7]

Fourth, the emergence of electric vehicles (EVs) will add further pressure on the grid. This is more an opportunity than a problem, because EVs are flexible loads and there is a lot of work that can be done to use them smartly—especially in terms of how, when, and where they are charged. This will also require investments in powerful software applications that can talk to charging stations, EVs, and the grid lines and feeders to spatially and temporally determine the maximum and least congestion in the system. EVs are touted as another smart source to balance out the variable nature of renewables.

Finally, it is useful to acknowledge that India's power demand is slated to increase. The average Indian consumes some 1,000 units of electricity every year. The world average is around 3,000 and, closer to home, both literally and figuratively, the average Chinese consumes 4,000 units a year. Clearly, we are an energy impoverished country in comparison to the rest of the world. As we increase energy consumption, the overall infrastructure will also expand; and DISCOMs will need to be able to cater to the expanded needs of existing customers and those of the 300 million Indians who would come online onto the electric grid for the first time.

Where We Are Today

The crucial question we ought to keep asking ourselves is how do we get to this tech-enabled future that smartly and brilliantly integrates twenty-first- century trends into itself. There is a high probability that the answer lies somewhere in the distribution side of the electricity value chain, given that DISCOMs are the only part of the electricity value chain today that directly touch the lives of consumers.

What is challenging on the distribution side, though, is the sheer number of nodal points that need to be managed. Last mile delivery implies complexity—more number of lines, sub-lines, feeders, sub-feeders, transformers, sub-transformers, energy metres, millions of submetres, a host of other equipment, and of course, managing the expectations of millions of customers. All these heavy moving parts increase the probability of errors, failures and breakdowns. Spread across many thousands of miles, the scope for theft, inefficient equipment, improper maintenance, collections-related issues, and the inability to charge a fair price for services, discourages distribution companies from making long-term investments to upgrade their infrastructure and related service offerings.

Coupled with these systemic challenges are two fundamental operating issues viz aggregate technical and commercial losses (AT&C) and revenue realization problems, both of which stymie any DISCOM's ability to make strategic long-term investments for the future.

AT&C Losses and Revenue Realization Issues

AT&C losses demonstrate the efficiency of electrons in the electricity system as a whole—how many electrons were generated at source, and by the time they reached customers, how many were actually delivered.

These loss numbers are important because they show wastage, both avoidable and unavoidable, along the value chain. As every unit of electricity sold provides marginal revenue, avoidable AT&C losses should be minimized to boost DISCOM top line. The average AT&C loss—electrons getting lost due to system inefficiencies—in FY15 was approximately 25 per cent.[8]

The accepted theoretical floor of AT&C losses is generally in the range of 8–12 per cent for Indian networks, given that there will always be certain unavoidable technical losses along the path of electricity.[9] Everything above and beyond this can and should be reduced. So if average FY15 AT&C losses were 25 per cent, somewhere between 13–17 per cent of losses could have been eliminated.

Assuming that avoidable losses were, in fact, avoided in FY15, savings of anywhere between 12,000 crore and 17,000 crore units of electricity could have been salvaged that year. At an average tariff rate of ₹4 at the time, this would have amounted to ₹50,000 thousand and ₹70,000 thousand crore in marginal—alas lost revenue.

Then there is also the problem that DISCOMs lose money on every unit of electricity they sell. As it is perceived to be politically suicidal, state governments rarely allow DISCOMs to revise tariffs beyond a point, and because DISCOMs rely on state government subsidies, they rarely challenge state governments on these matters.

In FY15, the number of units that DISCOMs collectively sold (minus AT&C losses) was about one lakh crore where the average cost of supply was ₹5 per unit, and tariff ₹4. If the 20 per cent delta between cost and revenue were to be reduced to 0 per cent by increasing the average tariff by ₹1 per unit, then that would increase revenue by ₹1 lakh crore.[10]

Revenue realization coupled with the minimization of avoidable AT&C losses would not only wipe out all DISCOM losses, but, in fact, would put DISCOMs on a very healthy path of profitability. This 'lost' money is important because it is what will enable DISCOMs to get their houses in order, and make investments to shape the grid of the future.

Success of UDAY and the Urgent Need for Privatization Reforms

To be fair, the problem is seemingly understood. In fact, the Ujjwal DISCOM Assurance Yojana (UDAY) scheme launched by the central government is like the phase one of the overall reforms needed in this space. UDAY has refinanced DISCOM debt through accounting ingenuity that will reduce interest payments by approximately ₹16,000 crore annually.

What is needed in the second round of DISCOM reforms, post UDAY, is the privatization of DISCOMs, away from the control of election-cycle-focused state governments. To deal with and resolve the large number of operational problems, and have the strategic ability to make long-gestation cycle investments for tomorrow, requires the grit that only private management teams can bring to the table.

One of the best examples of the successes of privatization is the case of Delhi. Privatization took place in 2002–03 and control of the distribution company's monopoly was handed over to two companies controlled by the Tata and Reliance Groups respectively. Within a decade, AT&C losses climbed down from over 50 per cent to under 15 per cent through a combination of better metering, crackdown on theft, tariff revisions, and proper maintenance of infrastructure. Delhi is also leading on piloting battery storage projects, demand response programmes, energy efficiency measures, and others, and shows its management's foresight in keeping itself abreast of the trends.[11]

The same holds true for American, European, Japanese, Korean and Australian utilities. In nearly all cases, utilities are run by private enterprises and regulated to some extent by government authorities. The argument for privatization is the same as it is across other sectors: Management is always under pressure to deliver alpha returns, and is therefore, almost with a sense of paranoia, on the lookout for opportunities to improve customer service and operations.

Recommended Next Steps

Overhauling a deeply entrenched system will not be easy. However, continuing the reforms that started with Delhi and Mumbai, and with UDAY, should be a good first step. Here is a five-step strategy to build momentum around this policy.

First, form a lean government appointed committee—comprising a couple of central lawmakers, state lawmakers, academics, DISCOM officials, private industry players, and senior bureaucrats—to submit a SWOT-analysis on DISCOM privatization vis-a-vis grid upgradation. The committee should also take into account the interests of all Indians. We must ensure that those Indians at the bottom of the energy (and social) pyramid are not brick-walled from energy access because of any potential private-market practices, and that suitable checks and balances are institutionalized from the get-go.

Second, if the view of this committee is favourable to privatization, which it most likely should be, the central government should set targets for DISCOM privatization. It should concurrently invite industry experts, academics on energy markets, industry professionals, and investors to a forum where the messaging for both privatization and attracting investments for building future capabilities is clearly delivered.

Third, invite the 3–4 of the most promising state governments and DISCOMs to begin laying the groundwork for regional privatization pilots. These initial pilots could be conducted on DISCOMs that predominantly serve urban centres or those that are under crushing financial stress. The central government could allocate other central funds, under the principles of federalism, to incentivize states to get on board.

Fourth, initiate a tendering process for private investors and industry participants to purchase ownership rights in these select DISCOMs. For the initial pilots, provide government-backed guarantees on the minimum return on capital that private market participants could make for the first five years of operations to ensure robust participation and interest. This exercise should be conducted with the clear objective that interested private companies would need to demonstrate an action plan to build the grid of the future.

Finally, prepare rigorous assessment criteria to measure progress specifically for grid upgradation. Metrics on AT&C losses, smart meter deployments, customer satisfaction, collections efficiencies, theft reductions, battery deployments, capital expenditures on infrastructure upgrades, successful tariff revisions, initiation of demand response programmes, creation of new EV charging infrastructure, etc., should all be quantifiably measured over 2–5 year periods. That data should then feed into policy debates around carrying out these reforms all across the nation.

The world is changing rapidly and the status quo will not work. To ensure we have the right electricity infrastructure in place to power our people's aspirations in this inherently technological twenty-first century world, we need to objectively debate what is working and what is not. For the betterment of the citizens of this country, DISCOMs should be put on a path of business sustainability so that they can make the right decisions and investments to create the grid of the future.

◆

Sumant Sinha is the chairman and CEO of ReNew Power, one of India's leading renewable energy developers.

Endnotes

1. 'Growth of Electricity Sector in India from 1947–2017', Central Electricity Authority, Chart 4, page 6. http://www.cea.nic.in/reports/others/planning/pdm/growth_2017.pdf
2. 'Growth of Electricity Sector in India from 1947–2017', Central Electricity Authority, Chart 4, page 6. http://www.cea.nic.in/reports/others/planning/pdm/growth_2017.pdf
3. Electric Power Consumption (kWh per capita), IEA Statistics © OECD/IEA, 2014, iea.org/stats/index.asp
4. 'EmPOWER Maryland Will Save Customers $4 billion on Electricity Bills', American Council for an Energy Efficient Economy, January 2017, https://aceee.org/press/2017/01/empower-maryland-will-save-customers
5. Patil, Mukta 'Why India's largest smart meter rollout may not be

very smart', *Business Standard*, 12 October 2017, http://www.business-standard.com/article/economy-policy/why-india-s-largest-smart-meter-rollout-may-not-be-very-smart-117101200177_1.html

6. 'Germany's Power Generation Mix 2016', German AG Energiebilanzen, https://1-stromvergleich.com/strom-report/renewable-energy-germany/#germany-power-generation-mix-2016

7. Chen, Olivia, 'Regulation and Resource Mix Drive a Demand Response Capacity Contraction of 2 GW', Greentech Media, 23 May 2017, https://www.greentechmedia.com/articles/read/regulation-and-resource-mix-drive-2gw-demand-response-capacity-contraction#gs.wRfirFI

8. 'Report on the Performance of State Power Utilities for the years 2012-13 to 2014–15', Summary for utilities selling directly to consumer, page iii. Power Finance Corporation, June 2016, http://www.pfcindia.com/Default/ViewFile/?id=1490186954263_Report per cent20on per cent20Performance per cent20of per cent20State per cent20Power per cent20Utilities per cent202012-13 per cent20to per cent202014-15.pdf&path=Page

9. 'What are AT&C Losses', Delhi Electricity Regulatory Commission, http://www.derc.gov.in/Consumer/Press per cent20Note/DERCE per cent20AD per cent20ENGLISH.pdf

10. 'Report on Short Term Power Market in India: 2015-2016', Economics Division, Central Electricity Regulatory Commission, Page 7, http://www.cercind.gov.in/2016/MMC/AnnualReport15-16.pdf

11. 'A Critical Review of the Performance of Delhi's Privatized Distribution Companies and the Regulatory Process', Prayas, May 2006, pp 4–5, prayaspune.org/peg/publications/.../275_10a6c1b418720e5371e8e1106d8a5bad.html

Special Economic Zones: A Key Driver of Good Job Creation

Vivek Dehejia and Pravin Krishna

The Indian economy is faced with two interrelated challenges: First, an inexorable demographic juggernaut, requiring job creation at the rate of roughly ten to twelve million new jobs a year—or a whopping one million jobs a month—and, second, a manufacturing sector that has been unable to increase its employment share over the last two decades, all the while recording low wages and poor wage growth for the vast majority of its workers.

The challenges facing the manufacturing sector have been variously discussed by analysts: A regulatory regime governing labour that disincentivizes the employment of workers and has, perversely, pushed Indian manufacturing into employing capital and skilled labour intensive techniques instead; challenges in the acquisition of land; and inadequate infrastructural support, inter alia. Taken together, these factors have conspired to ensure that Indian manufacturing has remained both small in scale and correspondingly inefficient: Nearly three-quarters of Indian manufacturing workers are employed in small firms (firms with less than twenty workers each) which collectively produce less than one quarter of Indian manufacturing output. More than a quarter century after the epochal economic reforms of 1991, Indian manufacturing output and export of manufactures fall close to just about 2 per cent of global manufacturing output and exports, respectively, far below the country's potential and its need to create plentiful 'good' jobs—well-paying, productive and durable jobs.

While addressing the manufacturing challenge in India evidently requires a multipronged approach, it is imperative to discuss the role that Special Economic Zones (SEZs) might play in combating the inefficiencies resulting from lack of economies of scale in manufacturing as well as the related issues of unemployment and chronic underemployment in the labour force. SEZs need to be a crucial component of the overall economic strategy of the government both to boost the importance of manufacturing in economic activity and to create good jobs. We would like to offer arguments for investment by policymakers in suitably designed SEZs, focusing on their potential to increase employment and efficiency in Indian manufacturing, while attempting to draw on the historical experience in India and other countries to avoid the mistakes of the past.

In this context, it should be noted at the outset that the concept of manufacturing or export enclaves is not new to India. As early as 1965, India established its first Export Processing Zones (EPZ) in Kandla, Gujarat. However, various models that India has attempted since then—EPZs, Export Oriented Units (EOUs), and indeed SEZs themselves—have fallen short of delivering satisfactory outcomes in export promotion, job creation and industrialization. While China's SEZs—especially Shenzhen—brought about a sweeping 'economic miracle', especially in the manufacturing sector, the zones in India did not generate much growth and became associated instead with recurring land scams and corruption. We do not believe that this represents a failure of the SEZ model per se, but rather the poor conceptualization and implementation of previous iterations.

State of Indian Manufacturing and Employment

A compelling rationale for the creation of one particular type of SEZ, a coastal economic zone (CEZ), was recently put forward by Arvind Panagariya (2017), then vice chairman of NITI Aayog, but the argument is applicable to SEZs more broadly construed. If the assumed policy goal is the creation of a large number of good jobs (a goal which makes political economy as well as economic sense for any incumbent government), a key problem is that firms in India are too small, employ too few workers, and productivity and wages are correspondingly low. As noted by Panagariya, research by economists Rana Hasan and Nidhi Kapoor of the ADB demonstrates that manufacturing firms with 20 or fewer workers accounted for 73 per cent of total manufacturing employment but only 12 per cent of total manufacturing output in 2010–11. Clearly, these firms are inefficient, and, although they employ several workers, the productivity of those workers and their wages are correspondingly low. An important reason that so many firms remain small is that rigid labour laws disincentivize the growth of firms. These are not the good jobs that India needs tomorrow, but the bad jobs of yesterday.

Further, research suggests that productivity, and correspondingly wages, rise with firm size. So why are larger firms more productive than smaller firms, ceteris paribus? One possibility is that larger firms are better able to exploit economies of scale and agglomeration economies. Another complementary hypothesis is that as larger firms operate disproportionately in the highly competitive global market as compared to smaller firms, they are forced to innovate to remain commercially viable, which tends to raise productivity and wages. This second explanation also suggests that smaller and medium-sized firms ought to benefit from the existence of some fraction of larger firms which are globally engaged, as this would tend to foster an ecosystem in which the competitive ethos spreads outward from larger firms. Panagariya (2017) concludes that 'substantial presence of large firms combined with an outward-oriented trade policy fosters high overall productivity'.

The apparel sector provides a vivid illustration of this point. Data on the size distribution of apparel sector firms in China and India in 2005 paints a striking picture. According to NITI Aayog/IDFC Institute (2017):

At one extreme, enterprises with less than eight workers employ more than four-fifths of the apparel workforce in India and less than 1 per cent in China. At the other extreme, nearly 57 per cent of the workforce in China is in enterprises larger than 200 workers but barely 5 per cent in India. The Chinese apparel industry is highly competitive with $187 billion in exports compared with just $18 billion for India in 2014.

As Panagariya (2017) notes, the absence of a significant mass of large firms has an impact on average labour productivity through two distinct channels: First, productivity levels in micro/small/medium enterprises (MSMEs) are low in India compared to other countries such as China; and second, MSMEs employ a disproportionately large share of total employment. A 2009 study by ADB, employing 2005, finds that firms with 200 workers or more accounted for only 10.5 per cent of total manufacturing employment in India as against 51.8 per cent in China. By contrast, firms with 50 workers or less accounted for 84 per cent of India's manufacturing sector employment while the corresponding figure in China is merely 24.8 per cent. The corollary is much higher average labour productivity in manufacturing in China as compared to India. China has good jobs while India has been managing with bad jobs.

Why SEZs?

It is clear from the above that the current state of the manufacturing sector in India is not conducive to the creation of a large number of durable jobs. How might SEZs help solve this problem?

To begin with, we note SEZs cover a broad range of managed industrial clusters including Free Trade Zones (FTZs), Export Processing Zones (EPZs) and High-tech Industrial Development Zones (HIDZs). While different SEZs may differ from each other in their particular design, they share in common the feature that they each receive a set of specific incentives from the government, so that economic activity within the SEZ is subject to a different fiscal and regulatory structure relative to firms outside the SEZ. Fiscal incentives can be in the form of lower levels of taxation or the provision of some tax exemptions and subsidies. They may also include tax exemptions on a temporary basis—for instance, an initial income tax holiday. Regulatory, non-fiscal incentives may include differential regulations concerning the hiring and firing of labour, government support in acquisition of land, simplified procedures for starting economic activity—such as registration, customs and other clearances. Further, the government may direct infrastructural investment to support SEZs to increase the competitiveness of firms within the SEZ.

In the Indian context, it should be clear that suitably designed SEZs could, in principle, address several of the most pressing problems limiting the competitiveness of Indian manufacturing. First, by relaxing labour regulations for workers employed in enterprises operating within SEZs, they could remove the disincentives to employing a larger workforce and achieving larger scale in production. Second, they could address the crucial issue of land acquisition by making available land to establish large scale manufacturing facilities and could do so speedily. Third, they enable focused infrastructure investments, allowing firms within the SEZ to have access to power and quality transport infrastructure, thereby addressing the two often cited concerns of Indian manufacturers.

Thus, in theory, the case for SEZs, in India and elsewhere in the developing world, seems a straightforward one. In practice, however, the experience with SEZs has been mixed. While countries such as China have been extraordinarily successful in catalyzing manufacturing growth through SEZs, others have experienced near total failure. It is imperative that we reflect upon the experience with SEZs in India, in relation to China, to isolate key features of these previous and comparative experiences. This would help avoid policy errors of the past and identify a better strategy for the future.

India and China—Comparative Experience with SEZs

How did China succeed in using SEZs to achieve sustained growth in manufacturing while India has heretofore failed? This is obviously a complex issue involving a variety of factors. We will consider what we believe are three key issues: Economic geography; industrial policy; and, relatedly, regulatory structure.

As part of China's economic reform and transformation, initiated by Deng Xiaoping, four SEZs were established in Shenzhen, Zhuhai, Shantou and Xiamen in 1980. The locations for these pilot SEZs were strategically chosen: They were on the eastern coast, allowing for more efficient access to global markets and were close to the developed economies that were geographically proximate and to which they were culturally linked—Hong Kong and Taiwan. Equally important was the issue of scale. Zhuhai and Xiamen were allocated about 30,000 acres. Shenzen, whose population then did not exceed 300,000, was allocated about 75,000 acres of land for its SEZ; today it has a population of over 11 million and generates output worth over $250 billion.

By contrast, Indian SEZs have been large in number and, generally, small in scale—with some SEZs being as small as ten acres in size. Due to the wide and generous incentives given, most states have wanted to have SEZs in their territory. As a consequence, Indian SEZs are spread around the country. The provision of supporting resources, especially transport infrastructure for widely dispersed SEZs—some of them located in landlocked regions with high transportation costs— is costly to do and has not been adequate in practice. Overall, the small size, dispersed locations and large number of Indian SEZs have constrained their basic competitiveness and brought into question the validity (or at any rate the implementation) of the SEZ model to generate growth and employment.

In designing SEZs, the question of industrial policy often arises at the outset. In an effort to exploit its huge labour force in the early 1980s, China's first few SEZs almost exclusively focused on labour-intensive manufacturing and their focus has gradually evolved with the deepening of capital and skills in the country. From heavily labour intensive goods, China's SEZs moved towards somewhat more capital and skill intensive production of machinery and telecommunications. This has evolved further. As Mao (2016) notes, 'The Xiongan New Zone (XNZ) near Beijing—which was announced in April 2017 as the SEZ to pilot China's latest reform of "sustainable urbanization and eco-friendly modernization"—prioritizes hi-tech industries such as integrated circuit, artificial intelligence and robotics.[1] Whether the Chinese evolution was the consequence of an active industrial policy can be debated. What must be recognized is that, active policy or not, the Chinese outcomes are consistent with their own evolving comparative advantage, as defined by their resources and technological capabilities.

The contrast with the Indian economy is striking. India too has an abundant labour force and the creation of productive jobs is the dominant challenge for the economy. However, India has found it difficult to expand low skill labour intensive activities. Its recent export successes have come instead in skill and capital intensive industries, defying India's natural comparative advantage.

According to Mao, 'Instead of conforming to its comparative advantage, India adopted a rather random industrial priority as far as SEZs were concerned. For example, many early EPZs, such as the Santa Cruz EPZ, promoted jewellery industry. However, given that for per ₹10 million of sales jewellery, industries only employ two workers, while textile industries employ as many as eighteen workers, this choice seemed rather economically unsound.'

Indeed, this is a continuing issue—'Among 192 operational SEZs as of August 2014, manufacturing SEZs (single- and multi-product) only accounted for about 30 per cent, within which labour-intensive industries had an even smaller share. In 2010–11, 75 per cent of the total exports from Indian SEZs were from three industries—pharmaceuticals, IT/ITeS, and jewellery, but none of them taps into India's supposed demographic dividend.'[2]

In view of the above, should an aggressive industrial policy in favour of labour-intensive manufacturing direct Indian SEZs? Our contention would be that in addition to any policies that nudge

SEZs towards low skill intensive production, we ought to reflect on the reasons for the inability of the Indian economy to use its abundant resources and grow in a manner that is consistent with its comparative advantage. The answer lies, in large part, in the inflexible labour regime, which has made it difficult to expand by hiring more workers. Thus, alongside any policy incentives to privilege low skill intensive in SEZs, firms within SEZs must be allowed to function under a different regulatory regime than the one to which they are subject outside.

The new CEZ initiative, currently under deliberation in India, aims to address many of these issues. NITI Aayog has proposed that efforts be focused first on just two large coastal zones. One should, nevertheless, expect many challenges in the implementation and many questions arise. Where should these zones be located? How can the necessary land be acquired? How can the process be managed without land-related fraud? In the past, it has been alleged that SEZs have acquired more land than is necessary (at discounted prices) and have used the excess land to develop residential real estate, which is then sold at market prices, thus defeating the purpose of the SEZ in the first place. Rules concerning the redirection of land initially acquired for legitimate SEZ related purposes appear to either be non-existent or weakly enforced. The actual usage of allocated land clearly needs to be vigorously policed. All this and a great deal more will have to managed well for the CEZs to succeed. But the need is urgent and success will be vital to India's growth trajectory.

♦

Vivek Dehejia is Resident Senior Fellow in Political Economy at IDFC Institute, Associate Professor of Economics and Philosophy at Carleton University in Ottawa, Canada, and Columnist, Mint.

Pravin Krishna is Chung Ju Yung Distinguished Professor of International Economics and Business at Johns Hopkins University.

References

1   Mao, Keji, 'Why Indian Special Economic Zones Do not Work Well? A Comparative Study of the Indian and Chinese SEZ Strategy', mimeo, Johns Hopkins University, 2016.

2   NITI Aayog/IDFC Institute, 'Ease of Doing Business: An Enterprise Survey of Indian States', http://www.idfcinstitute.org/knowledge/publications/ reports/ease-of-doing-business/

3   Panagariya, Arvind, 'Jobs, Growth and Coastal Economic Zones', NITI Aayog Blog, 1 February 2017, http://niti.gov.in/content/jobs-growth-and-coastal-economic- zones

Endnotes

1   Mao, Keji, 'Why Indian Special Economic Zones Do not Work Well? A Comparative Study of the Indian and Chinese SEZ Strategy', mimeo, Johns Hopkins University, 2016.

2   Mao, op. cit.

Towards Improved Land Titling: Pilot Approaches and Learning to Ensure Success

Shekhar Shah

Good land records and security of property rights are fundamental to well-functioning land markets required for sustained, robust economic activity in agriculture, manufacturing or services. India made a much-acclaimed climb up from 130th place to 100th place in the World Bank's Ease of Doing Business Index for 2018.[1] Unfortunately, on the sub-index on ease of registering property, India slipped 16 ranks from 138th to 154th, indicating the huge potential for improving India's investment climate by removing distortions in land markets and records.

India is among the world's most land-scarce countries relative to population. By 2050, land per capita in India will have declined four fold relative to 1960; by 2050, China will have four times more land per capita and Brazil some twenty times more.[2] Land market distortions in India have been estimated to reduce annual GDP growth by some 1.3 per cent a year.[3]

There is clearly much to be done to attain India's stated aspiration of moving to conclusive land titling from its current situation of presumptive titles. Land ownership in India is established largely through a sale deed recording the transfer of property, but there is no government guaranteed title, and the onus is on the buyer to check past ownership. Land ownership is therefore presumptive, and subject to challenge. Land-related disputes account for about 60 to 70 per cent of all civil litigation in India, and as much as 90 per cent of all land parcels are subject to legal dispute. Disputed land limits access to credit, since land is a collateral in a large proportion of loans in India.[4]

This paper shares the results of recent research on the ground-level performance of the government of India's flagship program on improving land records. Since 1987, the government has run a number of centrally sponsored schemes to improve land records. A network of three Indian research institutions came together in 2016 to produce a pilot assessment for three states of the government's 'Digital India Land Records Modernisation Programme' (DILRMP). Their research findings point the way to two things: First, the key considerations that the government should keep in mind in designing any national assessment of the DILRMP, and, second, the core reforms that the government should consider as it thinks about substantially improving the impact of the DILRMP.

The paper also has a second, process objective, which is to highlight the importance of piloting in public policy and state action. Too often in India, policymaking, implementation and assessments all go straight from the drawing board to national implementation for the world's soon-to-be largest population. The vital lessons that could be learnt from experimentation and piloting are often lost in the administrative or political hurry to roll out programs, resulting in both ineffective schemes that don't deliver when subjected to the test and, if politically important, schemes that undergo drastic changes in the very first few months of their being rolled out. Neither outcome bodes well for the effectiveness or stability of government action.

In this instance, the agency that manages the DILRMP, the Department of Land Resources (DoLR) in the government of India's Ministry of Rural Development, felt the strong need in 2015 for a national evaluation in order to understand the nature of the DILRMP reforms needed. DoLR, unlike many other sister agencies, decided to do a pilot assessment first before considering national effort. They felt that a pilot would greatly inform any nationwide evaluation and avoid the mistakes of a massive but uninformed national effort and of the policy prescriptions that might ensue from a poor quality evaluation.

Furthermore, DoLR also decided to have three nationally known, credible, independent research organizations working closely with each other to do the pilot assessment rather than do it departmentally with hired consultants. DoLR felt that the internal and external expert peer review processes among the three research institutions would further enhance the credibility of the findings and, as a side benefit, create new analytical capacity on land records issues in the country. Funding for the pilot was provided by the Omidyar Network. An external Technical Advisory Committee of experts was constituted for the continuous review and guidance of the research and met three times during the course of the impact assessment. Finally, stakeholder focus group discussions were held in each state and the findings discussed with the state authorities. The reports were released and discussed with policymakers and practitioners on 13 November 2017 in New Delhi.[5]

Indian Land Records and the DILRMP

The significance of good, verifiable land records has been self-evident in India for a long time. Under the Constitution, land falls within the jurisdiction of states. The central government released a draft 'Land Titling Bill' in 2011 as a model law for the consideration of states, but further action has been scarce. Starting in the late 1980s, the central government began incentivizing states to modernize and computerize their land records, principally through two centrally sponsored schemes—Strengthening of Revenue Administration and Updating of Land Records in 1987–88 and the Computerization of Land Records in 1988–89. The states unfortunately fared poorly in utilizing the funds released by the centre, with little progress towards the ambitious goal of conclusive titling, and little design recognition of how tough a challenge such a goal posed. DoLR then merged the two schemes, resulting in the National Land Records Modernization Programme (NLRMP, Figure 1) in 2008. NLRMP continued to be a centrally sponsored scheme and was renamed in 2014 after the change of government as the DILRMP, now under the nominal umbrella of the new 'Digital India' initiative.

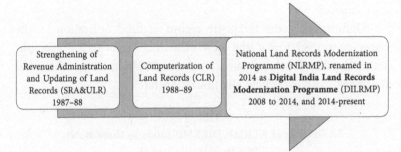

| Strengthening of Revenue Administration and Updating of Land Records (SRA&ULR) 1987–88 | Computerization of Land Records (CLR) 1988–89 | National Land Records Modernization Programme (NLRMP), renamed in 2014 as **Digital India Land Records Modernization Programme** (DILRMP) 2008 to 2014, and 2014-present |

Figure 1. Government of India's Initiatives to Modernize Indian Land Records

The main objective of the DILRMP (and the NLRMP before that) is to develop a modern, comprehensive and transparent land records management system in the country with the aim to implement conclusive land titling with title guarantee, based on four principles, (i) a unique identity for every property that will enable a common base for all land transactions, including the maintenance and updating of textual records, maps, survey and settlement operations and registration of immovable property; (ii) the 'mirror' principle, with cadastral records mirroring ground reality; (iii) the 'curtain' principle which makes the title the final proof of ownership, with mutation automatic following registration, and a curtain brought down on all past ownerships; and (iv) title insurance to guarantee title and indemnify the holder against losses from any title defects.

The DLIRMP's main components include:

- Computerization of the records of rights (RoRs) and digitization of cadastral maps to integrate the written and spatial data;
- Land survey and resurvey, and updating all survey and settlement records, including creating original cadastral records where necessary;

- Computerization of the registration process; and
- Integration of all three activities.

The programme also aims to develop a core GIS system and build state capacity.

Unfortunately, the lacklustre record of fund utilization by the states continued under the new schemes. Table 1, for example, shows the data for three states, Himachal Pradesh, Maharashtra and Rajasthan, with extremely low utilization rates.

Table 1
Utilization of NLRMP/DILRMP funds in three states,
2008 to 2016 (Rs lakhs)

	Central funds sanctioned	*Central funds released*	*Expenditures incurred*	*Utilisation (per cent of funds released)*
Himachal Pradesh	6,907	4,330	303	7.0 per cent
Maharashtra	8,420	6,536	1,674	25.6 per cent
Rajasthan*	753	550	264	47.9 per cent

Source: Department of Land Resources, Ministry of Rural Development, Government of India.

Note: *Data for Himachal Pradesh and Maharashtra are for the eight years 2008–09 to 2015–16 and for Rajasthan for the three years 2012–13 to 2014–15. These were the states used for the pilot assessment.

By about 2015, DoLR was of the view that its flagship programme needed adjustment and should therefore be evaluated to understand its functioning and challenges. A national impact assessment of the DILRMP was deemed imperative by government since the scheme and its predecessors had not been evaluated for impact. Given the immense diversity of land administration, record-keeping and registration practises across India, in discussions with NCAER and others, DoLR was persuaded that going to a nationwide evaluation at great cost without understanding the complexities of the situation on the ground to inform such an evaluation would be a mistake. DoLR therefore decided to support a pilot impact assessment in a small number of states that could provide a deeper understanding of the impact of the DILRMP. Furthermore, DoLR felt that there would be multiple advantages to requesting independent research institutions to do the task. The quality and rigour of the work might be higher, and it might create additional analytical and evaluation capacity in land economics outside government.

In consequence, with common terms of reference worked out with DoLR, pilot impact assessments were carried out for Himachal Pradesh (by NCAER), Rajasthan (by the National Institute for Public Finance and Policy, NIPFP) and Maharashtra (by the Indira Gandhi Institute for Development Research, IGIDR). These were deliberately designed as a learning exercise to explore the key potential areas of DILRMP reform and to also inform any national assessment that might ensue.[6] NCAER coordinated the effort and prepared the overall synthesis report.[7]

Evaluating the DILRMP

The impact assessment was designed in two parts—a state-level assessment and tehsil-level surveys, with some elements of the former needed as background for the tehsil-level fieldwork (Figure 2).

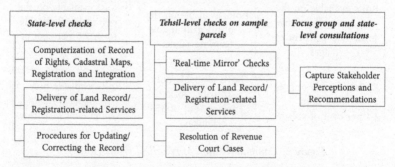

Figure 2. Methodological framework for the pilot DILRMP impact evaluation

A joint methodology was developed for the tehsil surveys, but with state-specific conditions and requirements being so different when looked at closely, the eventual sampling strategy for land parcel selection had to be modified by each institution and varied from state to state. Initially, this was considered to be a problem for interstate comparability, but as the teams worked together and drilled down into the results, it became obvious that this was indeed a plus point for the pilots, since it demonstrated the many different approaches that any large-scale assessment would have to take to get to important issues in each state. Comparability would have to be balanced by flexibility of evaluation design.

State-level assessments: All three states had digitized almost all their Record of Rights (RoRs) and made them web-friendly.[8] The key difference was the legal usability of the digitized RoRs on the web. In Himachal Pradesh (HP), they were almost 100 per cent legally usable, in Rajasthan less than 8 per cent, and not useable at all in Maharashtra.

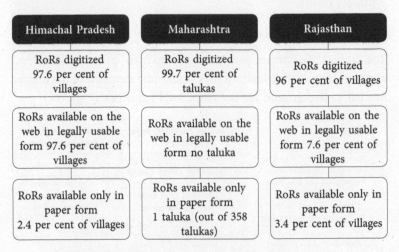

Himachal Pradesh	Maharashtra	Rajasthan
RoRs digitized 97.6 per cent of villages	RoRs digitized 99.7 per cent of talukas	RoRs digitized 96 per cent of villages
RoRs available on the web in legally usable form 97.6 per cent of villages	RoRs available on the web in legally usable form no taluka	RoRs available on the web in legally usable form 7.6 per cent of villages
RoRs available only in paper form 2.4 per cent of villages	RoRs available only in paper form 1 taluka (out of 358 talukas)	RoRs available only in paper form 3.4 per cent of villages

Figure 3. Computerization of record of rights (RoRs)

The computerization of cadastral maps (CMs) (Figure 4) has been delayed in all three states. HP is making some progress, but Maharashtra and Rajasthan are lagging substantially. It became clear that officials had started with the notion that without a de novo survey or resurvey using modern methods, there was no point in creating a digitized spatial record using old, possibly inaccurate maps. It was a painstaking process to scan, vectorize, verify and certify the digitization of old maps. More recently, officials have realized that digitized old maps are required even for finalizing the new ones after a resurvey so as to facilitate comparisons and sort out differences. They have also realized that fresh surveys/resurveys are extremely time-consuming.[9]

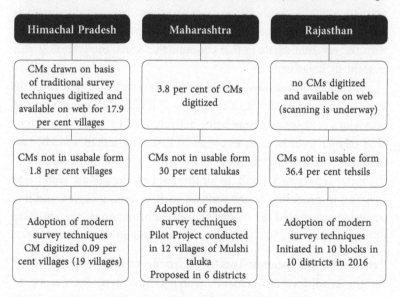

Figure 4. *Computerization of Cadastral Maps (CMs)*

Registration of land transactions is the most advanced in Maharashtra where much of the process is web-based, except for a few steps that require the registering authority to have greater access to verified records of rights. HP and Rajasthan have mostly manual registration or stand-alone systems. The final registration step of mutation that updates the RoR is manual in all three states. In HP, mutation is triggered digitally when a note of registration is made in the ROR, but to a much smaller extent in the two other states.

The full integration of RoR text, CMs and registration holds the potential for the true advantages of digitization. The most desirable outcome would be an automatic updating of the RoRs and, where required, the spatial record, when a registration happens. Just the integration of RoRs and CMs would permit visualization and two-way search on specific land parcels. Though still limited, integration seems the most advanced in HP, and Rajasthan is only just making a start. In HP, digitized CMs can be accessed using the digital RoR, and vice versa. In both HP and Maharashtra, before a document is registered, an officer can verify the registering parties and the property with the revenue database that contains the RoRs. Integration is still nascent in Rajasthan.

All three states have passed public services acts guaranteeing such services in quality and timeliness.[10] It did not appear that the provisions of these acts were being actively used by citizens to obtain land related records, such as copies of RoRs. Rajasthan and HP had no data on land related petitions under their acts, and in Maharashtra, the number was very small. In all three states, the private sector was involved in providing online services such as issuing copies, and this involvement seemed to be working well. Information on the updating of records was obtained to inform the subsequent tehsil-level checks.

Tehsil-level assessments: Two tehsils from each state were shortlisted for the tehsil-level assessment involving three types of checks for 50 land parcels chosen from each tehsil: A real-time mirror (RTM) check comparing the situation on the ground with the land records; a check on land records delivery and the difficulties citizens faced in obtaining them; and a check on the updating and correction of land records that measured how long corrections took.[11]

The RTM checks in each state were built around five features of each parcel: Ownership, possession, land use, land area and encumbrances. The situation on the ground was carefully compared with the RoR and CM on these parameters. On ownership, possession and land use, only the fully random stratified sampling strategy followed in HP yielded accurate results. On ownership, the mismatch between actual ownership and the ROR was 34 per cent in Shimla Rural and 6 per cent in Baddi. This was mainly because there had been a sale or a succession that had not been entered into the record. In many cases, the sale or succession had occurred more than five years back in Shimla Rural and two to four years in Baddi. An accurate record of land use leads to better estimates of agricultural production and property valuation. Inaccurate recording of land use was found in 34 per cent parcels in Shimla Rural and 32 per cent in Baddi. These errors were more than five years old in Shimla Rural and even 20 years old in one case in Baddi.

All three states suffered from considerable errors in recorded area, defined as more than a 5 per cent difference between the actual field measurement and the area recorded in ROR and/or the CM.[12] In HP, such errors were present in 65 per cent of land parcels, in Maharashtra, 78 per cent, and in Rajasthan, 68 per cent. Encumbrances, which are restrictions or conditions attached to ownership or land use, are usually recorded as remarks in a RoR. Incomplete records lead to disputes and litigation. The data showed that only mortgages were entered into the RoR; important information on ongoing litigation, land acquisition proceedings, revenue court cases and land use restrictions was mostly missing from the RoRs.

In HP, copies of computerized land records could be obtained without delay from Citizen Service Centres. In Maharashtra, the wait was from one to two days, and in Rajasthan, copies were available immediately or at most within the day. The studies also looked at how long it took to update and correct revenue entries, boundary demarcation and mutation, and to complete registration. For example, random samples from registers logging the correction of revenue entries in HP and Maharashtra suggested that this is a long, time-consuming process, ranging from 70 days to 270 days (Figure 5).

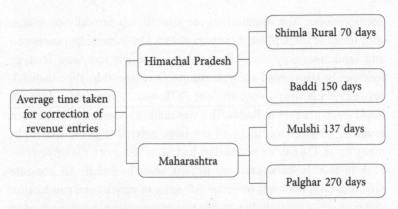

Figure 5. Time Taken for Correction of Revenue Entries

Reforming the DILRMP

The impact assessments show that while all three states have pursued the computerization of land records and the registration process, the emphasis has varied. HP has given the most attention to the digitization of handwritten records, while Maharashtra has focused on automating the registration process, and Rajasthan has made much less progress in both areas. But in all three states, the actual contribution of DILRMP to these efforts (mostly in its earlier incarnation, the NLRMP), has been well below expectations. The considerable potential of digitizing land records and their registration has so far been realized only partially, and much more needs to be done.

The pilot fieldwork done by NCAER, IGIDR and NIPFP offer a number of key suggestions, including better staff training and process flows to ensure comprehensive, accurate records that can be updated in near real time, linking disparate data bases and technological innovations that were simply not possible just a few years back. Such design and deployment improvements have the potential to dramatically improve land record services to the public and hopefully reduce property related litigation in India over time. They will also improve the value for money of the DILRMP.

The extremely important findings of this work present both the tremendous opportunities and the challenges for states to learn from best practices in other states and adapt them to their own conditions. The key weakness revealed by the pilot assessment is the substantial lack of updated and comprehensive land records after nearly three decades of running successive central schemes, of which DILRMP is the latest avatar. The procedural delays in disposing applications and legal cases for updating land records raise serious questions about state capacity despite the centrally sponsored schemes to build such capacity at the state-level.

These findings are of serious concern if India's ultimate aim is conclusive titling. Rushing to nationwide conclusive titling with the current foundations of still incomplete land records and inchoate state capacity to deal with them could spell disaster and push land markets into chaos, particularly for small-holder land parcels. Indeed, rather than reducing land litigation, a premature legislative jump without due preparation could lead to more land litigation. A much more measured, deliberative and long-term process of change is needed that resembles some of the most successful procedural digital reforms in India done smoothly and without disruption on a very large scale as, for example, the dematerialization of physical share certificates done starting in the mid-1990s, and the issuance of Aadhar biometric ID numbers to the entire resident population of India starting in 2009.

To enhance the effectiveness of DILRMP, states need action plans to streamline administrative procedures and build technological linkages and state capacity to ensure the focus on securing comprehensive accurate land records that can be updated in real time. The centre needs to incentivise states to formulate and implement such action plans.

Creating a Land Records and Services Index

NCAER's synthesis report suggests critical changes to the DILRMP funding design so that it is divided into two parts—input- and output-based. Input-based funding would disburse funds to states for computerising land records. Output-based funding would fund states based on their comparative performance on achieving comprehensive, reliable, and accurate land records.

To gauge comparative state performance, including how land buyers and sellers perceive this progress, NCAER is proposing to build a NCAER Land Records & Services Index (N-LRSI) for states and union territories. Such an index could then drive the output based central funding. The N-LRSI would be designed to capture the extent of computerization and the accuracy and real-time updating of land records. The index could be based on quick land parcel surveys using a set of easily available proxies of land records and their updating.[13]

The ranking of states on an index such as the N-LRSI could be used to reward better performing states. This should motivate all states to make more rapid advances towards the ultimate goal of more comprehensive, accurate record updated in real time instead of merely increasing the level of computerization. Such an incentive system would be consistent with India's current focus on cooperative and competitive federalism.

As a result of this work, NCAER is also considering a study on completed and ongoing land litigation in selected Indian High Courts. The idea is to categorize such litigation and then to relate different types of land litigation to the different dimensions of poor land records of the kind studied in this pilot assessment.

This pilot assessment of DILRMP and its legacy schemes in three states has highlighted the potential challenges in doing a national assessment of DILRMP. The pilot assessment can be a solid stepping stone for a nationwide DILRMP evaluation. The lessons learnt by the three participating institutions, NCAER, IGIDR and NIPFP, after months of fieldwork and the deep knowledge they developed of the different land administrative systems in each state has vastly increased our understanding of the complexity of any such nationwide assessment. These lessons suggest the need for extremely careful design of any such assessment. This design and its implementation should ensure that the assessment contains both a common core of data collection that can drive the comparative picture among states, but also have a number of flexible supporting data modules that cater to state differences and can help states formulate state action plans.

This pilot impact assessment can importantly help the Department of Land Resources make evidence-based design and implementation changes in the DILRMP that would encourage and support state efforts to make palpable improvements in their land recording products and services. This would be a big step towards the ultimate objective of conclusive land titling that the government has set out.

◆

Shekhar Shah is the Director-General of the National Council of Applied Economic Research (NCAER). Thoughtful contributions from Deepak Sanan, Devendra Gupta and Prerna Prabhakar at NCAER are gratefully acknowledged.

References

1   IGIDR. 2017. *Report on the Implementation o fthe Dl-LRMP in the State of Maharashtra.* IGIDR, Mumbai: IGIDR.

2   Kapur, Devesh, T.V. Somanathan, and Arvind Subramanian, 2014, 'Land-shackled-I & II', *Business Standard*, 21 July, Accessed 25 December 2017, http://www.business-standard.com/article/opinion/devesh-kapur-t-v-somanathan-arvind-subramanian-land-shackled-i-114072000708_1.html

3   Krishan, K.P.; Panchapagesan, V.; Venkataraman, M., 'Distortions in Land Markets and their Implications for Credit Generation in India,' *Economic and Political Weekly* LII (35): 48–55, 2017.

4   NCAER. 2017a. A Pilot Impact Assessment of the Digital India Land Records Modernisation Programme: Himachal Pradesh, New Delhi: NCAER.

5   NCAER. 2017b. A Pilot Impact Assessment of the Digital India Land Records Modernisation Programme: Synthesis Report, New Delhi: NCAER.

6   NIFPF. 2017. DI-LRMP Implementation in Rajasthan, New Delhi: NIPFP.

7   World Bank, Doing Business 2018: Reforming to Create Jobs, Washington DC: World Bank, 2017.

Endnotes

1   World Bank, 2017.
2   Kapur, Somanathan and Subramanian, 2014.
3   McKinsey Global Institute, 2001.
4   Krishnan, Panchapagesan and Venkataraman, 2017.
5   See http://www.ncaer.org/event_details.php?EID=205 or scan here for a video of the event.
6   NCAER 2017a, IGIDR 2017, and NIFPF 2017.
7   NCAER 2017b.
8   The data was collected from DILRMP website and land record offices for the time period till 31 March 2016.
9   This understanding has possibly led DoLR to issue a December 2016 policy note suggesting that for now fresh surveys/resurveys be restricted to situations where the record is torn, mutilated, or otherwise not available.
10 The Himachal Pradesh Public Services Guarantee Act, 2011; the Maharashtra Right to Public Services, 2015; and the Rajasthan Guaranteed Delivery of Public Services Act, 2011.
11 Shimla Rural and Baddi in HP, Mulshi and Palghar in Maharashtra and Girwa and Uniara in Rajasthan.
12 While NCAER used Electronic Total Station (ETS) for measuring land area in HP, IGIDR used both a hand-held GPS and ETS in Maharashtra, and NIPFP used only a hand-held GPS in Rajasthan.
13 As an illustration, a trial Land Records and Services Index was computed for the three pilot states based on the data obtained from the pilot assessments. On a scale of 0 to 100, HP scored 34.9, Maharashtra scored 30.8 and Rajasthan 9.5, consistent with the overall findings of the pilot assessment.

Epilogue

The Economic Survey, 2014–15, highlighted the constraints for implementing reforms in a country such as India, and in the process laid out the benchmark for evaluating economic performance.

'...Does India need Big Bang reforms? Much of the cross-country evidence of the post-war years suggests that Big Bang reforms occur during or in the aftermath of major crises. Moreover, Big Bang reforms in robust democracies with multiple actors and institutions with the power to do, undo, and block, are the exception rather than the rule. India today is not in crisis, and decision-making authority is vibrantly and frustratingly diffuse.

'Not only are many of the levers of power vertically dispersed, reflected in the power of the states, policymaking has also become dispersed horizontally. The Supreme Court and the Comptroller and Auditor General have all exerted decisive influence over policy action and inaction.

'Moreover, some important reforms such as improvements to tax administration or easing the cost of doing business, require persistence and patience in their implementation, evoked in Max Weber's memorable phrase, "slow boring of hard boards".

'Hence, Big Bang reforms as conventionally understood are an unreasonable and infeasible standard for evaluating the government's reform actions.

'Equally though, the mandate received by the government affords a unique window of political opportunity which should not be foregone.

India needs to follow what might be called "a persistent, encompassing, and creative incrementalism" but with bold steps in a few areas that signal a decisive departure from the past and that are aimed at addressing key problems such as ramping up investment, rationalizing subsidies, creating a competitive, predictable and clean tax policy environment, and accelerating disinvestment.'

How does actual performance in the last four years measure up against this standard? Have we heard Big Bangs? Or, have we seen persistent, encompassing and creative incrementalism? Or, some combination of both or neither? Consider some of the major reforms.

First, the GST is an unprecedentedly major reform with impacts on tax and tax buoyancy, creating one Indian market, improving formalization and tax compliance and above all, in the furthering of cooperative federalism. India has created one of the most effective institutional mechanisms for cooperative federalism, the GST Council. At a time when international events have been marked by a retreat into economic nativism and the attendant seizing of control, Indian states and the centre have offered up a refreshing counter-narrative, voluntarily choosing to relinquish and then pool sovereignty for a larger collective cause.

Cooperative federalism is of course not a substitute for states' own efforts at furthering economic and social development. But it is a critical complement, needed to tackle a wide array of difficult structural reforms that involve the states. For example, the 'cooperative federalism technology' of the GST Council could be used to create a common agricultural market, integrate fragmented and inefficient electricity markets, solve interstate water disputes, implement DBT, make access to social benefits portable across states and combat air pollution.

The spirit of cooperative federalism—defined by giving states the long-due recognition as equal partners driving the country's reform and growth agenda—has been the driving force behind two other reform initiatives. It was this spirit that led the government to promptly accept recommendations of the watershed 14th Finance

Commission (that submitted its report in December 2014) and increased the states' tax share in the divisible pool to a historic 42 per cent. Fiscal federalism was furthered as a result. Similarly, the creation of NITI Aayog was animated by the need to create cooperative federalism.

Second, the 2016–17 survey highlighted in chapter 2 that facilitating 'exit' has been one of India's most intractable challenges, evoking the generalization that over the last 50 years, India had gone from 'socialism with limited entry to capitalism without exit'. The IBC resolution process could prove a valuable technology for tackling this long-standing problem in the Indian corporate sector. The recently proposed Financial Resolution and Deposit Insurance (FRDI) bill would do the same for financial firms.

In the case of the TBS challenge, exit has proved particularly intractable because the objectives are many, conflicting, and politically difficult. Policymakers have had to find a way to reduce the debts of stressed companies to sustainable levels. At the same time, they have had to minimize the bill to taxpayers, limit moral hazard and avoid the perception of favouring controlling equity holders (promoters). The IBC aims to solve these problems through the expedient of transparently auctioning off stressed firms to the highest bidders, excluding those which are toxically blemished. This procedure is still a work in progress: Ensuring that timetables are respected and the bidding outcomes are accepted by all parties in the early cases is critical for establishing its credibility.

Next, a major plank of government policy has been to rationalize government resources, redirecting them away from subsidies towards public provision of essential private goods and services at low prices, especially to the poor. Government data suggests that progress has been made in providing bank accounts, cooking gas, housing, power, and toilets (amongst others), holding out the prospect that the lives of the poor and marginalized will improve in meaningful ways. The pace and magnitude of this improvement will depend upon the extent to which increased physical availability/provision is converted into greater actual use: Toilet building into toilet use, bank accounts into financial inclusion, cooking gas connections into consistent gas offtake, and village electrification into extensive household connections.

The government has created the JAM trinity—supplemented subsequently by the Unified Payments Interface (UPI) to implement this. An unprecedented impetus to financial inclusion was given by the PMJDY (about 316 million people have a Jan Dhan account).

The government's reform agenda—rationalizing subsidies, deregulating fuel prices, coupled with adoption of inflation targeting by the RBI and of the recalibrated FRBM path—have contributed to macro stability. As a result, after fourteen years, India's sovereign rating was upgraded by Moody's Investor services.

The recently announced 'Ayushman' health insurance scheme holds the potential to change the way healthcare is provided to the citizens, especially the poor in the country. This will address the long-term deficit reflected in the poor health outcomes and take away the major negative shock pushing people towards poverty.

The government has moved to reform governance. Now, all major public assets are auctioned transparently minimizing the scope for rent-seeking and corruption, thereby engendering faith in government.

With an aim to boost the economy's competitiveness, there has been a sharp focus on improving general ease-of-doing business. This has led to dramatic improvements in India's rankings on ease-of-doing business indicators produced by the World Economic Forum and the World Bank. The FDI regime has been significantly liberalized and now there are a few sectors in which serious restrictions remain.

However, despite coming a long way in moving forward on the reform and policy agenda, major challenges still lie ahead: From creating jobs commensurate with the increase in youth population, increasing the share of manufacturing in GDP, increasing exports growth, especially of labour-intensive manufacturing, addressing the twin balance sheet problem and making banks capable of lending credit to the private sector, to providing inexpensive and quality education and healthcare to each and every Indian.

With oil prices and inflation climbing up, growth still soft and an international environment increasingly marked by anti-globalization sentiments, the government has to keep up increased vigil on the macroeconomic front. We have learnt that all macroeconomic victories (such as that created after the Taper Tantrum of 2013) are provisional, and need to be sustained on an ongoing basis.

As reforms bear fruit, the aspirations of a young and ambitious India will soar. The economy has to continually meet these aspirations. For policymakers in India (and indeed everywhere), two good mottoes to follow are from Andy Grove, founder of Intel, and Robert Frost, respectively: 'Only the Paranoid Survive,' and there will always be 'miles to go before we sleep'.

Dr Arvind Subramanian
Former Chief Economic Adviser to the Government of India

Acknowledgements

The Path Ahead: Anthology of Transformative Ideas for India—would not have been possible without the contributions made by a rare and eclectic combination of industry executives, domain thought leaders and government officials. The diverse set of expertise brought on board by the contributors has helped me stitch together a comprehensive set of strategies for promoting and ensuring sustainable growth of various sectors in the country. Special thanks to Mr John Chambers and Dr Arvind Subramanian for their valuable contribution to the book in the form of a Foreword and Epilogue, respectively.

I would also like to thank my colleagues Urvashi Prasad, Vaibhav Kapoor and Devashish Dhar as well as my office led by Mr M.K. Talwar for coordinating and communicating with the contributors throughout the making of this book.

Special gratitude to Kapish Mehra, Managing Director, Rupa Publications, and the entire team for supporting me all along the process. In particular, thanks to Yamini Chowdhury, Senior Commissioning Editor, and Aparna Kumar, Copy Editor, for their diligent efforts in providing editorial inputs and giving the book its final shape.

To the reader, especially young leaders from all walks of life, I hope that this book inspires you to take forward some of the innovative ideas and solutions presented here which can put the country firmly on the path of unprecedented growth and development for all our citizens.

Amitabh Kant

Index